ATLANTA AND THE WAR

Other Books by Webb Garrison

A Treasury of Civil War Tales
The Lincoln No One Knows
Civil War Curiosities
Civil War Trivia and Fact Book
Great Stories of the American Revolution
More Civil War Curiosities
A Treasury of White House Tales
Creative Minds in Desperate Times
Lincoln's Little War

ATLANTA AND THE WAR

Webb Garrison

Rutledge Hill Press®
Nashville, Tennessee

Published in Nashville, Tennessee, by Rutledge Hill Press®, 211 Seventh Avenue North, Nashville, Tennessee 37219. Distributed in Canada by H. B. Fenn & Company, Ltd., 34 Nixon Rd., Bolton, Ontario L7E 1W2.

Illustrations on front cover: *Union Troops March into Abandoned Atlanta on September 2, 1864* by Currier and Ives, and detail from a portrait of William Tecumseh Sherman [Library of Congress]. Illustrations on back cover: "Confederate high tide at Atlanta; overrunning a Union battery" [Mountain Campaigns in Georgia] (top); Atlanta, just after its capture [Library of Congress] (bottom).

Typography by D&T/Bailey Typesetting, Inc., Nashville, Tennessee.

Cover design by Gore Studio, Inc.

Maps by Tonya Pitkin and reproduced from *Fields of Glory* © 1989, 1995 by Jim Miles.

Library of Congress Cataloging-in-Publication Data

Garrison, Webb B.
Atlanta and the War / Webb Garrison.
p. cm.
Includes bibliographical references and index.
ISBN 1-55853-414-8 (paperback)
1. Atlanta (Ga.)—History. 2. Atlanta Campaign, 1864.
3. Confederate States of America. Army of Tennessee. I. Title.
F294.A857G368 1995
975.8'231—dc20
95-17837
CIP

Printed in the United States of America

3 4 5 6 7 8 9—99 98

To Meredith

Contents

Part 4: Too Strong to Attack, Too Large to Invest

Part 5: New Gibraltar of the West

Introduction

Driving east from Atlanta on Interstate 20 today it takes less than half an hour to reach Covington. When some of Sherman's men followed approximately the same route in November 1864, it took them three days to reach the same small county seat.

No one born and reared in Covington could escape the impact of the Federal invasion of Georgia. One of my most vivid early memories comes from my little grandmother. Always dressed entirely in black, she was mentally and physically vigorous at age ninety-two. Over and over, she exulted in telling a small boy how she succeeded in burying "a side of bacon" so skillfully that marauding Yankees did not find it.

Her story, which may have been embroidered a bit as the years passed, deals with a single facet of a long and complex military operation. Most, if not all, accounts of it have viewed it in retrospect after it was completed. This reappraisal has been made from the perspective of 1864, while the invasion was under way.

For the most part, military reports about events of this period are limited in scope and formal in nature. They provide a record of troop movements, victories, and defeats, but do not reveal the thoughts and motives of their writers.

Military correspondence—telegrams, dispatches, and letters—are of quite a different nature. Many of them represent spur-of-the-moment documents; others seem to have been produced only after lengthy consideration. To a startlingly unexpected degree, this material gives insight into the passions, goals, frustrations, and exultations of the writers.

Federal lines of communication functioned much better than did the Confederate. Federal messages were preserved much more carefully than were those of their foes. Six volumes of the *Official Records* are full of communications issued in the western theater during the period from May 2 through November 15, 1864.

These include about 4,227 pages of Federal communications compared to only 1,672 of Confederate origin. Confederate reports deal largely with strategy and conduct of engagements. Many Federal communications, on the other hand, are rich in specific references concerning day-by-day activities and thoughts.

To get a good look at the action in Georgia during the period that began in May 1864 and ended in November it is essential to turn to the *Official Records* (volumes 1:32:iii; 1:38:iv, v; 1:39:ii and iii; 3:4; 4:3 [serials 75, 76, 78, 79, 125, 129]).

Memoirs, letters, and accounts by persons who were there are plentiful. Many of these appear in *Confederate Veteran* magazine plus the nearly one hundred volumes published under the auspices of state chapters of the Military Order of the Loyal Legion of the United States. Other first-hand material is found in the fifty-two-volume *Journal of the Southern Historical Society* and in the *Rebellion Record.*

A look at the invasion of Georgia through the eyes of those who staged it and those who resisted it yields conclusions that are unorthodox, even controversial. Hence all chapters that focus upon the military campaign are documented.

An immense amount of source material concerning the spot in the wilderness that became the city of Atlanta was accumulated while I was writing nearly five hundred historical features for the Sunday *Atlanta Journal-Constitution.* Chapters that deal with the prewar and postwar development of the city rest upon this body of evidence.

Grant and Sherman, newly elevated to higher rank, planned the thrusts of a coordinated east-west campaign. When they did so, neither commander was greatly interested in Atlanta. Their conference centered upon the strategy to be pursued in crushing the two largest Confederate armies. Robert E. Lee's Army of Northern Virginia constituted target number 1, while Joseph E. Johnston's Army of Tennessee was target number 2.

Atlanta was rarely mentioned by Sherman during the first sixty days of his invasion. The rail center emerged as a significant goal only as his forces approached the last of the three great rivers that lie between Chattanooga and Atlanta.

Sherman's capture of Atlanta had a dramatic impact whose magnitude was not anticipated when the plans for the joint operation were being made. Devastated and depopulated as a result of calculated measures, the city rose from its ashes more quickly than anyone would have predicted. Postwar Atlanta not only produced numerous significant leaders, but the city's industrial and financial base quickly became broader and deeper than it was at the time of its surrender.

In November 1864 Sherman believed he had written finish to the story of Atlanta, which he besieged and occupied when he failed to destroy the Army of Tennessee. Instead, the enormous publicity he generated helped to start the rail center on its way to world significance.

Atlanta's conqueror was a complex man, full of contradictions. William Tecumseh Sherman was sensitive but callous, kind but brutal, highly ambitious but consumed with guilt at failure, loud in protestation of respect for the law but eager and ready to indulge in flagrant violations of it. He said that he despised government, politicians, and newsmen. Yet he fought to preserve the central government, consistently turned to politicians for help, and learned to manipulate the news media. Despite these contradictions, and perhaps due to them, Sherman's name came to be inextricably intertwined with the railroad town known as Atlanta and the state that contained this great campaign of the Civil War.

TO CAPTURE the flavor of 1864 as much as possible I have used geographical names and other terms as they appeared then. For example, Peach Tree Creek is used rather than Peachtree Creek; instead of Kennesaw, Sherman and Johnston used Kenesaw; rather than using today's Jonesboro, the text deals with Jonesborough. Negroes and blacks, rather than African Americans, get considerable attention.

Quotations employ the exact language used by their authors, with punctuation and spelling following the originals. One concession to readability, however, has been made. During the nineteenth century it was not unusual for a paragraph to occupy most or all of a printed page. Here, paragraph breaks have been inserted to reduce the temptation to skip lengthy quotations.

I should also note that it is sometimes confusing to discuss troop movements of armies with similar names. Such is the case here. Like the Army of Northern Virginia, the second strongest Confederate army is known for the region in which it operated during the war—the Army of Tennessee. The North named its armies similarly, but for rivers rather than areas. Thus U.S. Maj. Gen. James B. McPherson's army was known as the Army of the Tennessee.

I hope that you will gain a new understanding and fresh appreciation of one of the world's great cities. At the same time, perhaps you will become better acquainted with the complex military genius who influenced modern warfare more than any other contemporary in blue or in gray.

Part 1

Three Armies Head for Dalton

1

Indian Country Seemed Just the Place for an Inland Port

TALL AND muscular, Stephen H. Long brushed aside offers of assistance. As chief engineer of the proposed railroad, he would direct the survey and building crews. The selection of the spot at which the line would terminate was too important an undertaking to be delegated. With an assistant and a railroad official looking on, Long drove the all-important stake himself.

Long's horse had taken him through much of the area east of the Chattahoochee River that he believed was on a line between Augusta, Georgia, and Birmingham, Alabama. Except for occasional hunters and traders, white men seldom ventured far from the region's rivers and creeks. Three ridges, each estimated by Long to be close to a thousand feet tall, converged at a spot not far from a solitary log cabin.

Two prominent geographical features, unique in the state, marked the surrounding countryside. Had the ground been level with forests cut down and thickets cleared, each would have been within an easy day's ride. Almost due east, a bald granite monolith was beginning to be called Stone Mountain. North of the selected spot lay a wooded eminence that some Indians called Chuquetah. Europeans stumbled over the name and mangled it into Kenesaw. By the standards of the state it deserved to be termed a mountain, but in 1837 no one knew it was the highest spot between the Atlantic Ocean and the Tennessee River. Five or six miles due north, the mighty Chattahoochee flowed on its way toward the Gulf of Mexico.

Long was convinced that he had found just the place for the southern end of a railroad designed to carry farm products and manufactured goods to the Tennessee River. Once upon navigable water, the cargo could proceed to the Ohio River and then down the Mississippi. When the Western and Atlantic Railroad was completed, a vast new market would absorb everything Georgia could produce.

After driving the stake into the ground, Long tossed his mallet into the wagon that held his tools and supplies. Having selected the terminus of the projected railroad, all he needed to do now was to plan its route toward Chattanooga. To him it seemed of little importance that a trickle of settlers would soon begin moving toward the place whose logical name at the moment was Terminus.

While Long was growing up and until Alabama was granted statehood in 1819, Georgia had been the southwestern tip of the United States. Trouble between settlers and Indians started long before then and had not been resolved when the point known as Terminus was but a new addition to the map of the state.

After nineteen separate treaties between Georgia and the Cherokees and Creeks, an agreement for the removal of the Indians was reached in 1825. Some Indian leaders then balked, and the issue was referred to Washington. All Indian claims to land within the state had been extinguished, or so the state insisted, and plans were made to distribute former Indian land through a statewide lottery.

State leaders formally denied the power of the president and Congress "to pronounce upon her [Georgia's] rights." Gov. George M. Troup announced that duty would require him "to resist to the utmost any military attack which the President of the United States shall think proper to make upon the *territory, the people, or the sovereignty* of Georgia" (emphasis added).

While the issues were being debated, the Georgia legislature authorized the formation of new counties from the land acquired by the 1825 treaty. Eventually an agreement was reached between the state, Washington, and tribal leaders, and the removal of Indians from Georgia was begun in May 1838.

BY THE time the exodus that became known as the Trail of Tears began, John Thrasher had looked over Terminus and had found the area promising. He made plans to build a store not far from the log cabin in which Hardy Ivy and his family lived as the only settlers.

Yet work on the railroad to Tennessee proceeded much more slowly than its architects had anticipated. Months of planning and labor went into constructing a bridge over the Chattahoochee. During three years of hard work, only a few miles of track were laid—from Terminus to Marietta, the seat of Cobb County.

After the two settlements were linked by iron, a locomotive was found near Madison, at least fifty miles to the east, but there were no rails on which it could steam to Terminus. Undaunted, the state leaders and executives of the Western and Atlantic contracted to build the largest wagon ever seen in that part of the country. With the locomotive aboard, it was pulled to Terminus by a team of sixteen mules.

Christmas 1842 was a day of special celebration two times over. Pulling one empty boxcar, the scavenged locomotive chugged the distance to Marietta and back to Terminus. A handful of men and women gathered in front of Thrasher's relatively new store, cheering as the iron horse puffed into sight.

Before the end of the following year, Terminus had shown substantial growth: ten or twelve families were scattered through the woods. Someone suggested that the town should have a charter, so an application went to the capital in Milledgeville. Clerks there, however, decided that Terminus was not a suitable name, so in honor of a former governor's daughter they substituted the name Marthasville. No protest by the settlers went into the record; it made little difference to them what the place was called. They celebrated again when completion of the Georgia Railroad in 1845 brought the first "through" train from Augusta. It consisted of a locomotive, three or four freight cars, and a caboose. Had a passenger car been included, it would have been empty. Few people wanted to travel to a clearing in the woods that held only one store, a handful of log cabins, and a few twisting dirt roads.

By this time Stephen Long had been succeeded by J. Edgar Thompson. Tradition says that the new chief engineer of the Georgia Railroad didn't like the name of the town to which trains now occasionally ran from Augusta. Proud of his fast locomotives, he suggested that the place should be called Atalanta in honor of the fleet-footed maiden of Greek mythology. Railroad files recorded that name for a few months before it was modified to Atlanta when settlers—nearly three hundred strong—received a new charter in 1847.

Officials repeatedly promised that the Western and Atlantic Railroad would soon be completed, but a hill of solid rock just south of

Chattanooga accounted for another year's delay. Eventually a tunnel was cut through it, causing the place to be known as Tunnel Hill. When a train actually arrived on the tracks of the new Macon and Western Railroad, it connected with the Georgia Railroad. To the settlers this meant that a depot was now needed.

Numerous cities to the north were served by two or more railroads. Since they had been established long before ribbons of iron reached them, it was the custom of the time for each railroad to erect its own depot. Freight and passengers were transferred from one line to another through the city streets.

Yet youthful Atlanta didn't have a single street, so it seemed sensible to build only one depot. A tract of one hundred acres was secured for four hundred dollars, and all railroad officials were instructed to extend their lines to this central spot. Soon the Atlanta and West Point Railroad was in operation, branching off from the Macon and Western at a crossroads locally known as Jonesborough.

By the middle of the century, Atlanta was a hub at which four lines connected at a single switching yard and passenger depot. Some choice town lots were bringing more than ten dollars a front foot, and the population had soared past twenty-five hundred. According to the census of 1850, 1,063 white males and 997 white females called Atlanta home. Female slaves outnumbered males 277 to 216, and there were 13 free black females, but only 6 males in that category.

Before the decade ended some of the free blacks set out to find more hospitable places to live. An ordinance passed by the city fathers in May 1859, however, stipulated:

> All free persons of color, coming within the limits of Atlanta to live, shall, within ten days of their arrival, pay to the clerk of the council $200. Failure to make payment shall result in arrest by the marshal, deputy marshal, or other police officer, who shall put him or her in the guardhouse for the term of five days, during which time the marshal shall advertise in at least one public gazette that such person or persons of color will be hired out at public outcry at the city hall, to the person who will take such free person of color for the shortest time for said sum.

Throughout the nation the electorate was then made up of white males twenty-one years of age or older who owned property or had served in the military. Only 174 Atlantans cast votes in the election of

1848 despite the fact that newcomers were starting to pour into their town at the rate of nearly 1,000 per year.

In the census year of 1850, a tin shop opened. Twelve months later, increasing railroad traffic was perceived as a splendid opportunity. Plans were executed to erect a machine shop "for the purpose of mending cars and other railroad work."

Atlanta grew so rapidly that an unofficial census was taken in 1854. To the surprise of no long-time settlers, it revealed that the population had more than doubled since 1850, with 6,025 persons now calling the place home. It seemed appropriate to erect a building to serve as both the city hall and the courthouse. Two stories high and measuring one hundred by seventy feet, it was completed in 1855. Nineteen brick stores went up during the same year.

IN 1854 most owners of these and other business establishments backed a plan to move the state capital from sedate, old Milledgeville to the brash young railroad center. Growth of the middle Georgia town then serving as the capital had been very slow, Atlantans pointed out. Though established in a county laid out as a result of the 1803 land lottery, Milledgeville had only 3,546 free residents in 1850. Its slave population, also static for years, hovered near 4,500.

Young as Atlanta was, it had much to offer in addition to railroads. Not counting retail liquor shops, more than sixty stores were in operation. Huge quantities of cotton could be kept in four large warehouses having easy access to the depot. The car shop easily represented a capital investment of $30,000. A modern mill, powered by steam instead of running water, was estimated to turn out $150,000 worth of flour per year.

Although the city formally was included in DeKalb County, the county government was viewed as too stodgy to suit Atlanta's merchants. They began to work toward creating a new county around the rail center and had gone so far as to select a name. It ought to be Fulton, they said, in honor of the inventor of the steamboat. After all, steam was fast turning Atlanta into the inland port that had been envisioned when the state legislators had voted to build the Western and Atlantic line.

Fulton County soon came into existence, wholly independent of DeKalb. Voters throughout the state, however, had a say concerning the location of the capital, and many of them didn't like what they heard about Atlanta. By an overwhelming majority the state's rural residents turned down an offer from the city's merchants and capitalists to erect "a splendid new capitol near the point of juncture of four great railroad lines."

POLITICAL DEFEAT did nothing to slow the growth or dampen the hopes of those who were determined to make Atlanta their home. The population reached or passed 8,000 at the end of 1856. Twelve months later the figure, probably inflated, was reported as 11,500.

Money seemed to pour into Atlanta and its "neighbouring villages." Against cotton in transit to Augusta, Savannah, Charleston, and New York, bank agents advanced $1.25 million in 1850. Every year the number and size of these transactions jumped within what would now be termed a metropolitan area; sometimes the total doubled in twelve months.

Not far away in Roswell, two large cotton mills, a wool factory, and a flour mill stood close to the Chattahoochee River. In 1850 the older of the cotton mills employed 2,208 fly spindles that produced number 6 to number 12 yarn at the rate of one thousand pounds a day. Roswell Manufacturing Company's new mill held 5,184 Danforth cap spindles, 32 thirty-six-inch cards, and 120 looms. At least 250 women worked in the two factories when the census of 1850 was taken. A 20 percent jump in employment, anticipated for the following year, was followed by other large annual increases.

Since many workers in the outlying towns had no transportation, a number of Atlanta merchants took goods to them, usually at inflated prices. The cash flow generated by their business a half-day's drive from the rail center gave a significant boost to Atlanta's booming economy.

PARTLY BECAUSE of the state's size, Georgia's leaders very early became obsessed with transportation. Port cities had always dominated the Atlantic seaboard, major rivers, and the shoreline of the Gulf of Mexico. To boost cities far from navigable water, a great deal of work had to be done. By 1830, when railroads were envisioned by a few as the transportation mode of the future, Georgia had invested an estimated $350,000 in canals and improvements to rivers.

Soon steam power was applied effectively to engines capable of running on narrow iron rails. The cost of building twenty miles of track proved to be a fraction of what was necessary to cut a canal of the same length. Thus, steam-powered transportation by rail became the passion of Georgia's capitalists and lawmakers.

Completed in 1833 as the first railroad in the state, the Central of Georgia linked Macon with seagoing vessels at Savannah. The building of the Georgia Railroad was started in 1833, and its trains ran regularly between Atlanta and Augusta before 1850. At the eastern end of this line, the navigable Savannah River offered shippers connections with all Atlantic ports.

Older and wealthier states such as New York and Pennsylvania failed to match railroad expansion in what citizens proudly called "the Empire State of the South." By 1860 Georgia's ratio of railroad miles to inhabitants was 1 to 744 while the national ratio was 1 to 1,083. In Georgia and the rest of the Cotton Belt, railroads were designed to serve two functions: transportation of cotton to the coast and importation of manufactured goods and foodstuffs to the interior.

After giving birth to Atlanta, the Georgia Railroad built branch lines to Washington, Athens, and Warrenton. At its eastern terminus, Augusta, goods could be transferred to other railroads serving Richmond, Wilmington, and Charleston. The city's second line, the Atlanta and West Point, provided service to and from Mobile and much of the rest of Alabama by means of its connection with the Montgomery and West Point line.

Atlanta's third railroad, the Western and Atlantic, ended at Chattanooga. With other lines it linked Georgia's farms to significant markets in Memphis, Nashville, and Cincinnati. The Macon and Western extended northward from Georgia's capital almost to Atlanta, joining the Atlanta and West Point just south of the growing rail center. At Macon the Central of Georgia was a conduit for freight between Atlanta and Savannah, whose cotton exchange was second in size only to that of London.

In April 1861 most major railroads of the state were financially sound. Capital stock of the Georgia Railroad was just over $5.5 million, with a bonded debt one-fourth as high and a surplus listed at $1.3 million.

Most revenue was derived from freight charges. Those passengers who rode the 171 miles from Augusta to Atlanta in nine hours paid fares of $5.50 each; the 102-mile journey from Macon to Atlanta cost $4.50. For the ride between Atlanta and Chattanooga at an average speed of fifteen miles per hour, a passenger paid $5.00.

Georgia had numerous rail centers by midcentury; six lines converged at Macon. Yet no other inland transportation hub in the Deep South was equal in importance to Atlanta. Goods and passengers moved to and from this four-line junction in ever-increasing volume. Once the Civil War began, the importance of the Atlanta rail network was quickly boosted.

Much of the rolling stock of the Western and Atlantic was seized by the Confederate government just before the battle of Shiloh in April 1862. New cars, many of them built in Atlanta, were purchased as rapidly as they could be produced, and demands for freight service increased astronomically.

Heavier trains played havoc with the light iron rails. Therefore to decrease maintenance costs and to serve the needs of the military, the Atlanta and West Point stopped accepting freight from private concerns in May 1862.

Supplies for Confederate forces in the eastern theater rolled constantly northward on the Western and Atlantic. Sometimes trains traveled so closely together that from a distance observers saw only one continuous line of locomotives and cars. By 1864 the importance of these trains was magnified by Union victories. Lee and the Army of Northern Virginia could no longer depend upon sugar from Louisiana, beef from Texas, or grain and pork from Tennessee.

Even after normal passenger service was suspended, military personnel more than made up for this loss of revenue. Conscripts from throughout the lower South were likely to roll through Atlanta on the way to their posts. Especially during 1863 and 1864 citizens of the growing town saw so many cars arrive crowded with sick and wounded soldiers that they ceased to be a source of wonder. In addition to an estimated eighty thousand such men who poured into the overcrowded town, carloads of the dead and trainloads of prisoners came to or through Atlanta.

SOUTHERN LITERATURE consistently identifies Atlanta as a center of manufacturing for military purposes. Yet the railway center never had a plant close to the size and importance of Richmond's Tredegar Iron Works or Augusta's Powder Works. Though numerous, factories in "the Gate City of the South" were small.

Gov. Joseph E. Brown called gunsmiths together in 1861 and asked them to make Atlanta a center of their industry. Forges from a railroad machine shop were allocated for the manufacture of gun barrels. Many small establishments also turned out knives, buttons, spurs, bridles, belt buckles, and canteens. A work force of nearly one hundred men produced shoes. Numerous revolvers and a few cannon were manufactured in the rail center. A foundry was supplemented by four machine shops. Suitable metal became so scarce that appeals were made to churches to relinquish their bells to be melted down.

An arsenal turned out substantial quantities of small military gear such as swords, cartridges, and friction primers. When the proprietor of the Atlanta Machine Works refused to produce shells, Confederate authorities confiscated the plant. A limited number of shells were turned out, but most proved to be of poor quality.

For military purposes, by far the most significant manufacturing enterprise in the city was the old rolling mill. When William Markham of Connecticut launched the enterprise in 1856, it was the first of its sort in the South. In spite of shortages, artisans often produced thirty tons of railroad iron during a single day.

The care of soldiers and their needs was a basic concern during 1861–65. Four small hotels and the buildings that housed the Female Institute and the Atlanta Medical College were used as hospitals. Eight months after Fort Sumter, diarist S. P. Richards lamented, "Our city is now full of sick soldiers."

As the number of ill and wounded men swelled in Atlanta, other structures such as Kile's Building and the Concert Hall were converted to hospital use. When an epidemic of smallpox struck in 1863, a special treatment center was constructed on a 155-acre tract of land. Partly because the railroad center was a major hospital base, authorities in Richmond had a pharmaceutical laboratory constructed there.

Months earlier, Atlanta was chosen as the site of a Commissary Department depot. Later the rail center housed the Quartermaster's Department of the Army of Tennessee. Even though it was home to many outspoken Unionists, before the end of 1862 Atlanta was dominated by the needs of Confederate military forces.

MANY SOUTHERN aristocrats had considered Atlanta to be populated entirely by newcomers, whom they regarded as raw and vulgar. Numerous adventurers and some solid capitalists had come to Atlanta from the North. To them, the city seemed to offer more opportunity than did the older, more sedate population centers. Claiming about twenty thousand residents in 1860—vulgar or not—Atlanta had become a vital link in the transportation network of the Cotton Belt.

Urged to make Atlanta the permanent capital of the Confederacy after it left the temporary capital at Montgomery, Alabama, Southern lawmakers turned instead to Richmond, Virginia. Resentment created by this decision evaporated on April 12, 1862, under the impact of news so startling that it was first dismissed as false.

A civilian from Ohio, James Andrews, was reported to have nearly succeeded in disabling the Western and Atlantic Railroad. Hours after the first rumors were received in Atlanta, the news was found to be true. Using a hijacked locomotive, Andrews and his men headed toward Chattanooga in an attempt to tear up track and burn bridges. Most of his followers, members of the Army of the Ohio dressed as civilians, were captured. Tried and convicted as spies, Andrews and several of his followers died in Atlanta's first mass execution. Andrews and his men did no significant damage, but their exploit created a temporary panic in Atlanta.

A year after Andrews's raid, Col. Abel Streight led a daring foray aimed at Rome, Georgia, and its important iron works. His cavalry rode mules rather than horses for their surefootedness in rugged country. Close to their objective, the men in blue surrendered to a small force of Confederates under the command of Nathan Bedford Forrest.

Neither Federal incursion accomplished its objective nor was significant in the growing sectional conflict. Both, however, suggested

LOUISVILLE AND NASHVILLE RAILROAD

The locomotive *General*, preserved as a legacy of the war, symbolizes the role railroads played in the founding of Atlanta and the city's importance to the Confederacy.

that Atlanta might someday be threatened. To influential leaders elsewhere as well as the city's residents, the time seemed near to prepare by erecting fortifications. Already accustomed to growing numbers of people reared in the North, Atlantans were confident that a railroad engineer from Maine could protect them.

Lemuel P. Grant had come south to work on the Georgia Railroad. Completed, the line stretched 140 miles from Augusta to Atlanta, which investors lauded as the world's longest. When John C. Calhoun visited Marthasville, he predicted that "trails of iron" would some day make it the South's chief inland city.

After spending nearly a decade in Georgia, Grant became chief engineer of the Atlanta and La Grange Railroad, which soon became the Atlanta and West Point line. At the outbreak of war his northern background was generally forgotten or ignored, and he was regarded as a Southerner. Civic leaders of the growing town therefore turned to him when Union activities began to create fear and uncertainty.

Congressman Lucius J. Gartrell, who later raised and led a regiment, called the attention of Richmond to the importance of Atlanta in May 1863. Vicksburg's fall to U. S. Grant on July 4 magnified the significance of the inland center. Twelve days after the siege of the Mississippi River port ended, authorities in the Confederate capital instructed Lemuel Grant "to examine carefully with a view to a proper system of defense, the approaches to, and the vicinity of Atlanta."

Grant surveyed the hills and valleys surrounding Atlanta carefully, making maps that Sherman would have prized in 1864. Using an estimated one thousand slaves, for whose service their owners were paid twenty-five dollars per month, the man from Maine erected "a cordon of enclosed works within supporting distance of one another" that ran for ten miles. Nineteen strong redoubts, each designed to hold five guns, were distributed among rifle pits.

Before this defensive line stretched four rows of chevaux-de-frise fashioned from pine. With their branches sharpened and pointing outward, felled trees were placed in such fashion that attacking forces would have to claw or crawl their way through. Land in front of the fortifications was cleared for an average of one thousand yards for sharpshooters to have clear fields of fire.

IN LETTERS to his wife, William Tecumseh Sherman occasionally made passing mention of Atlanta. Clearly, he was aware of its importance. Yet when he launched his invasion of Georgia, the Confederate Army of

Tennessee was his primary target. Joseph E. Johnston's army maintained its strength for many weeks and eluded Federal attempts to be drawn into a decisive battle.

After having marched his troops southward from Chattanooga, Sherman saw Atlanta in a new light. Without giving up attempts to crush the Army of Tennessee, he believed that in Atlanta he had found a target he could hit so hard that it would be his at the cost of only a few days of effort. How wrong he was he did not discover until he unsuccessfully tried to mount a full siege.

In the early summer of 1864, Sherman abandoned his primary goal of crushing the Army of Tennessee and turned his forces on the fortified rail center. Viewed as a strategic move, the conquest of Atlanta was the result of Federal defeat rather than of victory in the invasion of Georgia. Then and only then did Sherman's pursuit of Johnston and his clashes with Hood come to be known as the Atlanta campaign.

2

Hit Hard on Both Fronts at Once!

DISTINCTLY RED, William Tecumseh Sherman's sharp nose punctuated his wrinkled face. Wearing his usual field officer's brown coat without shoulder straps, the slender Union soldier bearing the name of a Shawnee warrior loped steadily toward the Nashville headquarters of Lt. Gen. Ulysses S. Grant. Something big was afoot, otherwise the new field commander of U.S. forces would not have stressed the urgency of a private conference on March 17, 1864.

Known to some of his men as "Uncle Billy," but called "Cump" by relatives and friends, including Grant, Sherman had an awkward gait that stemmed from his habit of carrying his hands in his pockets. To casual passersby the man in a hurry did not look at all like the commanding general of the Division of the Tennessee. Rather, he seemed to be a nondescript soldier of the military force that occupied the city. A newspaper correspondent who had seen the Ohio native in action described Sherman in this way:

> He was rather tall and slender, and his quick movements denoted good muscle added to absolute leanness—not thinness. His uniform was neither new nor old, but bordering on a hazy mellowness of gloss, while the elbows and knees were a little accented from the continuous agitation of those joints.
>
> The face was one I should never rest upon in a crowd, simply because to my eye there was nothing remarkable about it, save the nose, which organ was high, thin, and planted with a curve as vehement as the curve of a Malay cutlass.
>
> The face and neck were rough, and covered with reddish hair, the eye light in color and animated, but though restless and bound-

> ing like a ball from one object to another, neither piercing nor brilliant; the mouth well closed but common, the ears large, the hands and feet long and thin, the gait a little rolling, but firm and active.
>
> In dress and manner there was not the slightest trace of pretension. He spoke rapidly, and generally with an inquisitive smile.
>
> To this *ensemble* I must add a hat which was the reverse of dignified or distinguished—a simple felt affair, with a round crown and drooping brim, and you have as a fair a description of General Sherman's exterior as I can pen.[1]

Careful scrutiny of a man's exterior reveals little or nothing about the inner man. Sherman considered himself a better soldier than Grant in some respects, but he never failed to remember that at times he showed what some called "signs of mental instability." Two years older than Grant and three years ahead of him at West Point, he disavowed a twinge of jealousy at Grant's sudden elevation despite the fact that when the War Department listed brigadier generals of volunteers on August 7, 1861, he was seventh and Grant was eighteenth.[2] Months later, it was the senior man who persuaded the "perennial failure Grant" not to resign under Henry W. Halleck's abusive treatment.

LIBRARY OF CONGRESS

William Tecumseh Sherman

LIBRARY OF CONGRESS

The view to the southwest from the capitol building in Nashville during the Union occupation. Sherman and Grant met here to devise the grand strategy for the last year of the war.

When it came time to talk about the future, however, neither man guarded his speech. Each respected and trusted the other; theirs was almost a conference between equals. Sherman was delighted that President Abraham Lincoln had passed over generals with solid and stable reputations in favor of a man whose past was seamy and smudged.

One of his vivid memories was pegged to St. Louis, where he had served briefly as superintendent of a street railway. He spied Grant hauling wood into the city for sale, looking down and out. Sherman turned his head and acted as though he had not seen the one-time U.S. Army captain who had been mustered out of the service because he had lost a bout with the bottle.

Neither of the West Pointers, then civilians, was quick to put on his uniform again to fight secessionists. When men from his native state approached Sherman about recruiting a regiment as soon as Lincoln called for seventy-five thousand volunteers to enter Federal service for ninety days, he rejected their offer almost contemptuously. "You might as well attempt to put out the flames of a burning house with a squirt gun" as to subdue the South with such a force, he snorted.

Some of his friends shunned him after they volunteered, but Sherman took no action until he received a telegram from Washington. "Come at once," his brother Charles urged before informing him that he had been appointed colonel of the Thirteenth Infantry Regiment.[3]

Sherman conducted himself with credit at Bull Run but soon ran into trouble while serving under Brig. Gen. Robert Anderson. Charged with recruitment in Kentucky and with holding the state for the Union, Sherman went through a period he later preferred to forget.

WAITING FOR the arrival of his immediate subordinate, Sam Grant didn't need to be reminded that in many respects he now seemed to be a favorite of Providence. His initial attempts to reenter the military service had been ignored or rebuffed by Col. Lorenzo Thomas, adjutant general of the army.[4] His more-than-casual friendship with Elihu Washburne had borne unexpected fruit, however.

Men of the Twenty-first Infantry Regiment of Illinois, headed for ninety days of service but facing a challenge to volunteer for "three years or the war," balked at going into battle behind the colonel whom they had elected. Washburne, a member of Congress with great political power, learned of the impasse. At the lawmaker's urging and without Grant's knowledge, Gov. Richard Yates appointed Grant colonel of the troublesome unit.[5]

Grant's regiment "embraced the sons of farmers, lawyers, physicians, politicians, merchants, bankers and ministers, and some men of maturer years."[6] Several refused to enter U.S. service, but the majority stayed with their new colonel. Visiting Springfield, Grant met two Democrats with whom his future was destined to be intertwined: Kentucky-born John A. McClernand and John A. "Blackjack" Logan. After Colonel Grant somewhat hesitantly assented to their request, both political leaders gave rousing patriotic speeches to the men of the Twenty-first.[7]

Soon becoming one of a host of new brigadier generals, Grant might have remained in obscurity had he not made a sudden decision at Fort Donelson, Tennessee. When besieged Confederates asked what terms he would accept if they laid down their arms, he instantly replied, "Unconditional Surrender!"

The defeated Confederate Brig. Gen. Simon Bolivar Buckner, who had at one time loaned Grant enough money to get home from

California, was taken aback but had no choice. Once news of Grant's ultimatum became public, it was linked with his initials and U. S. Grant suddenly found himself famous. Admirers throughout the North, ecstatic at the first significant Union victory of the war, showered "Unconditional Surrender" Grant with an estimated ten thousand cigars.

His fame was tarnished by poor leadership at Belmont, Missouri, and at Shiloh (or Pittsburg Landing), Tennessee. Already disliked by his commanding general, Halleck, Grant seemed headed back toward the obscurity from which he had emerged. Halleck made life so miserable for him that Grant contemplated resigning, but he was persuaded by Sherman not to act in haste. Grant was soon assigned to lead the Vicksburg campaign, perhaps because Halleck knew that the river city would be difficult, if not impossible, to conquer.

Though accustomed to vocal criticism of both his personal life and his military leadership,[8] Grant chafed when his initial attempts to seize Vicksburg ended in well-publicized failure. After taking a roundabout path that enabled his forces to creep up on the blind side of the Confederates, the siege ended in victory. It is possible, but by no means

LIBRARY OF CONGRESS

Ulysses S. Grant

certain, that Grant carefully timed the surrender ceremonies to occur on July 4, 1863.[9]

Whether or not Independence Day was shrewdly selected by Grant as just the right time to burnish his damaged career, it again elevated him to prominence throughout the North. *New York Herald* reporter Charles A. Dana, soon to become an assistant secretary of war, sent glowing reports about him to Washington. Once Secretary of War Edwin M. Stanton digested the contents of these documents, he passed them along to the White House.[10]

Vicksburg and Dana, as well as the battles of Chattanooga and Lookout Mountain, may have been responsible for the president's rather abrupt choice of Grant as general in chief of the heretofore lackluster Union armies. Elihu Washburne, who had Lincoln's ear, led the congressional movement to establish a new and higher military rank and to place his protégé in it.[11] Whatever the behind-the-scenes circumstances may have been, the man with a reputation as a hard drinker and whose record was marred by numerous failures was ordered to Washington on March 3, 1864.

GRANT MAY have been under the impression that he had been summoned to the capital to discuss his plans for the remaining conduct of the war in the West. Writing on January 19 to Lorenzo Thomas (who had ignored Grant's initial request to rejoin the Union army), he suggested that too much attention had been devoted to Richmond. Forget the Confederate capital, he said, and send sixty thousand men against Suffolk, Virginia, or New Berne, North Carolina. Destroy the railroad leading to Richmond from the south, then concentrate on Raleigh, North Carolina, he wrote. As for himself, he expected to remain in the West and tentatively believed that William F. "Baldy" Smith should head the Army of the Potomac.[12]

Arriving in the capital with his fourteen-year-old son, Fred, unheralded and seldom recognized, he checked into Willard's Hotel. Soon he learned that Washburne had assured Lincoln that his protégé had no intention of campaigning for the presidency.[13]

How his patron had learned of his correspondence with Ohio Democrats, Grant had no idea. Queried about having his name offered for the nation's highest office, he had posted an urgent and confidential letter of refusal. "Nothing likely to happen would pain me so much as to see my name used in connection with a political office," the soldier wrote.[14] Once the president knew that his commander in the West would not oppose him at the polls, Lincoln nominated him for the newly created post of lieutenant general with permanent rank.

The chief executive's choice faced only nominal opposition. Much of it was relayed to him by thick-chested, square-faced Sen. Benjamin F. Wade of Grant's native Ohio. Already at odds with Lincoln, Wade and members of his Joint Committee on the Conduct of the War constituted a vocal minority among the lawmakers but were virtually ignored at the White House.

When news of Grant's sudden elevation was announced, editors of the *New York Herald* pondered the question What if he should fail? and reached this conclusion:

> If Grant, who has never failed in the past, should fail in the future, it will be because there is treachery in Washington. It will be because in that spirit of partisan fury that forgets all else but its object the Washington men have determined to employ all their power to ruin another man who stands high with the people.
>
> At this hour the energy and ingenuity of the adherents of the President are intensely concentrated on the game for the next presidency. No scheme that can make capital for them is forgotten.[15]

Wade and his colleagues wanted Gen. George G. Meade removed from command of the Army of the Potomac and hoped that if they could not select the new general in chief, they at least could accomplish this objective. Grant, whom the president had never met before, had awkward meetings with his commander in chief.[16] Instead of dealing with personnel matters such as Meade's command, the two men concentrated on the grand objective of the conflict.

Perhaps to his surprise, Grant learned that Lincoln had long objected to the repeated strenuous attempts to move upon Richmond by water. While the Confederate capital was a significant objective, the president was convinced that Robert E. Lee's Army of Northern Virginia was a far more important target. Once this and other enemy armies were destroyed, he believed that the Confederate cities would fall with little or no struggle. On this fundamental issue the chief political official and the new supreme military leader of the Union were in firm agreement.[17]

Halleck, long Grant's nemesis, had been reduced to the role of chief of staff, which meant that he would serve as a liaison agent between the president and his general in chief. But Halleck would never again command an army in battle.[18]

Not counting the Army of the Potomac, Grant found himself suddenly at the head of more than a score of army corps. They were distributed among nineteen military districts, and each commander seemed to have his own notion about the course that should be pursued. Separate forces under Meade, Sigel, Butler, Thomas, and Banks were acting independently and without coordination—"like a balky team, no two ever pulling together."[19] This business of going off in several directions at once had to stop immediately, the new general in chief insisted.

Lincoln gave him total support, but Stanton let it be known that he expected to continue to make personnel decisions. Presidential secretary John Hay echoed the sentiment of many in Washington when he said that he "would rather make a tour of a smallpox hospital than ask a favor of Stanton."[20] Well aware that he faced "the most severely impressive member of the cabinet," Grant refused to budge. "I will make the military appointments without help or advice from any civilian," he told the secretary of war.

Before starting on his return trip to Tennessee, Grant received a lengthy letter from Sherman written on March 10 from "near Memphis." "You are now [George] Washington's legitimate successor [as lieutenant general]," he wrote. To Sherman this meant that his friend now held a post "of almost dangerous elevation." Unable to resist offering his advice, Sherman urged: "If you can continue, as heretofore, to be yourself—simple, honest and unpretending—you will enjoy through life the respect and love of friends and the homage of millions of human beings that will award you a large share, in securing to them and their descendants a government of law and stability."

After devoting three paragraphs to praise of Grant, his comrade in arms penned a confession followed by a warning:

> My only points of doubt were in your knowledge of grand strategy, and of books of science and history, but I confess your common sense seems to have supplied all these.
>
> Now as to future. Don't stay in Washington. Halleck is better qualified than you to stand the buffets of intrigue and policy. Come West; take to yourself the whole Mississippi Valley. . . . For God's sake and your country's sake come out of Washington . . . I exhort you to come out West. Here lies the seat of the coming empire, and from the West, when our task is done, we will make short work of Charleston and Richmond and the impoverished coast of the Atlantic.[21]

Sam Grant greeted Sherman warmly when he arrived for the conference he had ordered. Better than anyone else in uniform, he knew that his long-time friend and colleague had made enemies and was generally regarded as having a fiery temper.

What's more, Sherman could harbor a grudge for many years. His father, Charles R. Sherman, a justice of the Ohio supreme court, had died suddenly in 1829 leaving behind a house full of impoverished orphans. Family friends stepped forward to assume responsibility for each youngster. Tecumseh had to travel no farther than next door. Prosperous Thomas Ewing gladly assumed responsibility for the nine-year-old, but he struck sparks when he insisted that the boy add William ("properly Christian") as a preface to his name.

If Ewing and his foster son quarreled over major issues, both remained silent about them. Cump became so enamored with his foster sister, Ellen, that he made her his wife. Yet his resentment of her father ran deep. In 1864 he prepared a terse autobiographical sketch that included everything he considered significant about himself, but in it his benefactor's name was nowhere mentioned.[22]

SHERMAN WAS greeted warmly by Julia Grant, who then joined her children. Before he took his seat, Sherman learned from her husband that he was now in command of the vast Military Division of the Mississippi. His forces were spread from Cairo, Illinois, to Knoxville, Tennessee, and then westward to both banks of the Mississippi River. Four departments were included in the division: Ohio, Cumberland, Tennessee, and Arkansas.[23]

Sam Grant, who had relinquished the post upon becoming lieutenant general, indulged in no perfunctory remarks. He informed Sherman that though he would make his headquarters in the East rather than the West, he would spend as little time in Washington as possible. In consultation with Lincoln, he said, it had been decided that a major change of strategy must be implemented immediately. Sherman's aides, who learned of the conversation later, said it could be summed up in a single terse sentence: "Hit hard on both fronts at once!"

Sherman's top commanders in his new post were four experienced officers of varied backgrounds who held commissions, not in the regular army, but in the U.S. Volunteers. Maj. Gen. George H. "Slow Trot" or "the Rock of Chickamauga" Thomas had grown up in Virginia and differed from Sherman by favoring the use of black soldiers. Both Maj. Gen. Frederick Steele and Brig. Gen. John M. Schofield (soon to be promoted) had New York state backgrounds. By every standard the favorite of the new commander of the division, handsome Maj. Gen. James B. McPherson of Ohio was regarded as sure to surge to top leadership soon.[24]

Grant wanted to make sure that these men and most of their troops would be welded into a single fighting force with a clearly defined objective. Hence he invited Sherman to accompany him on his northward journey as far as Cincinnati, so that their plans could mature. Had an observer watched the two casually dressed commanders as they left Nashville, only their private railroad car would have hinted at their rank. As they rode they discussed the contemplated changes, which Sherman later said involved "many little details." They talked for hours in the Burnet House Hotel before they parted.

Grant expected immediately to direct Meade to move against Lee and the Army of Northern Virginia. It was vital, he stressed, that precisely coordinated action occur in the East and the West. Soon the

Sherman and his generals: from left to right, Oliver O. Howard, John A. Logan, William B. Hazen, William Tecumseh Sherman, Jefferson C. Davis, Henry W. Slocum, T. A. Mower, and Frank P. Blair Jr.

Army of the Potomac would cross the Rapidan River and strike the Confederates in Virginia. On that same day, Grant stressed, Sherman must move into Georgia to engage the Army of Tennessee under its new commander, Gen. Joseph E. Johnston.

Back in Nashville on March 25, Sherman was confident that he and Grant understood one another. Six months later, he wrote: "We had a full and complete understanding of the policy and plans for the ensuing campaign, covering a vast area of country, my part of which extended from Chattanooga to Vicksburg."[25]

Significantly, he made no mention of Atlanta. On March 25 he began a tour of inspection that took him to Athens, Decatur, and Huntsville in Alabama plus Chattanooga, Loudon, and Knoxville in Tennessee. Having briefed his commanders concerning the coming campaign, he then devoted his full time to the nearly impossible task of fulfilling the promises made to Grant.

3

Far Too Strong for a Frontal Assault

PICKETS OF the Army of Tennessee erupted into a spontaneous cheer on December 27, 1863. They had spotted a man about fifty years old riding into their lines with a token escort. Described as "compactly built and strangely jaunty," he wore a set of short side whiskers and a gray goatee. Only his hat, decorated with a star and a feather, identified him as Virginia-born Gen. Joseph E. Johnston. His arrival at Dalton, Georgia, seemed to many Confederates to signal a reorganization of the army to take the offensive. Soon after he entered camp, officers said that "cantonments rang with joy."

A few weeks earlier Gen. Braxton Bragg had relinquished command of the second most powerful Confederate force. Bragg's selection by Jefferson Davis as his chief of staff ostensibly stemmed from the fact that he'd have to take up residence in Richmond.

Major Gens. B. F. Cheatham and W. H. T. Walker knew better. So did their colleagues in command and many of the soldiers who served under them. Bragg's humiliating defeat at Missionary Ridge on November 25 had cost him the confidence of his army. He resigned because he knew his dispirited forces would not follow him toward another encounter with the enemy in blue. Even those who admired him as a leader often condemned him for the high-handed way in which he conducted his business.

Lt. Gen. W. J. "Old Reliable" Hardee of Georgia stepped briefly into the vacancy left by Bragg. He wanted nothing to do with the "poisoned atmosphere" left behind by Bragg but agreed to serve until a permanent commander could be found. Davis tentatively suggested that Lee take over the decimated army, but the leader of the forces destined to face U. S. Grant insisted that he was needed in Virginia. In his place, it is believed that Lee suggested P. G. T. Beauregard for the high-profile position.

Davis, whose dislike for Johnston was well known, had even less taste for Beauregard. Pressured by his cabinet to put Johnston, a West Point classmate of Lee, into the chief Confederate military post in the West, Davis reluctantly yielded and on December 16 ordered Johnston to Georgia.[1]

Five days after reaching his new command, Johnston received from Richmond a set of instructions dated December 23. Davis lauded "the encouraging condition of the army" and said that he hoped "active operations against the enemy" would soon be set in motion. Recovery of territory lost in Kentucky and Tennessee was essential, the chief executive wrote. Besides, success in such an "onward movement" would replenish "the supplies on which the proper subsistence of our armies" was dependent. Relying upon rough estimates probably provided by Bragg, the president voiced the conclusion—incorrectly—that the

LIBRARY OF CONGRESS

Joseph E. Johnston

Army of Tennessee now included more men than were "actually engaged on the Confederate side in any battle of the war."[2]

Johnston had no idea that one of his own subordinates, John B. Hood, was actively encouraging Bragg and Davis. On April 13 Hood, who was born in Kentucky but enlisted from Texas, wrote to the president: "I am sorry to inform you that I have done all in my power to induce General Johnston to accept the proposition you made to move forward. He will not consent, as he desires the troops to be sent here, and it be left to him as to what use shall be made of them. I regret this exceedingly, as my heart was fixed on going to the front and regaining Tennessee and Kentucky."[3]

A. H. Cole, who was responsible for the transportation of the Army of Tennessee, contradicted Hood. In a letter of April 11, he warned the Confederate inspector general of transportation, "We must get some aid from North Carolina for this army, if it is the policy of the Government for it to move."[4]

As late as May 2, Bragg seemed to have doubted that Sherman and his armies would take the offensive and move into Georgia. Federals, he wrote, were probably making a demonstration to conceal their real intentions.

Termed "a temperamental enigma" by at least one modern analyst, the small general whose whiskers framed "a wedge-shaped face" had no intention of moving into hostile territory until he was sure he had adequate strength to do so. Instead of concentrating on the invasion of Tennessee, Johnston took action on two fronts at once. Although he gave his men latitude to relax and play, he showed himself to be a severe disciplinarian and a critical analyst of his officers.

Once during a winter storm, Confederate soldiers had divided themselves into opposing battalions and engaged in furious snowball fights. Men of the Thirty-ninth Alabama Regiment even formed a line of battle and, led by a colonel, marched on their foes "with colors flying." During winter afternoons, many soldiers engaged in a gander pull—trying to snatch the head from a goose whose neck had been well greased.

Meanwhile, massive reenlistment of those whose terms of service were about to expire was pursued with great success. In postwar years, a number of units claimed to have been first to respond to Johnston's call. Regardless of whether or not men under Brig. Gen. Otho Strahl led the movement, thousands who were eligible to go home signed up for the duration.[5]

Admiration for Johnston and his record was so great that even his stern treatment of deserters failed to halt the tide of reenlistment. Years afterward, B. L. Ridley wrote:

> The scene above all that impressed me was the shooting of fifteen deserters. . . . Early in the morning a detail from the provost guard marched to Gen. [Alexander P.] Stewart's headquarters, stacked their arms and left.
>
> Staff officers were ordered to load the guns for their execution in their divisions, half with blank cartridges and the other half buck and ball. After this was done the guns were so changed that those who had loaded them could not tell the loaded from those with blank cartridges. The detail then returned and took them. . . .
>
> Doomed men were brought out, and to the tune of the "dead march" were conducted around the square, an ambulance following with their coffins. Poor fellows knelt at the foot of the graves dug for them, and the guards fired. . . .
>
> In some commands the guards made a "botch" of their work, and had to shoot the doomed men twice.[6]

While demonstrating to dispirited men that they would risk their lives by trying to desert, Johnston induced entire companies to reenlist. As a result, he managed to hold in the Army of Tennessee an estimated forty thousand effectives, that is, soldiers present and healthy enough to fight. Leonidas Polk was expected to arrive soon with another fifteen thousand men of the Army of Mississippi. Confederate strength would then be approximately two-thirds as great as that of Sherman's forces converging upon Chattanooga.

Oral tradition says that one of Johnston's officers joyfully concluded, "If two butternuts can't whip any three Yankees that were ever born, we ought to stack our rifles and go home."

Had anyone inquired of him, Johnston probably would have said that the capability of butternuts was far from uniform. Writing to Bragg on the last day of March, he gloomily insisted: "I was not favorably impressed by the little I saw of our officers [artillery]. They exhibited a childish eagerness to discharge their pieces. . . . We have no officer who has ever commanded more than twelve guns; I mean, of course, artillery officers."[7]

Despite repeated urging from Richmond, Johnston stubbornly refused to move into Tennessee until he had what he considered to be an adequate force.[8] Davis and Bragg wrote with optimism about providing him with seventy-five thousand men but repeatedly failed to take steps that would enable such a buildup. As a result, the president received tactfully phrased messages informing him that the Army of Tennessee would hold its entrenched position in and around Dalton and wait for the Federals to strike. In retrospect, Johnston believed that additional troops would have made it possible for him to win a major battle near Dalton and then pursue his foes into Tennessee.

Near Knoxville, Gen. James "Pete" Longstreet was in command of two divisions facing forces under Ambrose E. Burnside. Perhaps because the Federal leader had been dubbed "a notorious bungler," Longstreet was more optimistic than Johnston. His forces were woefully short of food and his horses were hungry, he told Richmond on March 19. Still, he believed, "If our armies can take the initiative in the spring campaign they can march into Kentucky with but little trouble and finish the war in this year."[9]

STUDYING THE intelligence gathered by his scouts and crude maps of the region, Sherman soon learned that his foes were heavily entrenched in Dalton. Worse, they were established in a broad valley that lay behind a group of small mountains. Any movement toward them from the general direction of the Chickamauga battlefield, roughly halfway between Chattanooga and the Confederate bastion, would find them protected by Rocky Face Ridge.

The single-track Western and Atlantic Railroad, snaking its way from Chattanooga, Mill Creek, and a rough wagon trail ran through the only large gap in the ridge: Buzzard Roost. Though Grant never saw the place, years later he vividly recalled the reports he had read about it. They described the manner in which hastily built dams had converted much of the valley of Mill Creek into a lake. Water of unknown depth would impede movement through both Buzzard Roost and Mill Creek Gaps. Even Dug Gap, a smaller passage about five miles south of Dalton, might be affected.[10]

Newspaper correspondents, most of whose dispatches were unsigned, agreed that "natural advantages" and the Confederates' defensive works placed attackers at great risk.[11] Sherman described the situation more bluntly. In a telegram to Thomas, he stressed, "Your troops cannot take Rocky Face Ridge, and also the attempt to put our columns into the jaws of Buzzard Roost would be fatal to us."[12]

In a private and confidential letter, without mentioning possible future action against Atlanta, Grant had given directions to Sherman: "I propose for you to move against Johnston's army, to break it up and to get into the interior of the enemy's country as far as you can, inflicting all the damage you can against their war resources."[13]

Dalton was far too strong for Sherman to risk a frontal attack; he would have to try to flank the enemy. To do so, he needed to know a great deal more about the terrain immediately south of Dalton. An ungraded pass through the rugged little mountains was essential; perhaps Snake Creek Gap.

Should that gap prove suitable for passage of the Army of the Cumberland, by far Sherman's most powerful force, his commanders still would be handicapped by inadequate maps of country intimately familiar to the enemy. They'd need to locate churches such as Salem, Pea Vine, Stone, and Rock Spring.[14] Grist mills—the nearest thing the immediate vicinity had to industry—would be important landmarks, provided the scouts could find those operated by such families as the Thatchers, Ellidges, Burkes, and Gordons.[15]

Even solitary farmhouses would have to be added to maps so that troop positions would be known. This would require officers to find the residences of the Widow Reed, Mrs. Swain, and farms operated by Justis, Thornton, Ray, Smith, Kincannon, and Dr. Millbanks. Dogwood Valley and Trickum Road were shown on some maps, but the location of the Pocket Road was not.[16]

Soon Sherman would find himself directing McPherson to encamp "about the head of Middle Chickamauga, near the word 'Gordon' on [the map showing] the Tavern road." It would become important, if not essential, to know whether to head toward Villanow by way of Gordon's Gap or Ship's Gap. Even if a road was shown on a map, that didn't mean it might not be impassable following the spring rains.[17]

Perhaps Johnston would risk sending his Army of Tennessee into all-out battle; that would be the best alternative from the Federal viewpoint. If he refused to accept the challenge and launch an attack, Federal armies could not risk an all-out assault upon Dalton from the northwest. They'd simply have to feint while moving around the fortified town, trying to get between the Confederate forces and the heavily wooded country to the south. Clearly, the objective assigned to Sherman during his conference with Grant could not be achieved in a matter of days.

4

Ready to Destroy Joe Johnston

JAMES B. MCPHERSON studied the eyes of his superior and friend. Like others who knew Sherman well, the commander of the Army of the Tennessee was fascinated by their color. It was often impossible to decide whether they were black or dark blue, dark brown or hazel. At Huntsville, Alabama, late in March 1864, they seemed literally to dance in their sockets as the man second only to Grant gave animated instructions concerning the Federal campaign soon to start.

Back in Tennessee, Sherman had stopped at Chattanooga long enough to lay out for Maj. Gen. George H. Thomas the future plans for the Army of the Cumberland. From Chattanooga, Sherman paid a quick visit to Knoxville to brief Maj. Gen. John M. Schofield, who headed the Army of the Ohio.

Plans for the immediate future were outlined in detail, while only broad objectives for the long-range future were briefly sketched. All three Federal armies were scheduled to come together at or near Chattanooga no later than the third week of April.

Back at his Nashville headquarters on April 2, but planning soon to make Chattanooga his base, Sherman put everything else aside in order to concentrate upon his most crucial need. He'd soon be able to put 98,797 men into the field, but he was not sure of having supplies and rations for them,[1] plus corn and forage for their 35,000 horses and mules.

Although facing tremendous obstacles, Sherman was supremely confident. During April, he wrote, he would accumulate at Decatur,

Alabama, and at Chattanooga "a surplus of seventy days' provisions and forage" for his entire force.[2] In his optimism, he ignored reports saying that in some parts of Tennessee there was such a shortage of "horses, forage, and commissary supplies" that Union troops found themselves "eking out a miserable existence anxiously awaiting relief."[3]

He hoped that Mobile would soon fall so that the Alabama River could become his supply line. Should this not happen, he had another option that he recorded in detail:

> Georgia has a million of inhabitants. If they can live, we should not starve. If the enemy interrupt my communications, I will be absolved from all obligations to subsist on our own resources, *but will feel perfectly justified in taking whatever and whenever I can.* [Emphasis added.]
>
> I will inspire my command, if successful, with my feeling that beef and salt are all that is absolutely necessary to life, and parched corn fed General [Andrew] Jackson's army once on that very ground.[4]

Facing a critical shortage of strong and healthy animals, before the end of April he found himself taking them wherever they could be found. "I must imitate [Nathan Bedford] Forrest's example, and help myself," he informed Washington. "I began here [Nashville] yesterday, and at once have got here 1,000 good horses."[5]

Col. William B. Stokes of the Fifth Tennessee Cavalry was provided with a list of four counties where horses were said to be plentiful. "These must be taken without exception, until you are fully provided," he was instructed.

A shipment of 3,000 mules went to him from St. Louis,[6] but his own raid upon Meridian, Mississippi, had left that state "severely exhausted of horses." From Washington he learned, "Operations last fall and winter destroyed or broke down in Tennessee and Georgia no less than 30,000 draft animals and an unknown number of cavalry horses."[7]

In this dilemma, Sherman fell back upon brief and specific orders from Grant whose telegram directed: "We must equip the best we can and do without what cannot be got. . . . Dismount quartermasters's employees, orderlies, infantry officers, and all unauthorized persons at every station, and take their horses to mount the cavalry."[8]

Responding to a proposal that horses be driven from Kentucky to Tennessee, along with corn-bearing mules, S. D. Sturgis gave a reasoned reply. A mule, he pointed out, can't carry a load of over 240 pounds but eats at least 12 pounds per day. Since a round trip would require at least 20 days, every mule sent with a load of corn would add to shortages in and about Chattanooga. Since roads were "in most terrific condition" and expected to get worse because of spring rains, he said horses sent to Tennessee from the Blue Grass State "would arrive already broken down."[9] To make matters worse, forage was already scarce in the middle and eastern sections of the state.

Unless all Alabama could be quickly mastered, Sherman would have no great river to serve as an artery of transportation. Nevertheless, one supply route still lay open, he assured his aides. Therefore he would create supply depots at Nashville and Chattanooga—considered to be the most vital points—and Huntsville and Decatur in Alabama.[10] While warehouses were being constructed, he would devote much of his attention to the railroads that he expected to fill them.

Locomotives and boxcars had for months constituted the lifeline for animals used by Federal forces in the region. During the five months that began on November 1, one line had shipped 138,000 bushels of corn from Louisville along with 572,000 bushels of oats, and 16,000 tons of hay.[11]

This flow of supplies, called a mere trickle by Sherman, must and would be doubled and redoubled, he said. With the backing of the railroad's president, he took over the Louisville and Nashville Railroad. Single-track rails that stretched 335 miles from Chattanooga to Louisville had to be made to transport a minimum of 1,300 tons of rations, forage, and supplies every twenty-four hours.

"Even with this calculation," Sherman later wrote, "we could not afford to bring forward hay for the horses and mules, nor more than five pounds of oats or corn per day for each animal." He could take risks concerning forage, he believed, because he "expected to find wheat and corn fields, and a good deal of grass, as we advanced into Georgia."

When the 138-mile distance from Louisville to Cincinnati was added, Sherman calculated that he was "in supreme control" of what he called a "single stem of a railroad" that stretched for 473 miles. Since lines within his jurisdiction didn't have enough cars to do the job, he seized those that entered it from the north.

By the time he was approaching his transportation goal, he said that he regularly saw on his tracks under his jurisdiction boxcars carrying such labels as: "'Pittsburg & Fort Wayne,' 'Delaware & Lackawanna,' 'Baltimore & Ohio,' and the names of almost every [other] railroad north of the Ohio River." As a result, Allan Nevins called Sherman's campaign into Georgia the "first great railroad war of world history."

Getting enough locomotives pulling sufficiently loaded cars was an essential first step, but it did not complete the task faced by the commander of the Department of the Mississippi. Throughout Tennessee and much of Kentucky his men built blockhouses and entrenchments at bridges and tunnels. Lt. Col. W. E. Merrill, an engineer in the Army of the Cumberland, helped to design and erect many of these defensive positions. He later wrote that no other army, Federal or Confederate, "acquired so great an experience in the art of defending railroads through hostile territory."

At intervals of about eight miles, sidings were erected and a telegraph operator was assigned to each to expedite the flow of traffic and to warn of impending Confederate attacks.

While the blockhouses were being constructed, loaded boxcars rolled south twenty-four hours a day; empty cars returned north. Late in April, Sherman reported to Grant: "I have materially increased the number of cars daily. When I got here they ran from 65 to 80 per day. Yesterday the report was 193, to-day 134, and my estimate of 145 per day will give us daily [a surplus of] a day's accumulation."[12]

By May 1 that "accumulation" was highly visible; new warehouses at Nashville bulged with "five months' supplies of all kinds" for one hundred thousand men plus thirty-five thousand horses and mules.[13]

Beef was considered an essential part of a fighting man's diet, but it was seldom transported by rail or stockpiled in warehouses. Animals were driven to concentration points on foot and nearly every corps had its own drove of them. In St. Louis a commissary officer protested that cattle to be shipped by water from Cairo, Illinois, would cost "7 cents gross." Sherman fired one of his typically brusque telegrams in reply: "The price is nothing. I want the Army of the Tennessee to have beef-cattle on the hoof at or near Huntsville by May 1. The easiest way is to send them up to Clifton, on the Tennessee, and drive across. They should come up the Tennessee at the same time with the troops from Cairo."[14]

From Cincinnati he simultaneously demanded "beef cattle on the hoof" in number sufficient "for a month's supply for 75,000 men." Since that would take quite a bit of doing, he authorized Col. Charles L. Kilburn to "order what is necessary in my name."[15]

AT DALTON, Johnston had his own problems with supplies, but he had the advantage of the Western and Atlantic Railroad as a conduit from the heartland of Georgia. During 1863 central depots in Richmond had relied on Georgia corn since Virginia was producing very little of it.[16] Near Knoxville, forage for both draft animals and Confederate cavalry mounts was not to be found.

Supplies not readily available included "knapsacks, bayonets, small-arms implements, navy-pistol cartridges, spurs, and harness leather." An estimated six thousand men of the Army of Tennessee had no shoes, and nowhere could makers possibly produce them fast enough to meet the demand.[17]

In the Confederate camps food was abundant, however. Officers of the adjutant general and inspector general's offices ruled that "85,000 rations daily are more than necessary for the subsistence" of the Army of Tennessee.[18] By the middle of April, men bracing to meet the Federal onslaught had ten days' reserve at Dalton.

FIGHTING MEN in gray and in blue would usually be well fed, and most of the latter would be well shod. Some, however, began to wonder what would happen to civilians in the areas that were already contested or likely soon to be.

Foraging, sometimes disguised under the label of "impressment," was already a standard course of action among both forces. During the recent Meridian campaign, many plantations had been so "completely stripped of everything" by Union soldiers that McPherson expressed sympathy for the destitute. In East Tennessee, "both man and beast" had relied largely upon "foraging" for their necessities.

Sherman's calculations concerning accumulated supplies did not take into account the corn, oats, and hay his animals would need. He had already decided to feed them largely from the crops growing in enemy territory. As he had done in Mississippi, he would seize horses and mules wherever they were found. In addition to augmenting his own strength, this policy afforded a special kind of satisfaction that the red-bearded commander remembered with satisfaction many years later. Persons who permitted "their country to be used by the public enemy" were getting a dose of strong medicine designed to persuade them to abandon the Confederate cause.[19]

In Richmond, Quartermaster General A. R. Lawton was perturbed by Sherman's high-handed railroad seizures. With passenger trains no longer running, he wanted to know "what becomes of the furloughed soldiers, conscripts, &c., coming into the army every day."[20]

At his Chattanooga base, the commander of the Division of the Mississippi had little interest in civilians, regardless of whether they were secessionists or Unionists. Persons not in uniform were systematically banned from railroad cars. This policy extended even to workers of the U.S. Sanitary Commission and other societies formed to aid Union soldiers.

East Tennessee, perhaps including more Unionists than any other region within the Confederacy, had largely depended upon the military for food. In a single month, nearly three thousand rations were purchased from Federal warehouses at Chattanooga and Nashville alone. Twice as much food was issued to indigent families and individuals during the same period.[21]

Early in the first week of April, Sherman "made orders to stop all civil business and freight, and the cars to be devoted exclusively to dead freight."[22] Two weeks later, a blunt directive was more specific. "It is idle for us to be pushing forward subsistence stores if they are lavished and expended upon any persons except they belong to the army proper," the document concluded.[23]

Lincoln, busy planning a political campaign for an uphill fight that might bring him a second term in office, found time to interject his views concerning this policy. To Sherman, a telegram emphasized that he was not interfering with military affairs. He said that he would, however, be made glad by "anything you can do consistently with those [military] operations for those suffering people."[24]

Probably with his hackles raised, the commander of the Union's second strongest force responded at length from a post "in the Field, Chattanooga." He retorted:

> We have worked hard with the best talent of the country, and it is demonstrated that the railroad cannot supply the army and the people too. One or the other must quit, and the army don't intend to, unless Joe Johnston makes us. . . .
>
> I will not change my order, and I beg of you to be satisfied that the clamor is partly humbug; and to test it, I advise you to tell the bearers of the appeal to hurry to Kentucky and make up a caravan of cattle and wagons and come over the mountains by Cumberland Gap. . . .
>
> Every man who is willing to fight and work gets a full ration, and all who won't fight or work should go away, and we offer them free passage in the cars.[25]

Saying that his crews needed the iron in order to repair the Nashville and Chattanooga Railroad, Sherman ordered the confiscation of the rails of the Paducah line. Gov. Thomas E. Bramlette voiced a strong protest. To the Kentucky executive, the man preparing to move into Georgia replied, "My experience convinces me that the citizens of Paducah, almost to a man, are disloyal and entitled to no favors from the government."[26]

Earlier having been denounced publicly as insane, Sherman was now obsessed with a cluster of interwoven goals. Neither hungry civilians nor worn-out horses nor dilapidated railroads would make him miss the timetable that Grant would soon frame. Many of the men in Alabama would have to march to Chattanooga on foot.[27] "I want everybody here possible on the 5th of May," he informed his subordinates after having earlier circulated an order to move on May 1.[28]

Among four objectives that Sherman tried always to keep in mind, the overwhelming defeat of the Army of Tennessee took precedence. Grant was equally concerned, of course, about smashing the Army of Northern Virginia.[29] A dual victory would surely bring the South to its knees.

A major battle at Dalton was just what the red-haired Federal commander wanted, though he didn't intend to be in such a hurry that he might make a costly mistake.[30] While dealing with Johnston and his forces, Sherman also expected to follow another of Grant's instructions. "If the enemy in your front shows signs of joining Lee," the lieutenant general ordered from Virginia, "follow him up to the full extent of your ability. I will prevent the concentration of Lee upon your front, if it is in the power of this army to do it."[31]

Never forgetting Johnston or Grant, Sherman expected to destroy a significant portion of the Confederacy's resources. This special kind of punishment would bring him the same satisfaction he experienced earlier in Mississippi. From Vicksburg he had come close to self-righteousness as he expounded at length upon his philosophy of war:

> Treatment of inhabitants known or suspected to be hostile or "secesh" . . . is the most difficult business of our army as it advances and occupies the Southern country. It is almost impossible to lay down rules. . . .
>
> If any one comes out into the public streets and creates disorder, he or she should be punished, restrained, or banished. . . .

> [Residents of the South] have appealed to war and must abide by its rules and laws. . . .
>
> The Government of the United States has in North Alabama any and all rights which they choose to enforce in war—to take their lives, their homes, their everything—because they cannot deny that war exists there, and war is simply power unrestrained by constitution or compact. . . .
>
> Satan and the rebellious saints of Heaven were allowed a continuous existence in hell merely to swell their just punishment. To such as would rebel against a Government so mild and just as ours was in peace, a punishment equal would not be unjust.[32]

As a result of planned mutual protection, it was expected that victorious Federal forces would "unite for a final consummation" of the conflict. Sherman's complex goal therefore had four constituent parts: (1) a decisive victory over the Army of Tennessee, (2) protection of Grant, (3) punishment of rebellious citizens, and (4) union of the victorious Federal bodies.

During the first four months of 1864, hundreds of Federal reports were filed and thousands of messages were exchanged. Mobile, Memphis, Huntsville, Decatur, and other cities far from Chattanooga rated frequent mention while references to Atlanta were rare and terse. Sherman's four-pronged consuming goal did not as yet include the Gate City of the South as a significant target.[33]

5

Orderly Withdrawal in Lieu of All-out Combat

HIS GOATEE and sideburns led some of Joseph E. Johnston's men to call him "the Gamecock," despite the fact that his hair was turning gray. On Sunday, May 1, 1864, he preferred to think of himself as a Virginia gentleman rather than as a Confederate rooster about to be equipped with gaffs before entering a Federal pit. Bowing graciously to one woman after another who had gathered at his request, he tapped for silence. Tersely but firmly, he informed the officers' wives that all of them had to leave for Atlanta no later than Tuesday.

No explanation was needed or offered; throughout the Confederate camp everyone knew that the hills would soon be swarming with Union troops. Many of Johnston's men vowed that they were ready to fight; a vocal minority insisted that they were itching for the action to start. Most were eager to avenge the humiliating defeat suffered under Bragg at nearby Missionary Ridge.

SHERMAN REACHED Chattanooga on May 2. A newspaper correspondent exulted that his arrival "gave every division of the army a mysterious impulse." There was no mystery about the readiness of his troops to go into action on the following day, which initially had been designated by Grant as the date on which he would cross the Rapidan River and Sherman would head toward the Oostenaula.[1]

Six hundred miles to the north, Grant acted after a forty-eight-hour delay. When he learned of the new schedule on May 4, Sherman wrote to his wife, "We are now moving. I will go to Ringgold tomorrow, and will then be within five miles of the enemy."[2] Ellen Ewing Sherman may have known that the tiny village was named for a Georgian who had died at Palo Alto, the first battle of the Mexican War. None of her surviving correspondence indicates that she also realized that it had been occupied by Confederates just six weeks earlier.

Standing on the Western and Atlantic Railroad near the health resort of Catoosa Springs, Ringgold was barely visible from a distance of two miles. Three-fourths of the land in the surrounding countryside was covered with dense growths of oaks, hickories, poplars, and pines.

Prior to 1864 the hamlet had only one claim to fame. When Bragg was in full retreat after the debacle at Missionary Ridge, one of his subordinates halted a division near Ringgold. Fighting defensively at Taylor's Ridge, Patrick R. Cleburne's men trounced the pursuing Federals under Joseph E. "Fighting Joe" Hooker.

Ringgold was about to gain new prominence. All three of George H. Thomas's corps were encamped near the village by May 4. It was from this point that skirmishers moved upon Tunnel Hill and fired the first shots signaling that a new invasion of Georgia was under way. More importantly, Sherman established his headquarters in the village and later used it as a supply depot.

When Grant set May 5 as the new date for the simultaneous action of Federal forces in the North and in the South, troops would be

LIBRARY OF CONGRESS

A view of Chattanooga from the north, the assembly point for the invasion of Georgia.

Ringgold, Georgia, the site of the first fighting of the invasion and the initial engagement between Sherman and Johnston.

expected to pull out of Culpepper, Virginia, and Ringgold at about the same time.[3] Sherman had earlier gone on record as considering their "common plan, converging on a common center" to constitute "enlightened war."[4]

His officers were positive that the complicated two-pronged attack would be executed precisely as planned. One of them, J. L. Donaldson, wrote to Quartermaster General Montgomery C. Meigs, "Sherman will move if he has to eat his mules [to do so]."

Sherman's basic strategy was developed and communicated long before the first shot was fired. Each of his three armies would be responsible for guarding its own communications. Men in regiments whose terms of service were about to expire would usually be chosen for such guard duty. With about forty-five thousand men, the Army of the Cumberland under Thomas would "move straight on Johnston." Schofield and the thirteen-thousand-man Army of the Ohio would take the left of the line. McPherson's Army of the Tennessee, with at least twenty thousand effectives, would be on the right. This pattern proved to be so effective that as they moved south it was seldom altered, and then only briefly.

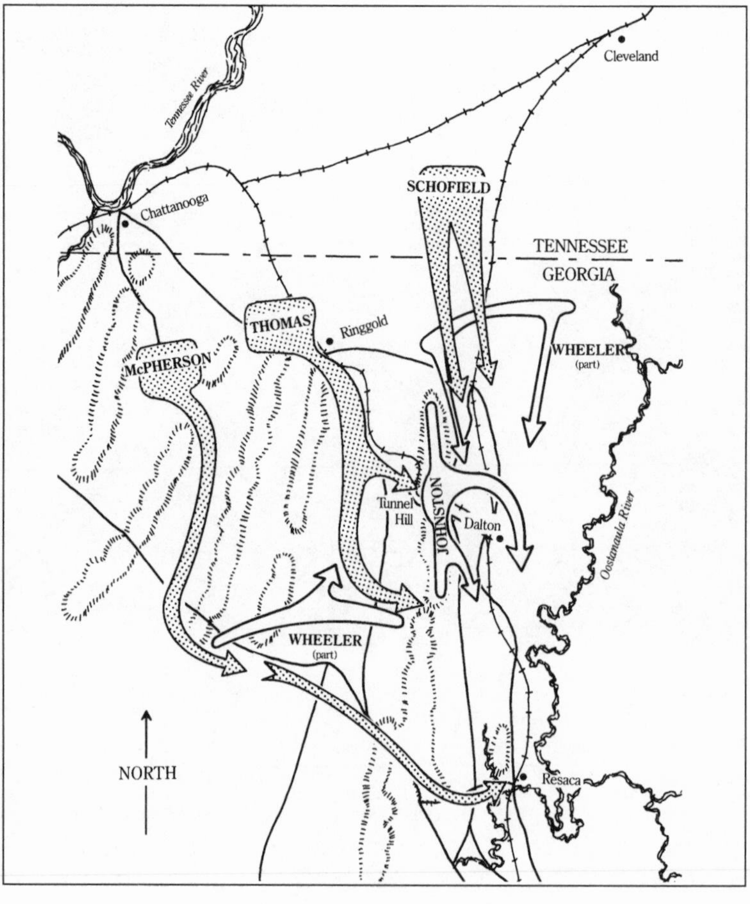

Union forces moved along a three-pronged front, while Wheeler's cavalry tried to protect Johnston's flanks.

HISTORIANS OF the Civil War have not agreed in their efforts to devise a precise terminology to describe the military action in Georgia and elsewhere during 1861–65. As a result, literature concerning the campaign launched against the Army of Tennessee deals with skirmishes, demonstrations, engagements, and operations in addition to battles. It is difficult or impossible to say definitively whether the thirty-mile Federal move against Dalton from Chattanooga constituted a "significant action" or "a minor battle."

The initial resistance by Confederates was so slight that some participants regarded it as a skirmish. Whatever it is called, it took place close to the hole blasted through a small mountain for the Western and Atlantic Railroad. Aptly named Tunnel Hill, for weeks it had been guarded by cavalry under the command of Joseph "Fightin' Joe" Wheeler. When overwhelming forces in blue drew near, the exchange of shots resulted in some casualties. To Wheeler's lifelong regret, his men quickly fell back to Dalton. Their withdrawal was disorganized and they failed to attempt to blow up the tunnel and thus disable the railroad on which their foes were dependent.

If Wheeler was humiliated, Sherman was disappointed. While approaching the site on May 8 he paused long enough to let Washington know his sentiments: "I hope Johnston will fight here, instead of drawing me far down into Georgia."[5] He wanted quick and decisive action, perhaps dealing a deathblow to the Army of Tennessee immediately. As a result, the Federals who made up the largest army left Catoosa Springs with specific orders:

> Major-General Thomas requests that when we move from this place toward the enemy that it be done with the least possible number of wagons.
>
> To carry out this request, there will be allowed one wagon each to corps, division, and brigade headquarters. A small supply train, sufficient for two days' forage and rations, ammunition train, and the wagons with tools, will constitute the train for the march. The rest of the wagon train will move to Ringgold, via Parker's Gap, filled with rations and forage at that place, and be ready for further orders.[6]

SIMILAR INSTRUCTIONS went to the commanders throughout the Federal force. Only wagons loaded with ammunition would accompany troops in abundance.

Sherman did not ask his men to do anything he was unwilling to do. "My entire headquarters transportation is one wagon for myself, aides, officers, clerks, and orderlies," he informed Washington. "I think that is as low down as we can get until we get flat broke." Apparently in a jovial and expansive mood, he explained his unusual actions:

> Soldiering as we have been doing for the past two years, with such trains and impediments, has been a farce, and nothing but absolute poverty will cure it.
>
> I will be glad to hear Uncle Sam say "we cannot afford this and that—you must gather your own grub and wagons, and bivouac and fight, not for pay but for self-existence."

> Old men as auditors can control the papers to the rear, but the causes are here.[7]

In keeping with the philosophy of their commander, men of the Fourteenth Corps left Ringgold on May 6 with three days' worth of cooked and five days' of uncooked rations. Their comrades in the artillery units of the Army of the Ohio took along only two days' forage for their animals—piled upon caissons. Officers and men of this army were allowed rations for four days.[8] Commanders were told: "Not a tent will be taken with the army, and officers will govern themselves accordingly. All surplus baggage must be thrown out and disposed of at once."

McPherson took an additional step calculated to guarantee the swift movement of his men. A special circular, addressed simply to "Soldiers of the Army of the Tennessee," concluded with the order: "If any of your comrades fall wounded do not leave the ranks to take them to the rear; an ample corps of men with stretchers and ambulances will follow close behind you to pick up the wounded. . . . Many a regiment on the battlefield has been sadly reduced in numbers at the critical moment by men leaving ranks to take wounded to the rear."[9]

In Virginia, the battle of the Wilderness began while Sherman was moving toward Dalton half-believing that Johnston might come out of his lair to stage an attack. Soon Lee and the Army of Northern Virginia would convince Grant that it was easier to frame a grand plan than to execute it.

Sherman, who seemed almost casual in his readiness to expose himself to Confederate fire, knew before he reached Rocky Face Ridge that he would not attempt a major assault. Still he must seem to be willing to have his men scale this immense natural fortification, whose top he described as "a perfect couteau, knife edge, a sharp ridge."[10] If he did not put up a bold front that would persuade Johnston that he expected to move directly upon Dalton, any flanking movement he might attempt would prove futile.

One newspaper correspondent was awed by the rocky barrier faced by the Federals. It stretched from about eight miles northwest of Dalton to a dozen or so miles south of the town and military camp, with few gaps or passes. On Wednesday, May 11, he wrote: "The verdant, but treacherous ridges of Buzzard Roost are dim and gloomy through the cold and clouded atmosphere. . . . I cannot but name a wish that God grant that the order for assault may not be given. My heart beats faster at the bare thought of standing near and gazing on it, convinced as I am that all the armies ever marshalled could not successfully storm the position if occupied by thirty thousand determined men."[11]

No general in blue believed that thirty thousand Confederates were massed upon the heights. According to Albert Smith, who was captured on May 8, Johnston had eleven thousand men posted in Buzzard Roost Gap. Smith may have been sent to surrender in order to exaggerate; Confederate accounts indicate that the place was lightly guarded.

Schofield later estimated, "One thousand men would be a strong garrison for the works I saw."[12] Andrew M. Sea, serving with a Confederate artillery company posted at the ridge, said that their orders were explicit: "'Fight them to the muzzle of the guns,' [which] simply meant to die or be captured in your tracks; sacrifice yourselves and guns to gain a little time, and that, too, absolutely without support."[13]

Whatever their number, the Confederates were short of ammunition or were conserving it for future use. Several eyewitnesses reported that the Southerners bombarded the Federals with rocks, clubs, and logs. Natural obstructions and artificial ones erected by the defenders

LIBRARY OF CONGRESS

Buzzard's Roost Gap was the primary passage through the North Georgia mountains. While McPherson began to flank Johnston at Snake Creek Gap, Thomas and Schofield forced Wheeler's cavalry to abandon Buzzard's Roost.

reduced the pace of the "Ohio Tigers," the Twenty-fifth Ohio Regiment, to half a mile an hour.

Sherman wished to encourage his men and enhance the impression that he intended to make this the point of his full-scale assault. Hence he was conspicuous on horseback, unprotected from the enemy at Buzzard Roost, directing operations personally. The Southerners could hardly fail to see him.

Federal generals had been instructed not to waste lives in all-out charges against entrenchments, but some could not control their men. As a result, skirmishes became pitched battles on little more basis than the unbridled zeal of the troops and the subordinate commanders.

In this situation, McPherson's exhortations concerning the wounded were not heeded. When the fray ended, "a long row of dead men [were] laid out for burial near the foot of the ridge." They represented only a fraction of casualties, however, according to a newspaper report: "In front of Logan's line even more ghastly sights were seen than on the enemy's right. The dead that lay here had lain for two days, and were badly swollen. They were lying in the ditches, on the knolls near the works, in the ravines, in every conceivable place, and in every possible shape."

While carnage prevailed at Rocky Face Ridge, McPherson and his Army of the Tennessee were racing toward Snake Creek Gap, about a dozen miles to the southwest. They hoped to penetrate the broad valley below Dalton in order to move upon the unfortified south side of Johnston's camp.

The Confederate commander was not then aware of the Federal move to flank him. Later, however, he was censured for having failed to attack at Rocky Face. Johnston's defense consisted of a single sentence: "Napoleon once said, the General who suffers his communications to be cut deserves to be shot."

Sherman, who pinned his hopes upon McPherson while leading the assault above Dalton himself, was making good upon a dual promise. Clearly, he was keeping Johnston so occupied that he couldn't possibly send any part of his army against Grant. Like Grant, he was also hammering continuously against the "armed force of the enemy and his resources."[14] How effective his hammering and the resultant Confederate busyness would be, only time would reveal.

As late as May 11, the Federal commander was convinced that Johnston "can't afford to abandon Dalton for he has fixed it up so nice for us, and he observes we are close at hand waiting for him to quit."[15] Unwilling to stage a full-scale frontal assault but hoping for a fight to the finish somewhere near his opponent's base,[16] Sherman could not devote all of his time and energy to Johnston and Dalton.

The Division of the Mississippi extended from Kentucky through Tennessee and west to Arkansas. During the week in which he led his troops into Georgia, Sherman and his aides dealt with a flood of messages from and to Alabama: Decatur, Florence, Huntsville, Athens, Larkinsville, and Tuscaloosa.[17]

Vexatious questions or simple problems arose in Tennessee at Athens, Charleston, Clifton, Prospect, Pulaski, and Nashville.[18] Coming as they did after his departure from the state, these matters demanded immediate attention. In Mississippi, Columbus remained a trouble spot; so did the city of the same name in Kentucky. Even Cairo, Illinois, could not be neglected for a single week.[19]

Meanwhile, it was of utmost importance to learn as much as possible about Grant's advance in Virginia. Not until May 9 was Sherman heartened by word that during his movement upon Dalton, Grant had pursued Lee for ten miles. He was already familiar with Grant's pledge to "fight Lee between Culpeper and Richmond if he would stand." Not until long afterward did he learn that during three days in the Wilderness, Grant lost more than eighteen thousand men while Lee's casualties were eleven thousand.[20]

It was impossible to get an accurate count of the dead and wounded along the eleven-mile Federal front before Dalton. Compared with the slaughter in the Wilderness, however, the Georgia total was very small. One factor in the dual equation was sometimes overlooked in the heat of battle. Grant and Sherman could "afford" their losses; Lee and Johnston could not.

Still, Sherman was surprised to learn about 1:00 A.M. on May 12 that his foes seemed to be pulling out of Dalton. Well before daybreak the movement was confirmed. O. O. Howard and his men entered the mountainous town about 9:00 A.M. on May 13 and ruefully reported that they discovered "nary a man in a gray uniform."[21]

Deeply disappointed that his quarry seemed to have slipped through the net prepared for him, Sherman decided to "interpose between Dalton and Resaca," an estimated fourteen miles below the abandoned camp. He had already moved more than thirty miles from Chattanooga but could not claim victory. Should Confederates retreat to the east, he was sure that his own forces would have an advantage over them.[22] If they moved in a different direction, the entire situation might be altered.

Sherman realized that he faced a situation he had hoped to avoid. It was now clear that Johnston, a skilled and cautious strategist, wouldn't risk sacrificing the Army of Tennessee if he could help it. Having failed in their objective of scoring a smashing victory as the climax of a brief campaign, Federal forces must now pursue the enemy somewhat deeper into Georgia.

Part 2

Slugging It Out, Mile by Mile

6

Over the Oostenaula

LEANING FORWARD from his railroad car seat to chat with John Bell Hood, fifty-eight-year-old Leonidas Polk was more comfortable than he had been for days. He had pushed his Army of Mississippi mercilessly to bring William W. Loring's division to Resaca on the evening of May 11. This meant that the head of the Episcopal Church in Louisiana, who wore the insignia of a Confederate lieutenant general, was not too late to help upset the plans of Grant and Sherman.

During a jolting eighteen-mile ride to Dalton, Hood lapsed into silence. One arm, useless after a wound at Gettysburg, dangled much of the time. A state-of-the-art cork leg made in France protruded from the tip of his right trousers leg. Polk had watched aides lift the heavily bearded thirty-two-year-old commander into the saddle and strap him in place. Because there was a danger that his artificial leg might be hit during an exchange of fire, Hood usually carried along a two-thousand-dollar spare that was tied to his saddle.

For the youthful Kentuckian as well as for Polk, their slow railway ride northward meant relaxation that could never be achieved on horseback, even by a rider with two good arms and two sound legs. Breaking their silence, Hood blurted out a request. He had for some time wanted to be baptized, he said, and would like for his comrade in arms to perform the ceremony as soon as possible. Taken by surprise, the only bishop to become a general in either of the opposing forces expressed pleased assent. He'd be glad to officiate just as soon as he reported to Joseph E. Johnston, he said.

It was nearly midnight before Polk and a few members of his staff reached Hood's headquarters. Absolved from kneeling because of his handicap, the baptismal candidate shook his head when given permission to remain seated. Pulling himself erect, he stood while the bishop scooped up consecrated water—reputedly from a horse bucket commandeered for duty as a font. Once the sacred formula was uttered, naming the handicapped commander as "a child of grace," even in dim candlelight subordinates saw his face suddenly become radiant.

There is no record that either of the principals or any of their staff members suggested that Hood might meet his maker the following day, Thursday. Soon, however, Joseph E. Johnston's wife learned that one lieutenant general had received baptism from another. She immediately wrote a hasty note to Polk in which she said: "General Johnston has never been baptized. It is the dearest wish of my heart that he should be, and that you should perform the ceremony would be a great gratification to me. I have written to him on the subject, and am sure he only waits your leisure."

During the following week, with the sound of Federal guns heard faintly from a distance, North Georgia was the site of the second baptism of a general by a general.

SHERMAN KNEW nothing of these events until long afterward. How he would have reacted, had he heard the news at the time, remains—like much concerning Grant's co-commander—a matter of conjecture.

His official reports and personal letters make it clear that he loathed newspaper correspondents, but he never explained his attitude. An order issued a few days before moving into Georgia caused some acquaintances to think of the past and shake their heads with wonder. Ostensibly as a move designed to clear the way for a rapid advance once Grant gave the signal, Sherman directed: "We cannot be too strict about prohibiting citizens on our roads. I will make no exception in favor of correspondents, who are mere traders in news, like other men who would make money out of the army. If any are here they stand a good chance for being impressed for soldiers or other labor."[1]

Only one correspondent is known to have been expelled as a result of this order, and several went along and issued reports that appear in the *Rebellion Record*. The exclusion of newspaper representatives from Federal forces would have resulted in a news blackout in the North. In sharp contrast to Sherman's attitude toward journalists was that of the Confederates, who seldom scolded or reprimanded newsmen.

Months earlier, Thomas W. Knox of the *New York Herald* had written a scathing critique of Sherman's actions at Chickasaw Bayou. As 1862 came to an end, this phase of the Federal campaign against Vicksburg, now generally forgotten, was dramatized by a direct assault against hellish fire. Sherman's forces suffered 1,776 casualties—compared to about 200 among Confederates. Their commander, who was leading troops in combat for the first time, had experienced a tragic defeat.

A week before the debacle, Sherman had issued detailed orders to Brig. Gen. George W. Morgan and other brigade commanders in the Thirteenth Army Corps.[2] Afterward, Sherman said that a road intentionally left unobstructed by his foes served as a trap that accounted for many of the casualties. He blamed Morgan for the defeat. Years later, Morgan published a spirited defense in which he declared that the basic errors in judgment were made by his commander.

Once Knox's account of Chickasaw Bayou came to Sherman's attention, he took quick and drastic action. He ordered that a court-martial be convened and that the journalist, who had been a New England schoolteacher, be given a speedy trial. When Knox was brought before the men who would decide his fate, Sherman labeled him as a spy who had provided information for the enemy.

The officers heard Sherman as the only prosecution witness before pondering the evidence. They rejected his accusations but convicted Knox of having violated orders and required that he stay outside army lines.[3] For the first time in U.S. history, a journalist had undergone a military court-martial and been sentenced for his activity.

Sherman's treatment of Knox after his own failure may have been motivated partly by a desire to get even with the press for earlier treatment of him. In September 1861 he had gone to Kentucky as an aide to Robert Anderson, the Federal hero of Fort Sumter. By then a brigadier general, Anderson was charged with holding Kentucky in the Union and raising regiments of volunteers. Too ill to function effectively, Anderson delegated many functions to Sherman.

Bombarded with demands and questions from many quarters, the volatile Sherman responded with tantrums. Newspaper reporters who were offended by this treatment described him to their readers as "a visionary, unstable and even mentally deranged" leader. One correspondent cited his appearance in uniform, wearing a stovepipe hat. Another mocked him for having borrowed a burning cigar in order to light his own and then tossing the borrowed one to the ground.

Public denunciation intensified his emotional problems, which became so serious that Don Carlos Buell was sent to relieve him of the post he had held for only two months. Ellen Sherman wrote long and furious letters to Lincoln, blaming the malice of Lorenzo Thomas for the affair and begging, with no avail, that her husband be transferred to the East.

In Cincinnati, the editors of the *Commercial* considered Sherman to have displayed "absolutely repulsive" ways and a few days later called him "a perfect monomaniac" in his hatred for journalists. His self-control gone, Sherman raged, "Our Govt is destroyed . . . and no human power can restore it."

Having botched his first major assignment, Sherman was ordered to St. Louis and given a few weeks' leave after reporting. In the familiar city where he had numerous friends, he was accepted by Henry W. Halleck as a staff member but asked to perform only minor services at first.

Halleck showed genuine fondness for the officer five years his junior who had suffered what would today be called a mental breakdown. It was his fraternal concern that helped Sherman fight his way to full recovery. Unlike the Chickasaw Bayou incident, Sherman's bouts with journalists in and below Tennessee seem to have cost him no sleepless nights. He remained in full control of himself and of his three armies.

Military records do not include the name of journalist Benjamin F. Taylor. A fellow reporter, however, said that Sherman had Taylor arrested in Chattanooga for writing that Federal lines "now extend from Nashville to Huntsville." Using the same tactics employed earlier in Mississippi, the commander reputedly expected Taylor to receive a "drum-head court martial, and execution." There is no record that he went on trial, but soon Taylor was described as having "gone North under the ban of the Commanding General."

In his latest bout with the press, the redhead was clearly the winner. Yet millions who lived in the North were disappointed that they learned so little from their newspapers. Some were downright angry. They hoped that Sherman was bringing Joe Johnston to his knees among the gullies and hills of the state heralded as "the breadbasket of the Confederacy." They had no way to know whether or not this was taking place, however. Was Sherman succeeding in this difficult task? If so, why didn't someone inform the public about what was taking place south of Chattanooga?[4]

THERE WERE hours and sometimes days in which Johnston and Sherman were equally ignorant of each other's actions and intentions. Johnston appeared to be invulnerable on two sides of his camp that lay at the head of the Oostenaula River valley—but was he ready to engage in a fight to the finish? Sherman seemed to be intent upon taking Dalton from the northwest—but could his action on this front be a ruse to conceal plans to strike hard somewhere else?

Scouts sent out from the Army of the Cumberland discovered what seemed to be the Achilles' heel of the positions held by the Army of Tennessee. Well to the south of Dalton, near the end of Rocky Face Ridge, a narrow defile could serve as a back door to the Confederate stronghold. If a substantial force could pass quietly through the gap cut by Snake Creek, Johnston would be finished.

George H. Thomas considered Snake Creek Gap to be so promising that he requested the honor of leading his men through it. His proposal was rejected without explanation, and Sherman directed his favorite officer—McPherson—to explore the place thoroughly. He was told to spare no effort in cutting the railroad that brought Johnston his supplies from the south.[5] Once this vital task was accomplished, artillery could knock down the bridges across the broad Oostenaula River, neatly trapping many or all of the Confederate units.

McPherson's probe went astonishingly well at first. He met only token opposition from Kentucky cavalrymen and cadets of the Georgia Military Institute as he neared the gap. After dispersing them, he passed through the gap and moved within about five miles of the railroad station of Resaca. When news of his exploit reached Sherman, he is said to have banged upon a table with his fist while shouting with glee, "I've got Joe Johnston dead!"[6]

His exuberance, however, was premature.

Later described by Johnston as not even being a town, Resaca lay within a great bend of the Oostenaula River, well south of Dalton.[7] Just above the depot, the Atlantic and Western Railroad swung sharply to the east. In order to reach it and rip up long sections of track, McPherson would have to put his men almost squarely between Dalton and Resaca.

Scouts had found freshly built, well-prepared roads connecting the two sites. Using these roads, the Confederates could move from the north much faster than the Federals could ease their way back toward the Army of the Cumberland. Forced to decide upon a course of action in an ambiguous situation, McPherson reacted cautiously. He fell back toward the gap and directed his men to busy themselves preparing entrenchments at a spot in Sugar Valley about thirty miles from Dalton.[8]

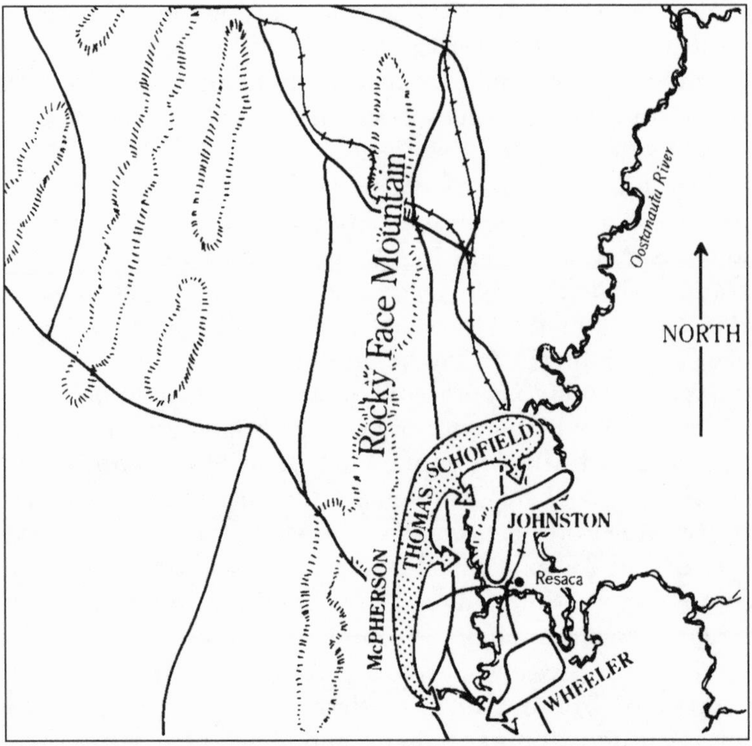

The three Union armies converged on Johnston's forces at Resaca.

He had failed to disable the Western and Atlantic Railroad, but his troops occupied an important pass without firing a shot.

McPherson's satisfaction with his accomplishments lasted only until word of what he had done reached his commander. To pass through a gap largely "unfortified and unguarded" was nothing, even though it was the only pass through which Federals might hope to flank the enemy.[9] Sherman blamed McPherson's overcautiousness for his bitter disappointment and to Grant confided that he "would have disposed of [Johnston] at one blow if McPherson had crushed [Confederate forces at] Resaca, as he might have done." To his wife he wrote only that "McPherson was a little overcautious."[10] With this off his chest, the Federal commander said little more about the failure of his favorite general.

He pored over his maps and concluded that the gap held by the Army of the Ohio could be made to serve another purpose. Most of the Army of the Cumberland could be sent through the tiny pass. Once the chocolate-colored land in Snake Creek Valley was firmly held by the Federals, Sherman wrote, "Johnston will then have to retreat below Resaca, or we shall interpose between him and Georgia."[11]

Inspection showed the gap to be so narrow that it had to be widened "with axes and spades" so that Federal wagons could pass through it. This job was so imperative that Daniel Butterfield assigned three men to each tool. With men of three brigades working hard, a suitable road was fashioned.

Sherman demanded "extreme quiet" on the part of work crews and men who went through the gap hoping for a battle. A silent march toward Resaca was scheduled to begin at 1:00 A.M. on May 13. Fighting men were ordered to carry filled canteens and cooked rations for three days.[12]

Should Johnston learn of the movement, the Federals believed that their foe would be forced to make a difficult march through the mountains to Allatoona. They also knew that they might need pontoons to cross Snake Creek.[13] With the spring rains pelting the countryside, a

LIBRARY OF CONGRESS

The battleground at Resaca, the scene of the first heavy fighting of the campaign.

watercourse could become impassable in a few hours. Tiny by comparison with many of Virginia's streams, the Oostenaula was at some points fifty to seventy-five yards wide and ten to fifteen feet deep.[14]

Even after having been enlarged, Snake Creek Gap delayed Sherman and his staff several hours; they did not pass through until noon on Friday. By then, the Federal commander noted, Johnston—considered to be demoralized—might be south of Resaca. Skirmishing was already well under way in the valley.[15] Meanwhile, some Federal units marched directly upon the desolate place by way of now-deserted Dalton.[16]

HAD SHERMAN been superstitious, he might have hesitated to let his subordinates initiate military action on Friday, May 13. Fighting was desultory until halted by darkness, but it became fierce soon after first light on Saturday. To the men in blue, the cutting of the Western and Atlantic Railroad was almost as important a goal as a battlefield victory.[17] In their eagerness to fight a real battle, men of the Sixteenth Infantry Regiment dropped their knapsacks to the ground as they spewed from the gap—a course of action soon labeled as "unfortunate."[18]

Sherman established his headquarters post in a patch of small trees. To observers he seemed totally at ease seated on the ground, leaning against a tree, a map on his knees, his coat unbuttoned, and his hat antiregulation.

A handful of correspondents were on hand to describe for readers what some of them called the battle of the Oostenaula. J. A. Daugherty, who watched from a spot in the hills, called the struggle "grand beyond description." His report continued:

> Lifted above a line of battle the musketry seems like hammers, and the sea of sparks that fall from the flame as it leaps from the muzzle like so many sparks from the anvil. To see a whole line firing, not by volley, but as rapidly as the men may load, and at night the line of flame looks like glowing chain-work that artisans are welding at the forge. Listen to it attentively and one would say that there are anvils of different weights. Some have a tinkling treble, and others have a hoarse dull bass. Mingle with this now the bellowing of the artillery, and the chime makes real music.[19]

By the time the fighting ended at dark on Sunday, a few Northern newspapers had received word of a Georgia battle said to be on the scale of First Bull Run.[20] Dozens of Federal officers later submitted written reports of their activities in Georgia, but few devoted more than a sentence to Resaca.

Casualty estimates vary from a high of fifty-one hundred Confederates and fifty-six hundred Federals to a low of twenty-six hundred Confederates and thirty-five hundred Federals. Present-day analysts tend to lean toward figures that show that Sherman suffered about one thousand more casualties than did Johnston.[21]

It was at Resaca, however, that Johnston lost four 12-pounder Napoleons of a Georgia battery commanded by Van Den Corput. These were the largest guns taken from him while he commanded in Georgia,[22] and their loss did not affect Sherman's approximate five-to-three advantage in artillery.

Editors of the *Charleston Mercury* informed their readers on May 18, 1864, that "no one knows what General Johnston's future plans are. He keeps them all to himself." No one was more keenly aware of this than was Sherman. Though the head of the Division of the Mississippi was glad to capture a few guns and to occupy Resaca, he was deeply

MOUNTAIN CAMPAIGNS IN GEORGIA

Union artist Alfred R. Waud's depiction of the battle of Resaca. Confederates thwarted a Union attack at Resaca on May 14 and 15, but Sherman was able to outflank the Southerners, causing them to withdraw.

disappointed that his quarry had again slipped away. Having crossed the Oostenaula and burned most of its bridges behind him, Sherman discovered no other Confederate forces in the upper reaches of Sugar Valley.

Sherman had hoped to dispatch triumphant telegrams announcing a great victory that soon would be followed by his marching to Virginia. Grant, entangled with Lee at Spotsylvania, needed all the help he could get. Sherman ruefully realized that his primary goals would not be achieved quickly. Instead, his three armies were certain to have to slug it out with Johnston's Confederates for mile after weary mile.

7

Three or Four Miles a Day

GRANT AND SHERMAN displayed imagination and daring in drawing up what the redhead called "The Grand Strategy of the Last Year of the War."[1] Despite their years of experience, both men soon learned that it was easier to develop a plan than to implement it.

George G. Meade, nominally at the head of the Army of the Potomac, took orders from Grant and seldom questioned them. During the first ten days after the joint East-West jump-off of May 5, the Army of Northern Virginia struck hard in the Wilderness. There the battle of Spotsylvania Court House had not been concluded when opposing forces clashed at Yellow Tavern and New Market and prepared to do so at Drewry's Bluff.

Along with most later analysts, Sherman considered Snake Creek Gap to have been a defeat. Dalton was evacuated, and the Resaca battle was a near-draw, perhaps tilted a trifle toward a Confederate victory. Three armies led by Sherman had advanced far into Georgia, yet Johnston, who had been reinforced by the arrival of Polk and his troops, was stronger than he had been on May 5. Hence Sherman did not share the elation of some of his comrades.

Headed toward a new assignment in Mississippi, one-legged Daniel E. Sickles stopped in Chattanooga, from which he accompanied the Federal armies in their advance upon Dalton and Resaca. Movements of the opposing forces led him to jump to a conclusion hastily voiced to his commander in chief in Washington. Since it was clear that Johnston and his Confederates were withdrawing, Sickles reasoned that they must have known that they faced early and inevitable defeat. From Resaca, the hero of Gettysburg informed the president: "If Georgia cannot be defended on its northern frontier it cannot be defended anywhere. . . . Johnston's retreat, out-maneuvered at Dalton and driven from Resaca, will demoralize his army to the level of Bragg's after Lookout Mountain and Mission[ary] Ridge. . . . Although the enemy destroyed the bridges over the Oostenaula to escape pursuit, Sherman is already after him and is close upon his heels."

Daniel Butterfield was less exuberant than Sickles. Yet he felt impelled to issue to his division a hearty commendation for their "gallant . . . splendid . . . [and] glorious" work at Resaca, "such that the army and the country will ever be proud of us."

WHILE SICKLES and Butterfield exulted and Sherman pondered, Johnston executed his second withdrawal because he was again being flanked. After abandoning Resaca, the Confederate commander got most of his men safely across the Oostenaula and then headed nearly straight south for Calhoun. Following a rest of about eighteen hours, his forces moved southward about eight more miles to Adairsville. There he expected to find terrain suitable both for strong defensive positions and the entrapment of Federal forces.

Every mile Sherman followed Johnston into Georgia widened his separation from Grant, yet he felt that he had no choice. He must run Confederate forces to the ground if he had to chase them halfway down the state. To his wife he reported a small source of satisfaction and word of his future plans: "One of my chief objects was to prevent Joe Johnston from detaching against Grant till he got below Richmond, and that I have done. I have no idea of besieging Atlanta, but may cross the Chattahoochee and circle round Atlanta breaking up its roads."[2]

Not quite sure where the Confederates went when they pulled out of Resaca, the Federal commander chose to stick close to the Western and Atlantic Railroad. He decided to probe toward Kingston and the Etowah River, hoping that there would be a fight to the finish long before that area was reached.

Many simplified maps show Federal forces moving to Adairsville, then splitting into two branches in order to unite near Kingston. Roads, bridges, and ferries of the region were not adequate for such an operation. As was his custom, Sherman decided upon a three-pronged advance.[3] He sent Thomas and the Army of the Cumberland straight down the rail line. Schofield and the Army of the Ohio swung well to the left of center. Meanwhile, the Army of the Tennessee—previously led by Sherman—moved to the right of center.

It was impossible to use all the troops in combat units; as armies advanced, it was necessary "to leave guards at bridges, stations, and intermediate depots" such as field hospitals and supply bases. Crews of experienced railroaders were assigned to tear up sections of track in the rear of the action if Confederates seemed likely to make use of them. Other units repaired rails and bridges that had been damaged or destroyed as the tide of battle moved slowly southward.[4] Sherman chafed that these essential operations resulted in "diminishing the fighting force" and told commanders that their troops must not wait for repairs.

THOMAS AND the Army of the Cumberland were given primary responsibility for repairing and defending the Atlantic and Western Railroad. Because his "head of column" was constantly skirmishing with the enemy's rear guard, the army moved slowly. Every delay created by the enemy gave Johnston "time to remove his stores" as well as to push ahead with his command.

Once his men were across the Oostenaula and Coosawattee Rivers,[5] Thomas believed that he would encounter no more significant geographical obstacles, and his Second Corps passed several potential trouble spots without incidents: Crane Eater Spring, Barrett's Creek, Oothcaloga Church, and Fritter. Joseph Hooker and the Twentieth Corps were delayed at the Coosawattee River by Federal artillery, but they gained time at the Connasauga River by striking it at Fite's Ferry.[6]

Men of the Fourth Army Corps were less fortunate; they found a number of bridges and ferries too small for their numbers and were hampered by narrow, twisting roads. Since Schofield balked at the idea of a night march, he went into camp at Big Spring and requested Sherman to send him orders.[7]

A few miles to the south at Field's Mill, he discovered Hooker's ordnance train to be blocking his path. Using the language of an officer and a gentlemen, Schofield sent word to his colleague, "I most respectfully request that your trains be ordered to yield to me either this ferry or the bridge you have constructed below." This message of May 17 ended on a somewhat plaintive note: "In no other way can I possibly fulfill General Sherman's expectation." Almost simultaneously, the wagon train of his Twenty-third Corps was ordered to stay "near the rear of center of the army, and not have it exposed on the flank."

Headed for Rome and its important ironworks, the Army of the Tennessee scurried past one water-powered mill after another: Oothcaloga, McDonnell's, and Robbins's. The overflowing banks of Dry Creek slowed the march only a trifle, and the shelves of Lacy Pinson's store near the Nannie Post Office were stripped bare without a halt. At Hermitage, the commander found himself far behind schedule. He sent Jeff C. Davis on to Rome, which he entered easily. Then the main body of McPherson's men swung directly toward Kingston, hoping to disable the Western and Atlantic Railroad.

Sherman, who was close to Adairsville on the evening of May 17, warned McPherson not to try to reach the town except by some route west of the railroad.[8] By midnight, the road on which Sherman had traveled was thoroughly congested with men, wagons, and all the accompaniments of an army.

His subordinate generals obeyed orders and engaged in daily skirmishes with the enemy. Not simply in battle, but every day and hour lives were at risk. Maj. Gen. D. S. Stanley summarized the march from Chattanooga to the south:

> But few days had passed that every man of the [First] division was not under fire, both of artillery and musketry. No one could say any hour that he would be living the next. Men were killed in their camps, at their meals, and several cases happened of men struck by musket-balls in their sleep. . . . So many men were daily struck in the camp and trenches that men became utterly reckless, passing about where balls were striking as though it was their normal life, and making a joke of a narrow escape or a noisy whistling ball.[9]

MANY GENERALS had no responsibilities outside of their commands. Unlike them, Sherman was concerned with a broad range of movements and policies.

Troops were needed somewhere above Eastport, Alabama, on the Tennessee River "to serve as a threat to North Alabama." Meanwhile, men under Brig. Gen. R. S. Granger were ordered to picket that vital waterway from Decatur to Stevenson. Near Athens, Tennessee, artillery fire had been heard near the flooded Elk River. Leading five hundred men with three guns, Josiah Patterson had descended on Madison Station, Alabama, and destroyed everything but the railroad. An estimated twenty-five hundred Confederates with ten guns were believed to be headed toward Whitesburg, Alabama.[10] Since Tennessee and Alabama were included in the Division of the Mississippi, all of these matters—and many more—were referred to Sherman.

Enlistments of many of his three-year veterans would soon expire; some of them would reenlist, but others would go home. Sherman repeatedly demanded effective operation of Federal conscription laws. A constant supply of fresh men was vital to the survival of his armies, he insisted, and he wrote an angry letter to Secretary of War Stanton stating, "If the President modifies it [the draft] to the extent of one man, or wavers in its execution, he is gone."[11]

Before leaving Tunnel Hill, Sherman learned that five thousand members of the Indiana militia had been ordered to report to him. He decided to put half of them at Tullahoma and the other half at Gallatin "for the purpose of affording protection to our communication"—thus enabling him to hold five thousand veterans in the fighting forces.

With manpower shortages believed likely to grow worse, Sherman didn't want some of the men he could have had. He didn't object to the use of free blacks or runaway slaves as laborers,[12] but he wanted no black soldiers in his command.

Here he found himself at odds with Lincoln and Lorenzo Thomas. Complicating an already delicate situation, Sherman soon forbade recruitment officers to "enlist as soldiers any negroes who are profitably employed by any of the army departments."

In addition to overseeing the troops in the field, exasperating conscription laws, and debating the use of black soldiers, Sherman also had to contend with Nathan Bedford Forrest. Since July 1861 the nearly illiterate, self-taught military genius had been a thorn in Sherman's flesh. Now he threatened to cut the railroad through Tennessee upon which Sherman's forces were absolutely dependent. For brief moments Johnston vanished from the thoughts of his pursuer. During the two months of May and June 1864 at least fifty-six federal messages dealt with some aspect of Forrest's activities.

By the time Sherman's forces were approaching Kingston on May 19, hoping to close in on Johnston, the head of the Division of the Mississippi admitted his frustration. "I feel certain that Johnston, after the affair at Resaca, does not want to fight us in the comparatively open ground this side of Cartersville," Sherman told Thomas. Almost as an afterthought he urged the head of the Army of the Cumberland to "connect with General Hooker, and, if possible, crush or capture any force that is, as I think caught between General [George] Stoneman [commanding cavalry of the Twenty-second Corps] and you."[13]

By the time all three Federal armies converged on Kingston and nearby Cassville, their commander felt they deserved two days of rest "to replenish and fit up." Sherman therefore scheduled the chase for Johnston to be resumed on May 23.

Ruefully counting days and calculating distances, Sherman realized that since leaving Resaca his men had marched only three or four miles a day. Worse, if possible, he did not know where "Gamecock" Johnston had halted. Regardless of what Butterfield and Sickles might say, Grant's comrade knew that his fighting men had not yet won a victory of any consequence in Georgia.

8

The Rubicon of Georgia

On ceremonial and formal occasions Joseph E. Johnston usually removed his light brown felt hat and revealed his balding pate. During the American Revolution his father was a lieutenant in the forces commanded by Henry "Light-horse Harry" Lee, father of Robert E. Lee. Many admirers insisted that his aristocratic Virginia background and courtly manners gave the Mexican War hero a Napoleonic look.

Subordinate generals, coming together at his call, knew the occasion was solemn as soon as they saw that their leader's feathered hat was not in place. John B. Hood, who spoke frequently and at length, urged Johnston to leave Cassville—the sooner the better. With Leonidas Polk occasionally nodding assent, the one-legged corps commander described his dilemma. Federal batteries recently placed on a hill near his right, said Hood, would enfilade his forces at daybreak. Once the guns opened fire, neither he nor Polk would be able to hold his ground, he insisted. William J. Hardee, whose combat experience dated from the Seminole War, strongly disagreed with his colleagues, but he realized that his was a minority voice.

Noted for his reluctance to sacrifice his troops, Johnston reasoned that "the commanders of two-thirds of the army" were sure to influence the thinking of their officers and men. A few hours earlier he had warmly commended the Army of Tennessee. Praising his troops for having "repulsed every assault of the enemy," he had promised, "You will now turn and march to meet his advancing columns." It was his plan, he said, personally "to lead you into battle."[1]

Despite his hopes and expectations, Johnston decided that it would be worse than futile to wage a doomed battle. He therefore yielded to Hood and Polk and agreed to leave Cassville for the Etowah River before daybreak on May 20. There was no other good position closer than Allatoona Pass, more than a dozen miles to the southeast.

Allatoona offered hope for a victory. Yet Johnston started there with a heavy heart. For the third time since the Federals pushed past the Tennessee state line, the Confederates were withdrawing from an entrenched position.

In 1864 the Etowah River was a significant barrier to those traveling on the dirt roads that led to its bridges and ferries. Fed by the Amicolola, its largest tributary, the river's current was swift. After a heavy spring rain, much of the runoff from the creeks around Dirtseller Mountain flowed just southwest of Adairsville. Federal soldiers who drank from the Etowah were likely to get water from the creeks such as the Pumpkin Vine, Raccoon, Pettile, Euharlee, Salacoa, Sweetwater, and Oothcalooga. Near Rome, about twenty miles west, the Etowah joined the Oostenaula to form the Coosa, which was navigable for nearly two

LIBRARY OF CONGRESS

Confederate defenses around the Etowah River bridge. Johnston's Army of Tennessee fell back on Allatoona after crossing the river.

hundred miles. Because it offered abundant power, the Etowah and its sister streams were dotted with water mills.[2]

By the time Federal advance guards moved out toward Adairsville at 5:00 A.M. on May 19, it was clear that the Confederates were gone. Near the town the road leading south split into two segments. Johnston had briefly hoped to trap one column of the enemy within the triangle formed by these north-south roads and the east-west connector, the Kingston and Cassville road.

When this plan failed, the Confederate leader expected to make a stand near Kingston, for his map showed that here the railroad ran through a narrow valley. To his disappointment, his information proved to be faulty. Soon he saw that "the breadth of the valley far exceeded the front of our army in order of battle."[3] Consequently his weary men were forced to press forward to Cassville. There they went into bivouac below Two-Run Creek, hoping to get a day or two of rest. Instead, they hurriedly built protective entrenchments stretching for more than four miles to the southwest.

A FEW miles away at Adairsville, while riding the skirmish line, Sherman attracted the attention of Confederate sharpshooters. Their fire wounded one of his aides and killed several horses. Though probably not affected by his near-death experience, like Johnston he decided that it was time for a brief stop. Many of his troops spent forty-eight or more hours at Kingston. While they rested and received issues of shoes and clothing, their leader concentrated upon the future.

Nothing would have suited him better than to have a major battle somewhere in the vicinity of Kingston, which he believed on May 18 was Johnston's destination. "Whether he proposes to fight there or not we cannot tell," he informed Washington, "but tomorrow will know, for I propose to attack him wherever he may be." Confederate deserters bolstered Sherman's hopes for an early showdown. Not knowing what course would be taken by the men in gray, he instructed Thomas to keep up pursuit "and order the enemy to be attacked if found."[4]

Though nothing came of the effort made by Thomas, good news was relayed by a black refugee. According to this native of the region, the Confederates planned "to give battle at Cass Station." Ordered immediately to move against the place, Schofield and the Army of the Ohio waited until "first dawn in the morning" to complete their march. As a result Johnston was well on the way toward Allatoona by the time the Federals approached Cassville.

This chain of events clearly caused the Confederates to maneuver for an advantage in position, yet Sherman insisted that he was eager to "fight like the devil." "Even at the hazard of beginning battle with but a part of our forces," he told Schofield, it was imperative that Thomas and his men should "follow his [Johnston's] trail straight, let it lead to the fords [of the Etowah] or toward Allatoona."[5]

In order to fight effectively in the near future, he needed more men at once. Because conscription was lagging badly, he had sent identical messages to four leaders of frontier states. Expecting to get an additional twenty thousand members of state militia units, but not having received them, he urged that "now is the time for superhuman energy."[6]

Sherman soon became convinced, correctly as events proved, that Johnston had taken refuge somewhere near Allatoona. Since that gave the Confederates the advantage of a defensive position on carefully selected ground, it would be extremely risky to stage an all-out attack at that point.

There seemed to be just one possibility of getting below the enemy forces and cutting the railroad that supplied them. The Federals could turn to the right, or west, and complete a march in the general shape of a half circle. That would take them fourteen or so miles south of the Etowah and close to Dallas, where the Western and Atlantic Railroad could be cut. Unless Johnston moved extremely rapidly, his forces would then be squeezed north of the main Federal body.

If such a move succeeded, it would leave Johnston with only two choices, Sherman reasoned. He could either do battle or turn toward the mountainous regions at his northeast. In either event, he would be soundly defeated and Sherman could accomplish three of the objectives in his four-point mission. There was an outside chance that Johnston might move north. Should he do so, it was unfortunately possible that he might thwart one of his opponent's objectives by hastily sending troops to strengthen the Army of Northern Virginia.

Johnston had quite different ideas concerning upcoming developments. According to Alexander St. Clair-Abrams of the *Atlanta Intelligencer,* word filtered through the Confederate camp that a long-expected major battle would soon take place below the Etowah River. It was expected to be so decisive that it would halt Sherman's move into Georgia.

TRYING TO take into account all factors and contingencies, the Federal commander arrived at the most daring decision he made while on Georgia soil. He would leave the Western and Atlantic Railroad behind and for a distance of about twenty miles depend entirely upon wagon trains for food, ammunition, and supplies.

To pull off such a "grand move,"[7] his men would have to travel rapidly and without impediments. All essential property would be under the care of an officer selected by his brigade commander; no one else would be permitted to take anything along. An enlisted man could carry nothing except a poncho, his weapon, and his ammunition box. Regardless of rank, no officer would be allowed more than a single valise or carpetbag. There would be no going back for rations under any circumstances. If forage was needed for draft animals or cavalry horses, it would have to be brought in on pack mules.

Federal operations in Tennessee and Georgia had already played havoc with the quartermaster corps. From Washington, Sherman and his colleagues were informed that "not less than 30,000 draft animals" had been destroyed or broken down during the preceding fall and winter. Wagons would have to be kept to an absolute minimum—or below that level.

Some veterans had complained at being forced to leave things behind when Federal armies moved into Georgia on May 5. Compared with the contemplated march, the drive southward from Chattanooga had been a casual stroll.[8]

Men unable to fight because of sickness or wounds were sent to the rear, along with "worthless men and idlers." Having accumulated at Kingston what he believed to be twenty days' rations, Sherman told his subordinates that their men must subsist without the railroad. If the estimated time required for the march should prove to be too optimistic, supplies for twenty days would have to suffice for thirty.

For the dramatic march, whatever its length might prove to be, each enlisted man and each animal was given allotments. A soldier's consisted of one pound of bread, flour, or meal per day and beef on the hoof. Once a week, he would receive "two days' allowance of sugar, coffee, and salt." If all went according to schedule, horses and mules would get four pounds of grain per day. Orders stipulated that "everything else must be gathered in the country [from civilians]."[9]

The Confederates were almost certain to strike at the wagon trains. Hence two regiments would protect each train from Kingston to Burnt Hickory. Subsequently, one regiment would accompany each hundred wagons as their guard.

From the perspective of the Federal camp at Kingston, these tough measures appeared to be satisfactory. In practice, they soon proved inadequate. When only a few hours out of Kingston, the wagon train of the Twenty-third was reported to have been destroyed. At midmorning of the same day Confederates made an unsuccessful attempt to raid a train belonging to the Seventy-ninth Regiment of Pennsylvania Volunteers.

A few miles to their east, not far from Cassville, Confederates burned about twenty wagons and drove off with twenty fully loaded ones. Thereafter Federal commanders issued orders to "arrest any officer or enlisted man connected with the trains who does not strictly attend to his duties."[10]

A less than exuberant Sherman reported to Washington on the evening of May 21. The weather was very hot and the roads were very dusty, he explained before promising, "We, nevertheless, by morning will have all our wagons loaded and be ready for a twenty days' expedition."

Attached to a May 23 message dispatched to the quartermaster general in Washington was a terse statement from Sherman, described as being "in cipher" and the last to be expected "till something decisive is known." Sherman's brief telegram, however, said a great deal: "Horse arrived all safe and sound. He looks well and I will ride him tomorrow across the Etowah, which is the Rubicon of Georgia. We are now all in motion like a vast hive of bees, and expect to swarm along the Chattahoochee in five days."

Robert L. Allen, an Ohio-born brigadier general and a career member of the quartermaster's corps, attached to the Washington message his own firsthand report: "He [Sherman] is provided with twenty days' supplies of all kinds. . . . Make yourself entirely easy. The emergency has passed. Sherman expresses himself as highly pleased, and says no army in the world is better prepared."[11]

Sherman planned to be on or near the banks of the Chattahoochee River on May 29. He was clearly delighted at the prospect of crossing "the Rubicon of Georgia." His effective strength was now boosted to about eighty thousand men,[12] yet he was still demanding more. "Back us up with troops in the rear so I will not have to drop detachments as rear guards, and I [will] have an army that will make a deep hole in the Confederacy." From Washington, the secretary of war warned, "There appears to be danger that you may count too much on the new troops for your support."

Bypassing the Federal central command, Sherman communicated directly with state governors and urged them to dispatch all soldiers possible, including men who had enlisted for only one hundred days.[13] He now planned to be on or near the banks of the Chattahoochee River before the end of the month, and to keep his schedule he'd have to have additional troops.

Sherman's timetable failed to take into account natural obstacles as well as Confederate destruction and entrenchments. Although he had crossed "the Rubicon of Georgia" as planned, many of his units were delayed. Confederates burned one bridge after another: on the road to Marietta, near Cartersville, at Etowah Cliffs, Milam's, and other points. On May 20 a good bridge was standing at Milam's, near the mouth of Euharlee Creek; two days later it had gone up in smoke.[14]

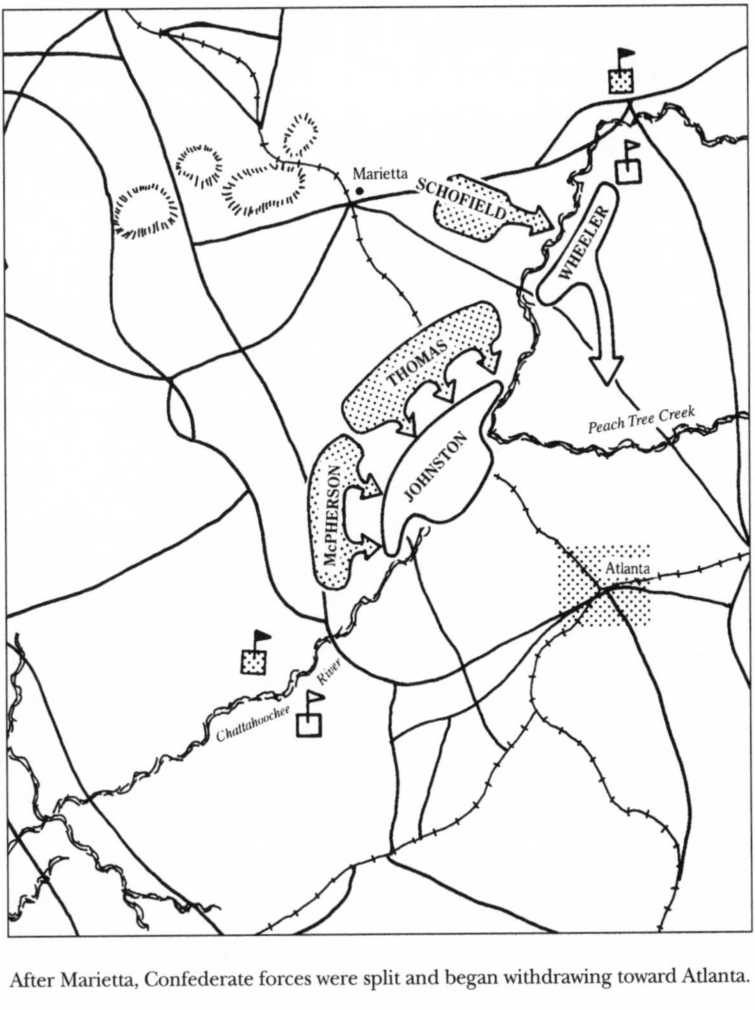

After Marietta, Confederate forces were split and began withdrawing toward Atlanta.

Some Federal units crossed the Etowah at its fords, but others sent frantic requests for pontoons. George Stoneman's cavalrymen, instructed to break the Western and Atlantic Railroad below Cassville "enough to take a couple of days to repair," were impeded by roads jammed with troops. When they tried to cross the Connesauga River at Fite's Ferry, a superior force of Confederates drove them off.[15]

Heading two thousand men of the Railroad Construction Corps, William W. Wright rebuilt the burned bridge at Resaca in just three days.[16] At the Etowah so many spans were involved that it was impossible to work upon all of them simultaneously. Stranded north of the river, many units of fighting men experienced substantial delays before starting to push rapidly toward the Chattahoochee.

Once across the river, the advance proved to be much more difficult than anticipated. Typical conditions encountered by the Fourth Army Corps were briefly described as "very pleasant day for marching; warm, but no dust. Hard to find safe roads through the country; full of heavy woods, cross-roads, &c, and could procure no suitable guides. All intelligent persons had left the country, or had been driven out by the enemy."

Soon Sherman and his troops would learn how well Johnston could make use of wooded terrain, hastily erected breastworks, and rifle pits.[17] No Federal troops would cross the Chattahoochee until July 9—nearly six weeks after the date set for this achievement by the head of the Division of the Mississippi.

IT REMAINED a primary responsibility of Sherman to "hold all of Johnston's army too busy [for Johnston] to send anything against him."[18] Grant had all he could handle on good days, and much more on bad days; soon he would be locked in a struggle along the North Anna River.

As Sherman's men inched their way toward Marietta,[19] a fresh emphasis occasionally received passing attention. Reporting about the crossing of the Etowah that was originally scheduled for May 23, John C. Van Duzer labeled it as a "movement against Atlanta." In transmitting one of Sherman's special orders, an aide-de-camp stressed, however, that "Marietta is the objective point."

Concerning Atlanta, when boasting that he had added one hundred miles to his "railroad communications," Sherman said only that he was now getting near the place.[20] To his subordinates, he emphasized, "We are now all in motion for the Chattahoochee."[21]

So far, losses in Georgia on both sides were approximately equal. Neither Sherman nor Johnston had a great deal to brag about. For the leader of the invaders, this was a stalemate rather than a victory. Men of the Army of the Cumberland, alone, had already expended 5.2 million rounds of ammunition, thus using about seventeen hundred rounds per Confederate casualty.

Sherman's move toward the Chattahoochee was designed to get Southern forces out of the woods and force them to wage a genuine battle. As May drew to a close, nothing in the record suggests that Sherman had begun to think of conquering Atlanta either in lieu of or in addition to decimating the ranks of his foes.

9

Into the Hell Hole

WHEN WILLIAM Tecumseh Sherman crossed what he called "the Rubicon of Georgia," the nature of his struggle with Joseph E. Johnston changed rapidly and drastically.

Since May 5 it had been marked by constant movement and almost ceaseless low-level strife that the Federal leader termed "one universal skirmish extending over a vast surface."[1] Perhaps because Jefferson Davis and Sherman agreed that the terrain covered so far was favorable to Confederates, Johnston asserted that it was not.

Johnston had repeatedly withdrawn in response to flanking movements by Sherman. Neither commander could report a significant victory to his president.

The losses of the two commanders since the Federals had departed Chattanooga were nearly equal. Many who had been counted as casualties suffered slight wounds and were soon back in the ranks. Hundreds who were listed as missing turned out to be stragglers who rejoined their units voluntarily or who were found and forced to return. As June drew near only approximately six thousand men in blue and in gray who were once effective were now dead or unable to fight.

Below the Etowah, the contest quickly became a struggle of entrenchment that meant the Federals could only creep forward at a snail's pace. The fury of combat escalated rapidly and promised that casualties in forthcoming battles were likely to be staggering in comparison with those of recent weeks.

Sherman soon realized that his goal of reaching the Chattahoochee before June 1 would not be met. About the time he had expected to be crossing the largest river in the region, he found himself stalled. His post was close to Pumpkin Vine Creek, which emptied into Allatoona Creek just below the settlement of the same name. To the secretary of war he lamely explained, "The country is most difficult, being of dense undergrowth and short steep ridges of flinty stone."

Brilliant strategist and coldly calculating thinker that he was, Sherman was not above offering an alibi for failure. Years afterward, he continued to insist that the physical nature of the theater of war gave his foes a "most decided advantage."[2] Some of his subordinates heartily endorsed this verdict,[3] but Johnston never ceased to challenge it. He said that he'd gladly have given "all the mountains, ravines, rivers, and woods of Georgia" for Sherman's supply of artillery ammunition. Some Confederate analysts argued that the rough country that sustained Johnston's defense "also aided his antagonist in movements to the flank."

Regardless of how greatly the terrain affected repeated flanking movements and withdrawals, the invaders were often frustrated by outdated or inadequate maps. Detailed instructions for the making of new maps were issued from near Dallas.[4]

Even after procedures began to be followed to the letter, commanders had to resort to points of reference such as "the blacksmith shop." Sherman decided, correctly as events proved, that the site marked as "*Court House* must be the Golgotha of our map." Joseph Hooker was less discerning; he relied upon a map so bad that he was forced to stretch his line dangerously thin. A site sometimes called Burnt Church and at other times known as Cross-Roads was briefly Sherman's headquarters.[5]

No major military leader on either side challenged the Federal reports that the Confederates excelled at quickly throwing up entrenchments and digging rifle pits. Relying upon his familiarity with classical literature, Sherman labeled "these field intrenchments" as distinctively American, though he said they were probably employed long ago by Julius Caesar during his wars in Gaul.

Recalling his struggle with Johnston's men after twenty years, the Federal commander wrote of his foes: "Troops, halting for the night or for battle, faced the enemy; moved forward to ground with a good outlook to front; stacked arms; gathered logs, stumps, fence-rails, anything that would stop a bullet; piled these to their front, and, digging a ditch behind, threw the dirt forward, and made a parapet which covered their positions as perfectly as a granite wall." Penned as a tribute to Johnston, that description is echoed many times in the correspondence of Sherman and his subordinates.

Federal soldiers also were not exempt from the manual labor required to prepare fortifications. According to an undocumented report, the Southerners said, "Sherman's men march with a rifle in one hand and a spade in the other."

Correspondents who reported the Federal movement southward from Chattanooga indicated that Union troops often stopped to prepare defensive works. However, their descriptions of Confederate installations suggest that the latter were frequently elaborate and very strong, built as though they were be held for days or weeks. South of the Etowah, many fortifications encountered by Sherman and his men seemed to have been erected for a long-term or even a permanent garrison.

Probing their way southward ("feeling" as they often labeled such movements), men in blue discovered the New Hope Church road to have been fortified all the way to the Villa Rica road. As a

LIBRARY OF CONGRESS

The New Hope Church battlefield, with four thousand casualties, was the costliest of a series of engagements many veterans described as "the Hell Hole."

result, Pumpkin Vine Church near Dallas became for a time a center of Federal operations. McPherson, stationed not far away, was told to loose a volley from his guns upon New Hope Church if he heard the sounds of battle.[6]

Entrenched at Allatoona Pass, more than one hundred miles below Chattanooga, Johnston was momentarily secure. While riding the Etowah River region in 1840, then-youthful Lieutenant Sherman had inspected the place. No one now needed to tell him that it was more formidable than "the terrible door of death" his men had faced at Buzzard Roost, above Dalton.

Some Federal units were ordered to be under arms and ready to march at 3:00 A.M. on May 27.[7] This movement, premature as it developed, launched actions that alternated between intervals of fierce conflict and near quiet. Even after Sherman shifted toward Allatoona on June 2, the region was marked by intervals of savage fighting that produced many casualties. Union forces used New Hope Church to label an entire series of clashes, some of which took place at Pickett's

LIBRARY OF CONGRESS

Allatoona Pass as it appeared to advancing Union troops.

The combination of mountainous terrain and wet weather boded ill for Sherman's army, which was dependent on wagon train supply lines, and underlined the significance of railroads.

Mill and near Dallas. Soaking wet for seventeen days because of incessant rain, the men in blue said that this was where they "descended into the Hell Hole."

REGARDING ALLATOONA Pass as too formidable to assault, Sherman again resorted to a flanking movement to "turn the position." Once many of his foes were south of the pass, Johnston responded by yet another orderly withdrawal. This time he chose as his new base a series of rugged little mountains—hardly more than hills—close to the Atlantic and Western Railroad and just north of Marietta.[8]

As the Confederate withdrawal began, Sherman sent some of Stoneman's cavalry toward the main bridge over the Etowah River, near

The Western and Atlantic Railroad passed through Allatoona Pass. Johnston's army held the pass in May 1864, and several months later Hood's army attacked Union forces here, trying to disrupt Sherman's supply line and draw him out of Georgia.

the pass. Almost simultaneously, troops under Frank P. Blair Jr. were withdrawn from Rome. Ordered to Allatoona, Blair's immediate mission upon arrival would be to oversee repair of the railroad up to that point.[9]

It was imperative to get back to the railroad; most Federal wagon trains were on the move, but some were running into major problems. Frequently it was difficult to find a place suitable for halting and guarding a train.[10]

Some roads were hard to find, and rain was making many of them so soft that they were sometimes impassable. When the roads were in good condition, the wagons were given priority and soldiers were forced to march "in byways and fields" so trains could have the use of the prepared surfaces.[11]

AMONG CAVALRY units of the Army of the Cumberland, the lack of supplies approached crisis proportions. Stoneman became angry because failure of wagon trains to maintain their schedule left him stranded, leading him to complain that "men and horses are entirely without anything to eat." He hinted that this was the reason his men had been driven off Laughing Gal road, and he insisted forage and food be sent to him at once. Cavalry commander Kenner Garrard went directly to Sherman with a report that his forage train hadn't reached him, so he requested a few days' rest for the animals.

Already having regained the railroad near Allatoona and pressing toward other points at top speed, Sherman had little time for minor issues. He told Garrard to let his horses "feed upon green feed and forage." To McPherson he suggested, "Empty wagons and caissons should be sent for growing wheat, barley, oats, or rye, as well as grass or such bushes as horses and mules eat." Stoneman was told simply to spare his horses as much as possible "and let them feed on grass."

Wagon trains loaded with rations for twenty days had rolled south in an orderly and systematic fashion and on schedule, but the return of troops to the railroad was chaotic and sporadic. Along a stretch of a dozen or so miles of track, Federal units pulled up to the rails as soon as they reached them. Some of McPherson's troops were at the semi-magical line of iron on June 5, but other units of his army did not reach it until four days later. Men of the Fifteenth Army Corps were at Burnt Church, a full day away from the Western and Atlantic Railroad, when it was reached by McPherson's advance guard. Troops of the Sixteenth and Seventeenth Corps were then equally distant from the sound of locomotive whistles and the sight of piled-up supplies.

Once the railroad was again firmly in Federal hands, the base of supplies was shifted southward repeatedly. By May 26 it was firmly established at Allatoona. Telegraph lines were repaired almost as rapidly, and by June 4 had only a few breaks between Acworth and Washington. It would take an estimated five days to restore the great bridge over the Etowah to its former usefulness; in the meantime, pontoons must be used, even though common sense said they'd soon be overwhelmed.

In an early version of his official report, Sherman devoted one-third of a column to praise those who repaired, defended, and extended his rail lines:

> I must bear full and liberal testimony to the energetic and successful management of our railroads during the campaign. No matter when or where a break has been made, the repair train seemed on the spot, and the damage was repaired generally before I knew of the break. Bridges have been built with surprising rapidity, and the locomotive whistle was heard in our

> advanced camps almost before the echoes of the skirmish line had ceased. Some of these bridges—those of the Oostanula, the Etowah, and Chattahoochee—are fine, substantial structures, and were built in an inconceivably short time, almost out of material improvised on the spot.[12]

THAT GLOWING tribute was framed by the man who made it possible. Sherman was the only top commander on either side who was totally committed to transportation by rail when possible.

During the three weeks in which he felt compelled to resort to wagon trains, Sherman must have been in constant emotional turmoil. Even during this period, one of his cardinal rules—never directly expressed—was repair, defend, and extend. Huge crews of workmen were kept busy at this threefold task during the entire invasion. Sometimes military units that included thousands of men were sent to assist trained railroad workers.

Sherman's Georgia lifeline, the Western and Atlantic Railroad, was complete with a tunnel and ran through enemy territory for the entire length he used. Normally, the telegraph line followed the route of the railroad. Simply to keep open these communications lines, as he called them, was a task of monumental proportions. With the exception of very large bridges that had been destroyed, the Federal commander was usually able to effect repairs within one or two days.

These accomplishments in the face of natural obstacles and Confederate opposition were enough to make any commander rejoice. In an exultant mood, Sherman dispatched a telegram saying that he was at Acworth and holding the road to within six miles of Marietta. Reversing his usual attitude toward the press, he gloated, "Johnston tried to head us off at Dallas but did not succeed. In all encounters we had the advantage. All is working well. You may give this publicity."[13]

As late as May 20, Schofield forbade men of the Fifteenth Corps to indulge in foraging. Not so his chief; so long as they were dependent upon wagon trains, Sherman's troops were encouraged and sometimes even ordered to forage off the land. He wrote that Johnston has "abandoned to us the best wheat-growing region of Georgia."

A correspondent reported that Sherman expected "supplies from the country" to augment those shipped from his bases of supply. This was an abbreviated way of ordering that the army should be subsisted as far as possible off the country. Men whose wagon trains had not kept pace with them could "safely rely on much meat, forage, and vegetables in the country to which we propose to go." Officers and men of every brigade were told to "organize foraging parties . . . for the purpose of collecting supplies from the country."

As had been the case during Sherman's Meridian campaign,[14] conducted before he became head of the Department of the Mississippi, destruction as punishment of the Southerners and destruction for the hell of it merged with foraging for necessities. Brig. Gen. Milo S. Hascall was so incensed by what he saw that he entered a formal protest on May 23:

> I consider it my duty to call the attention of the major-general commanding the corps to the terrible state of things that exists in different parts of the grand army under Major-General Sherman, so far as the wanton destruction of private property and works of art is concerned. It has not been my fortune to march a single day during the last week without being compelled to witness sights which are enough to disgrace and render worthy of defeat any army in the universe. . . . While I am willing that everything shall be taken that will be of service to our army or beneficial to the enemy, if done in an orderly manner, I have no desire to serve with an army where the fundamental principles of civilized warfare are so shockingly violated at every step in our progress.[15]

SCHOFIELD, HEAD of the Army of the Ohio, may have replied to his subordinate, but his reply about senseless destruction didn't get into the record.

Sherman refrained from officially sanctioning wanton destruction he couldn't avoid seeing. At the same time, he treated Union skulkers and stragglers almost as though they were Confederate civilians. Many a man in the Federal force ducked into a thicket and hid until he could no longer hear the tramp of marching columns. Sometimes such a fellow repented and caught up with his unit; often he took to his heels and raced to the rear.

"Shirking, skulking, and straggling in time of danger" were categorized by Sherman as "detestable crimes." Near Dallas he became angry at reports that some of these loafers could be found as far behind the lines as Kingston, Tennessee. Consequently he issued a special field order in which he stipulated: "The only proper fate of such miscreants is that they be shot as common enemies to their profession and country, and all officers and patrols sent to arrest them will shoot them without mercy upon the slightest impudence or resistance. . . . Officers, if found skulking, will be subjected to the same penalties as enlisted men, viz, instant death or the harshest labor and treatment."[16]

There is no record that stragglers and skulkers were ever executed; it was wiser to put them to hard labor. Near Allatoona, men "loafing about and pretending to seek their regiments" were made to build redoubts. This did not solve the problem; a few days later Cartersville was described as "infested with stragglers." Confederate scouts estimated that ten thousand such fellows were to be found near Dalton at the end of May.[17]

SHERMAN'S FURY at the conduct of some of his own men may have been triggered partly by bad news from the North. An early report had said that Grant had defeated Lee, who was in retreat across the North Anna River, and that Federal forces were within fifteen miles of Richmond. Soon, however, the Virginia half of the joint Grant-Sherman action was known to be bogged down. Grant had all he could handle and maybe more on the Chickahominy River.[18]

Sherman's half of the joint Federal operation now had all three of his armies deep inside Georgia. Though he had failed to provoke Johnston into a decisive battle, he would continue to seek such a meeting. A decisive victory probably would not come quickly or easily because the Confederate leader had shown himself to be a master of defensive strategy. Surely, though, Johnston could not slip past the throngs of his enemies near Marietta without a fight of consequence.

10

The Enemy Must Be in a Bad Condition

Acworth, Ga., *June 10, 1864*
(Received 12:20 P.M., 11th)
Major-General Halleck,
Washington, D.C.:

Our cavalry yesterday developed the position of the enemy in a line along the hills from Kenesaw[1] to Lost Mountain. We are now marching by three roads, all toward Kenesaw, and shall feel the position in force to-day, prepared to attack or turn it to-morrow.
All well.

W. T. SHERMAN
Major-General[2]

SHERMAN'S ELATION at having crossed the Etowah was premature, he realized. Yet the situation was now even more promising than it had been while he was approaching the Etowah River.

Only a few miles to the south lay the Chattahoochee, by far the largest watercourse of North Georgia. It was hoped that Johnston would come out of his defensive positions and stage a fight to the finish. If he refused to do so, it should be easy to get between him and the Chattahoochee. With three Federal armies poised to strike, no matter what direction the Confederates might take, they would be hammered with hard, decisive blows.

On Saturday, June 11, Sherman reached Big Shanty on the Western and Atlantic Railroad promptly at 11:00 A.M., as planned. Maj. Gen. John M. Palmer was already moving toward a group of hills; his mission was to gain the road between Pine Hill and Kenesaw Mountain. This and other operations were designed to "make the enemy spread out as much as possible on this his right flank."

Soon Federal lines were within four hundred to five hundred yards of the Confederate defenses, but the anticipated battle did not materialize. The rain-soaked roads were battered by more rain all day Sunday and again on Monday. It was impossible to move heavy artillery toward the enemy.

Three of the estimated five days needed to reach the big river to the south had passed before the Federals came to a reluctant conclusion. Soon after dark on Monday it was agreed that they would have to have three clear days in order to move artillery and wagon trains from Big Shanty.

Another set of coordinated plans was developed and put into action on Tuesday, June 14. Col. F. T. Sherman's division headed toward the left of Pine Top, followed by the divisions of David S. Stanley and Thomas J. Wood. By moving his men toward the Hardshell Church, Schofield hoped to mask the action designed to flank Pine Top. Blueclad columns moved out as directed, but their officers quickly found the Confederates unassailable with "every rivulet a line of defense."[3]

Earlier established on Lost Mountain, Johnston had abandoned that position in favor of a much stronger one anchored on a series of hills. Along with Polk and Hardee, Johnston rode to the summit of Pine Mountain at midmorning. Together, the three generals surveyed the surrounding countryside and planned their next move.

They decided to give up the site and started down just as a Federal battery opened fire. Two shots were harmless, but the third struck Polk, killing him instantly. Folklore perpetuates a story that Sherman directed the guns that ended the career of the Confederate bishop-general. But this account is without foundation. According to the commander of the Army of Tennessee, the Federal gunners were aiming at a Confederate battery and hit Polk by accident.

In addition to Pine Mountain, the Confederate line linking Gilgal Church with Lost Mountain was abandoned after dark on June 16. Three days later Johnston's men were in a new position. Under the guidance of Col. Stephen W. Prestman, a gray-clad semicircle stretched halfway around the town of Marietta. With the crest of Kenesaw Mountain its strongest point, Sherman decided simply to occupy the attention of the enemy. He was not yet convinced that a direct assault upon Kenesaw would be a wise move. To his subordinates, it seemed clear that "a very few days must give us possession of all this side of Chattahoochee."[4]

IN SPITE of the fact that he was once more far behind his schedule, Sherman shared this optimistic view. A message dispatched to Grant berated Garrard as overcautious and Stoneman as lazy. Thomas and the Army of the Cumberland, he said, continued to be "awfully slow." Yet an unusually long communication ended on a note of exultation: "I have all the high and command ground, but the one peak near Marietta, which I can turn."[5]

The Federal commander gave an even more optimistic summary on June 19: "Enemy gave way last night in the midst of darkness and storm, and at daylight our pickets entered his line from right to left. The whole army is now in pursuit as far as the Chattahoochee. I start at once for Marietta, and leave orders for railroad and telegraph to be kept up."

Thomas urged Maj. Gen. J. M. Palmer of the Fourteenth Corps to move forward rapidly with his freshest troops. "We must endeavor to follow the enemy up close," he urged. "He must be in a bad condition." Members of a Federal scouting party turned in a report that led their commander to summarize their findings in four words: "The rebels have gone." Simultaneously, Brig. Gen. E. M. McCook studied information from several sources and concluded that "the whole of the enemy's forces is falling back." Schofield received a terse order from his commander: "Push pursuit as far as the Chattahoochee."

Within twenty-four hours, a rueful Sherman was forced to notify Washington that he and his generals had been wrong. Impassable roads with fields and woods turned into quagmires made it impossible to advance as planned. He lamely concluded: "The enemy hold Kenesaw, a conical mountain, with Marietta behind it, and has retired his flank to cover that town and his railroad. I am all ready to attack the moment weather and roads will permit troops and artillery to move with anything like life."[6]

During twenty-seven days of bad weather, fighting men on both sides lamented that only musket and artillery fire was more continuous than rain. Hardly a daylight hour passed without a brief or an extended period of conflict. At least twelve clashes were of sufficient magnitude to be enumerated in official reports of 126 Federal officers: Brush Mountain, Cheney's Farm, Gilgal Church, Kolb's Farm, Lost Mountain, McAfee's Cross Roads, Nickajack Creek, Noonday Creek, Noses' (or Noyes) Creek, Olley's Creek, Pine Mountain, and Powder Springs. In Federal records, the more significant of these bear other names.[7]

Action close to an unidentified hill lying beside Kenesaw Mountain was described by Sherman as "one grand skirmish, extending along a front of eight miles." Only one day-by-day combat was mentioned by name in a lengthy report compiled by the Federal commander three months later. Of Kolb's Farm (sometimes called the Kolb House) he said that when the enemy "reached our line of battle he received a terrible repulse, leaving his dead, wounded, and many prisoners in our hands."[8]

With his headquarters "In the Field, near Chattahoochee River" on July 5, Sherman analyzed the month-long stalemate in retrospect. "We have a nice game of war and must make no mistakes," he wrote. "We ought to have caught Johnston on his retreat, but he had prepared the way too well." He found satisfaction, however, in concluding that "we have fought Johnston steadily back for 100 miles over very difficult ground, fortified at immense labor. I don't think our loss exceeds that of the enemy."[9]

By the time he realized that the condition of the enemy was far from bad, Sherman was bombarded with other concerns. Having been thwarted repeatedly in his bid to win a great victory and join Grant in Virginia, he may have excused his failure by stressing the magnitude of his task. In addition to directing the movements of three armies in Georgia, he hoped for an early move upon Mobile. At the Mississippi River, his responsibilities ended on the east bank. Yet vexatious problems of command continued to erupt from the west bank.

While watching over the division and making day-by-day decisions concerning his pursuit of Johnston that had turned into an invasion of Georgia, Sherman was forced repeatedly to wrestle with political issues. He realized that he had brought some of them upon himself by taking stands that ran counter to policies set in Washington.

On June 3, while still positive that he would soon fight and win a decisive battle, he issued a directive through an aide-de-camp: "Recruiting officers will not enlist as soldiers any negroes who are profitably employed by any of the army departments, and any staff officer having a negro employed in useful labor on account of the Government will

LESLIE'S

Gen. Joe Hooker's Twentieth Corps of the Army of the Cumberland engaged Confederate forces on Lost Mountain on June 14, 1864. After two days of skirmishing, the Southerners evacuated.

refuse to release him from his employment by virtue of a supposed enlistment as a soldier."[10] Despite this order he objected to sending black soldiers from Nashville to Kentucky. They might be needed at the Tennessee capital, he said.

ACTIVE RECRUITMENT of black soldiers was taking place throughout the North, and many states were sending agents into the South. Every former slave who donned a uniform was credited against the quota of the state whose ranks he joined. By inducing blacks to become soldiers, political leaders hoped to reduce somewhat the pressure of the draft upon their white constituents.[11]

From the beginning of the conflict, former slaves had constituted a problem for the North. Instead of diminishing, it increased steadily. Many commanders in blue initially refused to shelter these refugees; some tried to return them to their owners. Very early in his administration, Lincoln insisted that the Fugitive Slave Law must be upheld and that runaways were clearly fugitives.

In October 1861 Secretary of War Simon Cameron authorized Gen. Thomas W. Sherman to free slaves and equip them with arms. Lincoln struck out the clause concerning the granting of freedom and stipulated that no officer was authorized to engage in "a general arming of them [former slaves] for military service."

At Fortress Monroe, Benjamin F. Butler deftly cut a verbal loophole in the law. After sheltering a few runaways, Butler decided to stop calling his uninvited guests former slaves. Since their labor constituted an aid to the enemy, he labeled them "contrabands of war" and put them to work on projects of his own.

With the possible exception of an occasional black spokesman, Butler's solution of a delicate problem was happily accepted by Northerners. No white man objected to the use of black laborers; thousands of them could be used in the building of canals and railroads.

Use of blacks as soldiers, however, was a different matter. Many a Northern leader, including the president of the United States, had put his views concerning persons of African descent upon the record. Blacks were widely considered to be biologically inferior to whites and incapable of bridging the gap between the races. That being the case, it was self-evident that a black couldn't make as good a soldier as a white.

In the immediate aftermath of Fort Sumter, a minority of Northern radicals began clamoring to put free blacks and former slaves into uniform. Lincoln admitted that he had serious personal reservations about taking such a step. Such considerations aside, he insisted, he could not afford to do anything that might cause Kentucky and the other border states to sever their ties with the Union.

James H. Lane of Kansas, however, ignored the national policy and raised a regiment of black troops. In Louisiana, Confederate officials incorporated a number of such units into the state militia. After the fall of New Orleans, most of them transferred into the newly organized Federal Corps d'Afrique. Yet in the North there was no strong sentiment for use of black soldiers until the Emancipation Proclamation took effect.

Men of the First Kansas Regiment went into combat at Island Mounds, Missouri, late in October 1862. Immediately after Lincoln's most drastic and most effective single military step was taken with a stroke of his pen on January 1, 1863, these men entered Federal service. At Port Royal, South Carolina, abolitionists began raising a regiment of blacks in August 1862.

These pioneer efforts, largely symbolic, had no impact upon the war. On May 22, 1863, the War Department established a bureau for black troops, headed by C. W. Foster. Its purpose was to actively recruit and enroll black Americans in the Union forces.

Brig. Gen. Lorenzo Thomas became responsible for this new branch of the military service in March 1863. From the day of his appointment, progress was so rapid that before war's end an estimated 180,000 blacks entered Federal service. For many months, a black recruit's pay was only a little more than half that of a white comrade, however. This disparity prevailed until July 1864.

By the time Sherman and his troops crossed the Etowah River, few military or political leaders of stature publicly endorsed Sherman's practices and views concerning blacks. He had used slaves in both Mobile and Charleston during his early years in the U.S. Army. Unlike Lincoln, he felt that legislation aimed at making possible the westward extension of slavery was harmless.

In such territories as Kansas and Nebraska, he insisted, slavery would not be profitable and hence could not flourish. Instead of trying to take a neutral stand concerning abolition, Sherman openly opposed such a move by Union leaders. While fighting in Mississippi, he showed little interest in or sympathy for contrabands who flocked toward his forces.

Such views were no longer generally accepted in the North. Hence Sherman's refusal to permit recruitment agents to follow his forces as they inched southward in Georgia created a storm of indignation. Sherman acted as though he was not aware that he was being challenged. To his wife, he confided: "I would prefer to have this a white man's war and provide for the negroes after the time has passed. . . . With my opinions of negroes and my experience, yea, prejudice, I cannot trust them yet."

Months later he softened his stance a trifle. If "recruiting agents must come into the limits of my command under the law," he wrote, he still wanted nothing to do with civilians. Instead he proposed that "commanding officers or adjutants of regiments be constituted such agents."[12]

Though he nowhere said so, his low esteem for black soldiers seems to have been responsible for a major policy decision. Some units, then identified as colored, were attached to the Department of the Cumberland. But when George H. Thomas and his men moved out from Chattanooga in early April, all blacks were left in Tennessee for guard duty.[13]

No one knows how greatly or how little Sherman's attitude concerning recruitment affected events in the region then known as the West. However, a statistical report compiled in October 1864 is suggestive. During twelve months, the number of regiments made up of black soldiers increased from 58 to 140. Manpower of these units jumped from 37,707 to 101,950 during twelve months. Yet former slaves "enlisted and mustered into service at the several rendezvous established in the rebel States" numbered only 2,510.[14] This strikingly low rate of recruitment prevailed during a period when movements of a single Union army might be followed for days or weeks by thousands of contrabands.

A SECOND vexatious set of problems, again more political than military, centered upon the matter of prisoner exchange. When Maj. Robert Anderson surrendered Fort Sumter and lowered its flag, there seems to have been no thought of treating him and his men as prisoners. Unconditionally liberated, they were allowed to return to the North and in New York City were greeted as conquering heroes. So many prisoners were taken at Bull Run, however, that the question of what to do with them became a major issue.

Lincoln firmly insisted that no secession had taken place; so-called seceded states were simply in a state of rebellion, he said. According to him, there was no possibility of compromise or concession upon this fundamental issue. Any and all acts aimed at effecting so-called secession on the part of rebellious states were null and void, he stressed.[15]

This inflexible stance on the part of the president, who was also the commander in chief of U.S. armed forces, created a dilemma. To exchange prisoners between Union and Confederate forces would imply that the fighting men of the latter belonged to an independent nation. Matters were complicated by the prevailing view in Washington that captives should be treated as delinquents. According to this concept, every soldier in gray could be convicted of treason—a civil crime punishable only by death.

No formally approved exchange of prisoners could take place until the issue of Confederate sovereignty was somehow resolved. In practice, numerous commanders agreed to informal exchanges. Others simply ordered prisoners of war to swear that they would not bear arms again until "properly exchanged" and turned them loose—"on parole."

It took months of negotiation to arrive at an agreement, or cartel, that was signed by the belligerents on July 22, 1862. Federal authorities continued to stress, however, that this in no way implied recognition of the Confederate government. An elaborate system of exchange, with separate provisions for enlisted men and various grades of officers, seemed to promise that prison camps would soon be emptied.[16]

Col. Robert Ould was appointed to serve as the Confederate agent for the exchange of prisoners. Gens. Lorenzo Thomas, E. A. Hitchcock, and Lew Wallace, along with Col. C. C. Dwight, represented Federal interests at various times. On April 16, 1864, Washington officials reported that 121,937 Confederates had been exchanged for 110,866 Federals.[17]

Agents of the U.S. Commissary of Prisoners did not know it, but a new and hard position had just been reached by Federal authorities. One day after these statistics were released, all formally authorized exchanges of prisoners came to an abrupt halt.

Partisan followers of Grant tried, then and later, to blame the new posture upon Secretary of War Stanton. Months earlier, before assuming his new rank and post, Grant had made his position clear:

> It is hard on our men held in Southern prisons not to exchange them, but it is humanity to those left in the ranks to fight our battles. Every man we hold, when released on parole or otherwise, becomes an active soldier against us at once directly or indirectly. If we commence a system of exchange which liberates all prisoners taken, we will have to fight on until the whole South is exterminated. . . . At this time to release all rebel prisoners in the North would bring Sherman's defeat and would compromise our safety here.[18]

Two major factors, said Grant, should be taken into serious consideration. First there was the matter of approximately twenty-nine thousand Confederates who were released on parole after the July 1863 fall of Vicksburg. They were placed in the charge of Confederate Brig. Gen. Lloyd Tilgham, and there was reason to believe that thousands of these men had broken their word and returned to the ranks to fight.

A still more compelling reason to halt exchanges was found in the Confederate attitude. Furious at seeing black soldiers don blue uniforms and go into battle, Jefferson Davis and members of the Confederate Congress agreed upon a desperate measure. Under its terms, a black private who was captured would be returned to his owner, sold, or otherwise treated as a runaway slave. White officers of black units, who held nearly all positions of authority in them, would be treated as criminals.

The alleged breaking of paroles and the bitter enmity toward black soldiers and their officers fueled public sentiment in the North. Many people in and out of uniform became convinced that these factors alone accounted for the cessation of prison exchanges.

They failed to reckon with the fact that Grant had a virtually unlimited pool of manpower, while the number of potential new Confederate soldiers was shrinking. Moreover, great numbers of Federals presently held captive would soon reach the dates at which their enlistments would expire. It would be foolish to make exchanges for men likely to head for home as soon as they were released. These and other factors contributed to the crucial decision made public when Sherman and his generals were concentrating upon the decimation of Johnston's forces in Georgia. Stanton, Grant, Sherman, and Johnston were not at the moment aware that the new policy would have far-reaching effects for them.

Already a trickle of prisoners had gone to a newly established camp close to Americus, Georgia, not far from the Georgia-Florida state line. Formally known as Camp Sumter but generally called Andersonville, the facility went into operation shortly before Sherman left Chattanooga. In late February, a shipment of five hundred men from Richmond's Belle Isle reached the sixteen-and-a-half-acre stockade. Constructed to accommodate ten thousand prisoners, it was three-fourths full by the time Sherman crossed the Etowah River.[19]

Georgia's Gen. Howell Cobb, commander of the state's reserve corps, was already deluged with demands from Andersonville. Guards, guns, ammunition, and supplies of every kind were urgently needed at the camp, reported Col. A. W. Persons. To Richmond, he dispatched a plea for tools of any kind. Supporting that plea, he warned that "foul, fetid malaria and effluvia" caused by filth and disease, could lead to "a frightful mortality."[20]

Prisoner exchanges stopped regardless of who made the crucial decision: Grant alone, Stanton alone, or Grant and Stanton and Lincoln. At the same time, the South was experiencing a severe shortage of food. Soon there was not enough for both the military and civilians, to say nothing of prisoners already at Andersonville. Thousands more would immediately go there as a result of a terse directive issued in the Confederate capital: "Prisoners captured south of Richmond will be sent direct to Andersonville, Sumter County, Ga."[21]

Once the camp was packed with three times the number of prisoners it was built to hold, every man there experienced what one

Pennsylvania inmate described. He said that his "big intestines were eating his little ones up."[22] A combination of factors had converged to convert Andersonville into a bomb whose explosion was only a matter of time.

Unaware that the camp far to the south of his lines would be evacuated before he could join forces with Grant, Sherman seems not to have balked at the cessation of prisoner exchanges. Though some of his own men were sure to go to Andersonville, he continued to regard the defeat of Johnston as the central objective of his campaign. Gilgal Church and Olley's Creek would soon be forgotten. Though progress had been distressingly slow, the Federal commander reasoned that matters must soon take a different turn.

11

Judgment Day at Kenesaw

A TOP AIDE-DE-CAMP to Sherman, L. M. Dayton didn't ask for an explanation or clarification. He hurriedly but carefully noted what his commander said, knowing that within forty-eight hours he would learn that many of his comrades were dead.

Thomas and the Army of the Cumberland, McPherson and the Army of the Tennessee, and Schofield with the Army of the Ohio were given advance notice that all would "attack the enemy in force" at 8:00 A.M. on June 27. Sherman had already made plans to be on Signal Hill and to maintain communication with his generals by means of field telegraph lines. Using an oversize "glass," or telescope, from this high point he could view much of the action.[1]

Each attacking column would attempt "to break a single point in the enemy's line." This meant that success depended heavily upon coordination, with hour-to-hour movements being directed by Sherman himself. A terse clause stressed the urgency of preparing to act without letting the enemy know what was under way; "All commanders will maintain reserve and secrecy even from their staff officers," the order stipulated.

To officers who studied Sherman's carefully drawn directives, it was clear that he intended to force Johnston to stretch his line of defense. Once that was done, a series of hammering blows at the Confederate center would result in a breakthrough—and a splendid victory! To the Federal commander, it seemed possible at one blow "to cripple Johnston beyond the hope of recovery."[2]

Sherman's orders were not hastily improvised. On the contrary, they were drafted after deliberation and after he had weighed the risks involved. To his subordinate who was charged with breaking the center, he dispatched a terse message on the day before the attack: "I am willing to risk a good deal."[3]

Despite top-secret maneuvering by Union troops as they moved into position, by Sunday, June 26, the Confederates knew that something very big was afoot. It was too late for help to reach Johnston for the present crisis, but the Confederate commander knew that it would not be the last one he would face. While awaiting the attack, he dispatched a desperate but futile request that cavalry from East Tennessee or Mississippi be sent to Georgia.[4] An estimated one thousand members of the Georgia militia, lacking combat experience, increased his numbers but added little to his strength.

The Federals began moving well before daylight on Monday; J. W. Reilley's brigade obeyed instructions to "commence operations by 5 o'clock at latest." So many troops were involved that staggered starts were necessary; Brig. Gen. John Newton was told to "commence his movement for the attack at sunrise, keeping his troops as well concealed from the enemy's view as possible." Some men of the Army of the Cumberland waited impatiently, chafing that they were required to wait until 8:00 A.M. to get under way.[5]

As planned, a furious cannonade punctuated by the rattle of small-arms fire warned that men in blue would soon try to scale the slopes of Kenesaw. Sherman later said, "All along our lines for ten miles a furious fire of artillery and musketry was kept up."

Actually, firing of an estimated two hundred big guns ended about 8:30. While it lasted, the hill under attack (then and now called a mountain) was described as smoking and blazing in a fashion that transformed it into "a volcano as grand as Etna."

Big Kenesaw, tallest point in the region, was only about seven hundred feet high. Little Kenesaw, connected with it by means of a ridge about two miles long, was no more than four hundred feet in height. Nearby Pigeon Hill, named for migrating birds, was only half as high as Little Kenesaw.

Deep gullies, steep banks, and dense stands of chestnuts and other trees made the upward movement slow and painful. By fortifying all three raised positions, Johnston had extended his lines, abounding in abatis and rifle pits, to about four miles in length. Sherman correctly assessed the topography in a single sentence: "Kenesaw is the key to the whole country."

The peaceful farms and fields around Kenesaw Mountain were the stage for Sherman's worst strategic blunder of the campaign. During the two or three hours of "judgment day at Kenesaw," he lost three thousand men and seven commanders.

JOHN A. Logan, charged with breaking the Confederate line between Pigeon Hill and Little Kenesaw, was not optimistic. Earlier, he had opposed the assault and suggested that action again be taken to flank the enemy. McPherson, some of whose troops acted in concert with Logan's, made his main thrust against the right center of the long Confederate line.

Two brigades under Jefferson C. Davis aimed at Cheatham Hill, a knoll just high enough to make a splendid spot from which defenders could rake attackers as they clambered upward. Immediately dubbed the "Dead Angle" by the men in blue, this spot was enfiladed by Confederate cannon fire from both sides.

Some who survived the futile attempt to storm the hill later described themselves as having been like cattle driven into a slaughter pen. It was here that Brig. Gen. Edward M. McCook, of the famous "fighting McCooks of Ohio," was fatally wounded. Third of the clan to

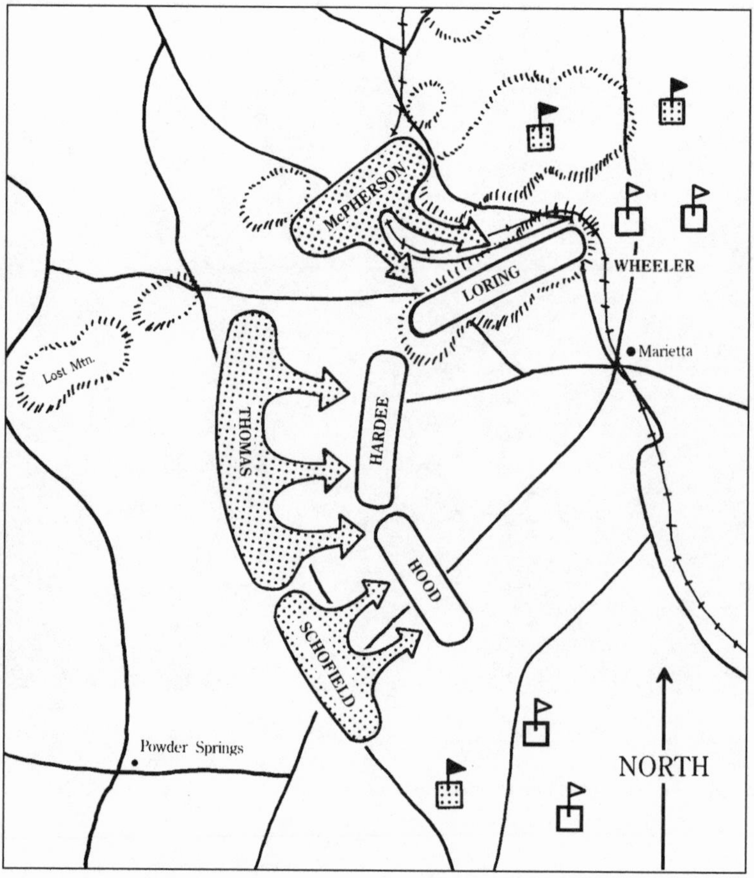

The Kenesaw plan of attack

die in action, he left fourteen brothers and first cousins behind in Union blue. Sherman made no attempt to conceal his grief at the loss; during his brief fling as an attorney, McCook had been one of his law partners.[6]

Men under George H. Thomas fared only a little better than those who were caught in the Dead Angle. Soon they found themselves using bayonets and musket butts against the Sixty-third Georgia Regiment. Brig. Gen. Charles G. Harker, a West Pointer who had won early distinction, led his five columns of troops against a brigade of Tennesseans. Confederate positions were so strong that only a handful of the attackers came close to their objective before being driven back. Awed by what he found when the battlefield was abandoned, Gen. O. O. Howard concluded, "The whole line was stronger in artificial contrivances and natural features than the cemetery at Gettysburg." When crossfire raked the steep slope, it became virtually impossible for the attackers to move forward.[7]

Half an hour after Sherman's men were exposed to withering Confederate fire, many of their officers knew that it was hopeless to keep moving. Communications directed to Sherman on Signal Hill or relayed by subordinates varied in language but conveyed a single message.

"I consider a successful assault of the work in my front impossible," reported Brig. Gen. John Newton. Davis said that his men "could not make the assault, if ordered." Hooker respectfully suggested that it might be possible to turn the enemy's left by means of a night march. Milo S. Hascall, making free use of artillery, discovered the Confederates so well fortified that he had "to give up hope of getting his works." Schofield concluded that there was no hope of reaching "the flank of the enemy's main line today." Dodge found the slopes of Kenesaw so steep that "no line could readily ascend it."[8]

Despite their realization that Sherman was eager for another attempt upon Kenesaw, his commanders wanted nothing more to do with the hill. By 1:00 P.M., men of the Fourth Corps were greatly relieved to learn that there would not be orders to make another attempt that day.

A few Federals were in full retreat within an hour of having begun their movement. Some units remained in action nearly three times as long. A Confederate estimate said that the battle lasted for two and one-half hours "at very short range." Correspondents who observed the combat lauded the gallantry of the troops. Yet one of them summarized the battle in a sentence: "The struggle lasted one hour and twenty minutes; regiment after regiment planting its colors on the ramparts, only to be driven back."

Sam Watkins of the First Tennessee Regiment described the fearful contest from the perspective of Confederates defending Kenesaw: "I was as sick as a horse, and as wet with blood and sweat as I could be, and many of our men were vomiting with excessive fatigue, over-exhaustion, and sunstroke; our tongues were parched and cracked for water, and our faces blackened with powder and smoke, and our dead and wounded were piled indiscriminately in the trenches."

In his brief initial report to Washington, Sherman admitted that the planned grand assault had failed but minimized the extent of his loss. He had suffered no more than fifteen hundred casualties, he said, and would now "aim to get to the railroad below Marietta by a circuit or actually reach the Chattahoochee." He confessed that from the Federal perspective, "the only advantage of the day" served to see Schofield's men push beyond the limits of Hood's left.

Already, some of his officers were sure that he would fail to file an accurate account of the struggle. One of them grimly estimated "2,000 will cover all casualties severe enough to take men out of the ranks."[9]

VERY SOON after having dispatched a message to the Federal capital, Grant's colleague doubled his casualty estimate. In postwar years, he insisted that his losses did not exceed twenty-five hundred men.[10] Most analysts now say that he lost McCook, Harker, five other commanders, and about three thousand men during the two or three hours that constituted "judgment day."

Kenesaw brought the Federal losses during June to about seventy-five hundred. Johnston, however, insisted that about six thousand Union troops fell at Kenesaw alone. Confederate analysts later conceded that the entire "twenty-six days of fighting before Marietta" cost Johnston about thirty-nine hundred men. Of these, about eight hundred fell during the repulse of attacks upon the hill that seemed like a mountain to the men trying to gain its heights.[11]

Resaca began a series of withdrawals and flanking movements so marked that some fighting men compared the two commanders to two dancers. If the comparison was valid, it was no minuet or ballet in which they were engaged. Rather it was the dance of death.

During three months of moves and countermoves, the Confederates had suffered an estimated fourteen thousand casualties, or one out of every four men engaged. Union forces suffered at least three thousand more casualties, but the size of Sherman's armies meant that only one man in seven was affected.

Many men and officers in blue later berated their commander for having attempted the impossible. Howard's summary was especially bitter. Viewing Kenesaw Mountain in retrospect, he wrote: "Our losses in this assault were heavy indeed, and our gain was nothing. We realized now, as never before, the futility of direct assault upon intrenched lines already well prepared and well manned."

During a seven-hour truce arranged on June 29 so that both sides could bury their dead, brush earlier ignited by cannon fire was fanned by strong winds. Soon flames flared over the Dead Angle and other areas in which hundreds of dead and wounded were intermingled. Confederate Col. William H. Martin led a joint effort to stop the fire, after which an officer in blue made a gesture of gratitude.

Martin accepted the matched pair of military revolvers that were offered to him—and smiled as he promised soon to use them against the Federals.[12]

Few officers in Sherman's three armies dared to growl about their commander's stubborn resistance to a general withdrawal on the day drenched with blood. George H. Thomas, sometimes derided by Sherman as "Old Slow Trot," was an exception. On Monday afternoon, Sherman had approached Thomas at 1:30 P.M. about renewing the hopeless fight. Certain that the Confederate works could not be carried by assault, Thomas suggested that they might try to "build saps," or dig tunnels beneath the enemy lines. Sherman scoffed at the plan and soon notified his subordinate to "make such preparations as you can" for more fighting.[13] Just before 2:30, he renewed an earlier idea, rebuffed by Thomas, that he should "secure what advantageous ground" he had gained. Again Thomas refused to act.

Reporting on the battle the following day to a subordinate in Chattanooga, Sherman insisted, "I will persevere, and think I can find a soft place. At all events, we can stand it as long as they."[14] As was his frequent practice, Sherman rationalized his failure and made excuses for it. A primary concern, he stressed, was his growing conviction that both his own men and the enemy had decided he wouldn't stage a real battle. Again, he argued that he was handicapped by the skill and speed with which the Confederates could throw up fortifications. "As fast as we gain one position," he said, "the enemy has another ready."

Another solace was the fact that he was losing men at a slower rate than Grant. This enabled Sherman to declare, "Our loss is small, compared with some of those in the East." Years afterward he stressed that in spite of his losses, a ratio of ten-to-six in Federal-Confederate strength was maintained. According to him, this preserved "our relative superiority, which the desperate game of war justified."[15]

Keenly conscious that his account of Kenesaw would be given to the press, the commander chose his words carefully when he framed an explanation for his actions: "The assault I made was no mistake. The enemy and our own army and officers had settled down into a conviction that the assault of line formed no part of my plan, and the moment the enemy was found behind anything like a parapet, why, everybody would deploy, throw up counter-works, and take it easy, leaving it to the 'old man' to turn the position."

Writing to his wife three days after the debacle, he was more candid: "I begin to regard the death and mangling of a couple of thousand men as a small affair, a kind of morning dash. . . . It may be well that we become hardened. The worst of the war is not yet begun."

Sherman had held no large independent command since his failure in Kentucky. Now he had sustained losses of three- or four-to-one during his first major battle in Georgia. Yet he took pains to stress what he labeled an achievement. "If nothing else had been gained," he reported to Washington, "I can press Johnston and keep him from reenforcing Lee."[16]

JOHNSTON AND his generals, however, had no thought of attempting to reinforce Lee. For three months they had effected one withdrawal after another, fighting defensively and losing fewer men than did the Federal forces. After their stunning victory at Kenesaw, it was time to move once more without concealing what they were doing.[17] Schofield's Army of the Ohio was already pushing past the Confederate flank. None of Sherman's other forces could claim even a token gain from their costly assaults of June 27.

Union troops, under orders to march at top speed, reached a point barely eleven miles from the Chattahoochee River late on the day of the battle. That put them in a position to slide behind the Confederate rear, forcing the enemy to retreat to new sites at or near the riverbank. Only one thing threatened to slow this new Federal advance: a severe shortage of essential supplies.[18]

As he had so often done since leaving Chattanooga, Sherman voiced plans for swift and decisive action. Two days after his defeat, he reported to Washington, "I will aim to get to the railroad below Marietta by a circuit or actually reach the Chattahoochee."[19]

Somehow, the weeks of June had seemed to fly even faster than those of earlier months. Sherman never admitted it in writing, but he must have been glad that no one appeared to be counting the days that had passed. He was eager and ready to cross the big river to the south—but to do so he must once more reckon with Johnston.

Part 3

A Fresh Target and a New Foe

12

Joe Johnston Can Withdraw; Atlanta Cannot

JOSEPH E. JOHNSTON knew that his smashing victory at Kenesaw had not crippled his enemies. Another withdrawal toward the south began almost as soon as burial parties finished their work. Unknown to Sherman, the Confederates had prepared two lines of defense upon which to fall back.

One was centered near tiny Smyrna campground, less than ten miles below Marietta. Johnston's second and much stronger line lay on high ground along the Chattahoochee River. By July 2 Federal officers were generally aware that Schofield's flanking movement had failed to catch the enemy in a trap.

Moving rapidly, Union troops staged a surprise attack on July 4. Without significant loss, they managed to turn the Confederate left. Until a few hours before the action began, Sherman knew nothing of this position or of the fortifications that guarded the railroad bridge over the Chattahoochee. Again flanked, Johnston moved away from the enemy to occupy his second line behind Marietta. Described as a *tête-de-pont* (bridgehead) at the river, Sherman remembered it as "one of the strongest pieces of field-fortification I ever saw."[1]

Brig. Gen. Francis A. Shoup, who was responsible for planning this six-mile defensive line, had placed redoubts less than one hundred feet apart. A stockade built with logs linked these installations. In addition to conventional field artillery, Shoup managed to secure and mount a few large-caliber siege guns.[2]

While making plans to cross the river eighteen miles to the north and ten miles to the south of the heavily fortified spot, Sherman took steps to reduce the flow of supplies to the enemy. Brig. Gen. Lovell H. Rousseau was sent to Opelika, Alabama, where he succeeded in cutting rail lines.[3]

Close to the vital Chattahoochee, Federal wagon trains rolled continuously for five days. With Allatoona and Marietta as major bases, huge quantities of supplies had been accumulated. Sherman, however, found himself too far ahead of his railroad and telegraph lines, so he paused while they were pushed ahead.

Dodge managed to lead two brigades in a rare but successful direct assault upon "heavy intrenchments." Sherman, who planned simply to "press Johnston hard until he is over the Chattahoochee," was surprised at the strength of the resistance he met.

One of the least familiar traits of the Federal commander was his firm insistence that he had the gift of "foreknowledge." His belief in this power was so strong that he often confided to his wife that he saw the future more clearly than the present. "I can't help but overlook the present and look ahead," he confided.[4]

Reports of scouts and what he considered to be an ability to see into the future convinced him that Johnston was likely to try to hold the river. "All the regular crossing-places are covered by forts, apparently of long construction," he noted.

As he had started to do while planning strategy with Grant, Sherman tried to second-guess the commander of the Army of Tennessee. Long before he passed Marietta, the Federal commander arrived at one conclusion after another only to scrap each in short order. Now he was feverishly concerned—virtually obsessed—with yearning to know what Johnston might do next. An outline of some of his notions constitutes a characteristic day-by-day chronicle of Sherman's thinking.

On Saturday, July 9, he decided that his foe "will be forced by the present situation either to attack or withdraw." During the following day he concluded that Johnston's actions would force him to weigh four options: "If he neglect his right or center we get on his Augusta road. If he neglect Atlanta we take it. If he assume the offensive we cover our roads and base and can make as good use of Peach Tree Creek as he. If General Stoneman could break the road [railroad linking Atlanta with Augusta], so much the better, but if he cannot I calculate that General Rousseau will do so within a week."[5]

On Monday, he decided that "Johnston will group his army around Atlanta, and wait for us to develop our game." Hours later, a rumor that the Confederate leader would fight for the place persuaded Sherman that he would not try to hold it. By noon, this verdict was spreading among his subordinates.

Having believed that Atlanta would be strongly defended, he now decided that unless Johnston received reinforcements, there would be no effort to retain the town. Far to the north, Grant was convinced that the Confederates would concentrate upon cutting Sherman's rail and telegraph lines rather than staging a full-scale battle. To him it seemed likely that some units of the Army of Tennessee would soon hurry to the eastern theater to reinforce Lee.[6]

Running in a general northeast to southwest direction before Atlanta, the Chattahoochee was a formidable barrier. Had there been no defensive works on either side, the river would have served to shelter the watershed, or low plateau, on which Atlanta stood. Under cover of darkness during the night of July 7, Schofield's artillery engaged in "the most tremendous cannonade of the campaign." Intended to draw the attention of the Confederates from the point at which Union troops

LESLIE'S

Brig. Gen. Grenville M. Dodge's Sixteenth Corps forded the Chattahoochee on July 10 at Roswell's Ferry.

Sherman viewed Roswell as a significant industrial center, having three textile mills. He was surprised that the Confederates had not fortified the town when he ordered his cavalry commander, Kenner Garrard, to seize it.

hoped to effect a crossing of the Chattahoochee, this exercise seems to have served its purpose well.

Since he had in his command "many old Lake Erie sailors," Schofield threw a pontoon bridge across the river without losing a man. His crossing, made at Sope Creek not far from Roswell, was described by his commander as having been executed "very handsomely." Almost simultaneously, Garrard and some of his cavalry moved past the river by "the shallow ford" at Roswell.

JEFFERSON DAVIS had warned Johnston not to retreat beyond the Chattahoochee, but Federal crossings north of his position left him no choice. A few of his units pulled out of their fortifications and went to the south bank of the river on June 5. Johnston did not follow until June 9, and when he moved out he had all nearby permanent bridges burned.

A pontoon bridge was cut in such fashion that its north end gradually floated to the south bank, making it useless to the enemy. This withdrawal, made in preparation for falling back upon Peach Tree Creek lines, left the Federals "in undisputed possession of the right [or north] bank of the Chattahoochee."

Sherman crossed the big river on July 12. Soon afterward it was reported that Gen. Braxton Bragg had reached Atlanta from Richmond. Precisely what his mission might be, no one knew. McPherson made his way across the Chattahoochee on July 17, charged with immediately moving toward Stone Mountain to destroy the railroad leading east from Atlanta.[7]

In Federal camps, there was some talk about the possibility that Johnston would now—finally—take the offensive. He clearly considered this possibility, and perhaps would have done so had it not been for decisions made in Richmond. Relayed to him on July 17, a directive from the Confederate president relieved him of responsibility for making such a momentous decision.

Much that took place among the ranks of the Confederates was almost immediately known to their enemies. Sherman and his generals employed a number of persons, mostly men, to gather information. Called scouts, they were spies who wore civilian clothing or Confederate uniforms in order to pass through battle lines with some frequency.

LIBRARY OF CONGRESS

Johnston proposed a stiff resistance to the Federals' crossing the Chattahoochee River, but Schofield's forces erected a pontoon bridge at Sope Creek, near Roswell, and outflanked the Confederates, forcing them to abandon their Chattahoochee defenses.

J. C. Moore, who reported the arrival of Bragg, said on July 14 that numerous civilians were leaving the region.

Sherman's effective force had been reduced to about seventy-five thousand men. Knowing that units of the Georgia militia had reinforced Johnston, he judged his foe to be more nearly his equal than at any earlier time.

Years of experience in the U.S. Army were meaningless if the Federal commander meant what he said. Every veteran knew that untried or "green" state troops were all but worthless in combat. At least one thousand "citizen soldiers" had joined the ranks of the Army of Tennessee, but they were useful only for guard duty.

OVER AND over—every day or so from Chattanooga to the Chattahoochee—Sherman insisted that the rugged terrain was an aid to the enemy. His verdict concerning the Federal disadvantage was repeatedly echoed in the reports of the men who led the Army of the Cumberland. Yet Johnston was positive that the "densely wooded character of the country" was an asset to his pursuers.

Terrain in which one set of soldiers withdrew again and again while their foes repeatedly flanked them was of major concern. They did not know it at the time, but both commanders were also vexed by the relatively minor issue of newspaper coverage.

Sherman was furious when a *New York Herald* reporter wrote that Sherman's men had learned to decipher the Confederate signals. At the drop of a hat, said the redhead, he'd arrest the correspondent and put him on trial. He also fumed, "The Atlanta papers contain later news from Washington than I get from Nashville." Then he added one of his frequent exhortations: "Absolute silence in military matters is the only safe rule. Let our public learn patience and common sense."

Johnston was less articulate but equally troubled by revelations he found in the media. During an earlier campaign he had tried to expel all reporters and correspondents from his army. That order had proved to be ineffective, so on June 25 he told corps commanders to prevent "statistical tables of our losses during specific periods" from getting into newspapers.[8]

Sherman's intense dislike of reporters and his willingness to adopt harsh measures with them may account for newspaper silence concerning an arbitrary decision that revealed the man's darker side. This silence prevailed in other quarters as well as in the daily press. Kenner Garrard was the active agent in an operation that included the ingredients of high drama, yet Sherman omitted mention of it from his official reports. Biographers tend to be equally silent concerning the affair of the Roswell factory women.

ROSWELL WAS nearly twenty miles northeast of Atlanta on a bluff overlooking the Chattahoochee and was locally derided as "a factory town." Until his men reached the place, Sherman knew little about it but believed that it had been a long-time cloth producer for the Confederate government.

Confederate Brig. Gen. Daniel C. Govan was captured a few weeks later. After having been exchanged, he told Brig. Gen. Benjamin F. Cheatham that during his captivity he conversed at length with Sherman several times. According to Govan, the Federal commander said that had Johnston attacked after the Roswell crossing, "he might have ruined him."

Since the Confederates made no aggressive move, Sherman went ahead with his plans. Because of its industrial significance, Sherman believed that Roswell would be fortified. Expecting that he would thwart Johnston if he had any plans "to molest our rear," he ordered Garrard to the village on July 4. His instructions to the Federal cavalry leader were to take it if he could. If that proved impossible, Garrard was to watch it closely and oppose any Confederate movements.[9]

Reaching the factory town on July 5, Garrard saw that it was not defended. He moved promptly, however, to burn a paper mill, flour mill, and machine shops. All buildings would be destroyed, he promised. On the following day he filed a detailed report about what he had done there.

Roswell was the site of a woolen factory capable of turning out 30,000 yards per month, he said. A "cotton factory" that he neglected to mention the previous day held 216 looms and could produce 191,086 yards of cloth, 51,666 pounds of thread, and 14,229 pounds of rope per month. About 400 women worked in the cotton mill alone. Since the output of the cotton mill was thought to be "exclusively for the rebel Government," he burned it without hesitation.

A French flag flew above the woolen mill, signifying overseas ownership; finding no U.S. flag beside the foreign emblem, Garrard put the woolen mill to the torch also. He was careful, however, to spare several thousand yards of cloth and some rope and thread. This he promised to "save for our hospitals." For reasons he did not explain, the cavalry leader had one man shot.[10]

Incidents of this sort occurred repeatedly throughout the Civil War. Had the usual attitudes prevailed, the destruction of the industrial complex—large for the time and place—would have ended the matter. That it did not was due to the temperament and inclination of the man whose primary mission was the destruction of the Army of Tennessee.

BEFORE 11:00 A.M. on Thursday, July 7, Sherman relayed an account of the affair to Halleck in Washington. Few of his communications reveal more about the man and his self-chosen goals that do these lines:

> General Garrard reports to me that he is in possession of Roswell, where were several valuable cotton and woolen factories in full operation, also paper-mills, all of which, by my order he destroyed by fire. They had been for years engaged exclusively at work for the Confederate Government, and the owner of the woollen factory displayed the French flag; but as he failed also to show the United States flag, General Garrard burned it also.
>
> The main cotton factory was valued at a million of United States dollars. The cloth on hand is reserved for use of United States hospitals, and I have ordered General Garrard to arrest for treason all owners and employés, foreign and native, and send them under guard to Marietta, whence I will send them North. Being exempt from conscription, they are as much governed by the rules of war as if in the ranks. The women can find employment in Indiana. This whole region is devoted to manufactories, but I will destroy every one of them.[11]

A lengthy set of instructions probably framed for the guidance of Garrard went forward before the telegram was sent to Washington. Sherman's message for his cavalry leader who was at or near Roswell included a special reference to the owner of the woolen factory. He told Garrard: "Should you, under the impulse of anger, natural at contemplating such perfidy, hang the wretch, I approve the act beforehand."

If Garrard submitted a written report concerning this stipulation, it was destroyed or lost. Records do not indicate what happened to the man above whose factory a French flag flew. Neither is there any evidence as to whether or not he really was a citizen of France. To compound the complicated and legally delicate situation, Sherman had no way of knowing how long this installation or the cotton factory had been selling to the Confederate government, or in what quantity.

Garrard was authorized to execute without pretense of trial an industrialist who may have been a foreign national. The language employed by Sherman can be interpreted as a direct suggestion that his subordinate should adopt this course.

Sherman's accusation leveled against the women workers is easily overlooked in the context of his emotion-charged order. On the presumption that the labor of these women helped the Confederate cause, he ordered them and their employers to be arrested as traitors. In doing so, he could not have been ignorant that the U.S. president had repeatedly declared secessionists to be "in a state of rebellion" (or insurrection) rather than of war.

Lincoln's first inaugural address stressed his firm conviction that "the Union of these States is perpetual" and cannot be broken. His office, he said, required him to see that "the laws of the Union be faithfully executed in all the States."[12]

Section 3, Article 3 of the U.S. Constitution stipulates that treason consists of making war against the United States "or in adhering to their enemies, giving them aid and comfort." It follows that since the United States had not declared war against the "so-called Confederate States of America," rebellion and insurrection could not be acts of treason.

William B. Mumford, a New Orleans gambler who tore a flag from the U.S. Mint in that city, was given a perfunctory trial. Convicted, he became the only citizen to be executed for treason against the United States during the eighteenth and nineteenth centuries. Perhaps a Roswell factory owner may have died under similar circumstances; what happened to him is unknown.

On July 9 at 2:00 A.M., men of the Union's Fourth Corps were notified to "move to Roswell Factory at daylight, and to move without wagons." Two brigades arrived at about 2:00 P.M., eight hours after Garrard had effected his passage over the nearby river.

Sherman did not suggest that the women whom he branded as traitors should be executed. Rather, he drafted specific instructions concerning them: "I repeat my orders that you arrest all people, male and female, connected with those factories, no matter what the clamor, and let them foot it, under guard, to Marietta, when I will send them by cars to the North."[13]

After two days of consideration, he decided that some of the people in Roswell were only "tainted with treason." It appeared to him that their work had been performed "almost exclusively" for the Confederate Army. "I will send all the owners, agents, and employés to Indiana to get rid of them here," he said. Almost as an afterthought, he tried to justify some of his actions by adding, "I take it a neutral is no better than one of our own citizens engaged in supplying a hostile army."[14]

On July 9 he reported his mass arrest and deportation of the civilians to Brig. Gen. Joseph D. Webster and instructed him: "When they reach Nashville have them sent across the Ohio River and turned loose to earn a living where they won't do us any harm. If any of the principals seem to you dangerous, you may order them imprisoned for a time. The men were exempt from conscription by reason of their skill, but the women were simply laborers that must be removed from this district."[15]

One of the correspondents despised by Sherman noted that the action concerning the Roswell civilians involved complex legal issues. He then reported how Sherman solved this entanglement: "[He loaded] them into one hundred and ten wagons and sent them to Marietta, to be sent north of the Ohio, and set at liberty. Only think of it! Four hundred weeping and terrified Ellens, Susans, and Maggies transported in the springless and seatless army wagons, away from their lovers and brothers of the sunny South, and all for the offence of weaving tent-cloth and spinning stocking-yarn!"

Thomas reported the arrival at Marietta of "Roswell Factory hands, 400 or 500 in number" on July 10 and noted that most of them were women. Scattered Confederate documents indicate that an undetermined number of children accompanied their mothers. Sherman replied to Thomas in a single sentence, saying that from Nashville the civilians under arrest would be sent to Indiana by Webster.[16] For the military record, that closed the case in which women and children were illegally deported after having been charged with treason. In his voluminous writings, Jefferson Davis never voiced a protest, presumably because he was so occupied with the war effort that he knew nothing of the incident.

The mystery of the Roswell women, whose ultimate fate remains unknown, is of major importance in its own right. Even more significant is its foreshadowing of the things to come. With the Army of Tennessee still virtually intact, Sherman clearly had a great deal more work to do. How much of his energy would be directed to the unconstitutional violation of civilian rights, only time would tell.

Had the Roswell incident not been followed immediately by major military developments, it might have made a lasting impact upon opinion. In this century, few analysts have given it the emphasis it deserves. Incredibly, one of them has gone on record as believing that the motive behind Sherman's mass deportation was concern for the women's safety.

DURING THE week following the arrest and deportation of the mill workers, a rumor reached Sherman's armies that Lee and his men, for the first time, were discouraged. Actually, the Army of Northern Virginia remained so strong that Grant was impelled to warn Sherman that Lee might send twenty-five thousand men to reinforce Johnston.

In Washington, Halleck was dreadfully uneasy about the situation in the East. He shared his concern with Sherman, saying, "*Entre nous.* I fear Grant has made a fatal mistake in putting himself south of James River. He cannot now reach Richmond without taking Petersburg, which is strongly fortified, crossing the Appomattox and recrossing the James."

For his part, Grant recognized that his forces appeared to be bogged down. His chance of winning a splendid victory that would change the course of the upcoming presidential election was growing smaller by the day. In this situation, he shifted the blame to civilians within the Union. Writing to an old friend, he confided, "If the Rebellion is not perfectly and thoroughly crushed it will be the fault and through the weakness of the people North."[17]

With the peace movement in the North apparently gaining strength every week, Lincoln's bid for a second term was in deep trouble. It would take a dramatic turn of events to cause a reversal in the trend of public opinion. In both the East and the West many observers agreed that Grant could not effect such a change of mood in time to affect the minds of voters.

That left the matter up to Sherman; in a real sense the fate of the nation as well as the conclusion of the war was in his hands. According to the Richmond newspapers, Confederate batteries were actually shelling the Federal capital. The Grant-Sherman plans for simultaneous East-West offensives leading to quick victories were now seen to have been futile.

WITH THE Chattahoochee River at his back and Confederate defensive lines along Peach Tree Creek ahead of him, Sherman believed he saw a wonderful opportunity. Nothing would please him more, he said, than to see Johnston suddenly take the offense.

Since such a change in strategy was improbable, Sherman hoped to send the Confederates running after a direct assault by his forces. He was confident that if Grant could prevent reinforcement of the enemy for a week, units of his combined armies could "dispose of it."

Yet during four months, his quarry had managed to slip away from him time after time. It was likely that the Army of Tennessee would withdraw once more—but the railroad hub that was the town of Atlanta occupied a fixed position. A target mentioned only rarely and briefly in the past suddenly began to loom as "the objective point" of Sherman's invasion of Georgia.[18]

13

John B. Hood Takes Command

Richmond, *July 17, 1864*
General J. E. JOHNSTON:

Lieut. Gen. J. B. Hood has been commissioned to the temporary rank of general under the late law of Congress. I am directed by the Secretary of War to inform you that as you have failed to arrest the advance of the enemy to the vicinity of Atlanta, far in the interior of Georgia, and express no confidence that you can defeat or repel him, you are hereby relieved from the command of the Army and Department of Tennessee, which you will immediately turn over to General Hood.

S. COOPER,
Adjutant and Inspector General.
[Indorsement]

Received [about 10:00 P.M. on the] night of July 17, 1864. Headquarters three miles from Atlanta, at Nelson's house, on Marietta road.[1]

THIS DECISIVE order closely followed exchanges between the Confederate commander and his president. After a month during which nothing of consequence was sent from the White House of the Confederacy to Georgia, Jefferson Davis suddenly became actively involved. On July 7, he stressed his apprehension for the future as a result of Johnston's having "fallen back to the Chattahoochee." This move was essential, his commander replied, because he had "found no opportunity for battle except by attacking intrenchments." Believing sixteen thousand Confederate cavalry to be defending Mississippi and Alabama, Johnston hoped that four thousand of them could be sent to his aid. By breaking the Western and Atlantic Railroad, he urged, they could compel Sherman to withdraw.[2]

A blunt telegram arrived for Johnston on July 16. "I wish to hear from you as to present situation," Davis wired, "and your plan of operations so specifically as will enable me to anticipate events."[3] If there had been any lingering doubts, this message dissipated them; Davis was furious and was at the point of making a drastic decision.

It was well known that he had not wanted to be chief executive of the Confederacy. With his West Point education and background as U.S. Secretary of War, he would have preferred to head the Confederate armies. Therefore, like Lincoln, he functioned actively as commander in chief of his armed forces. Both chief executives constantly made many difficult top-level decisions about military matters. Facing the dilemma of what to do about the seemingly bogged-down Army of Tennessee, Davis turned to an old friend and comrade.

Braxton Bragg, age forty-seven, had been a fellow cadet during West Point days. Later he fought in the Seminole wars and won distinction in the Mexican War. In 1856, Bragg, then a lieutenant colonel, resigned his commission to become a Louisiana planter.

He donned a Confederate uniform early in March 1861 and five months later was made a major general. Following another promotion, he headed the Army of Tennessee for a time. After his defeat at Chickamauga, he was relieved of command at his own request. Davis then brought him to Richmond as his personal adviser. Bragg, said the president, was just the right man to inspect the situation in Georgia and straighten it out.

The presence of Bragg provided Davis with a shield against the criticism sure to follow any decision he might make. After reaching Georgia's battle zone on July 13 without incident, Bragg informed the president that the Federals were across the Chattahoochee in force. "Our army is sadly depleted," he said. "I find but little encouraging."

Two days later, he was convinced that "we do not propose any offensive operations, but shall await the enemy's approach." According to him, Hood—supported by Polk until the death of the bishop-general—had continually urged an attack, but Johnston was "ever opposed to seeking battle."[4]

Bragg had informed Johnston that his visit was personal and unofficial, that he was en route to Montgomery, Alabama. To support that claim, he talked far more about events in Virginia than in Georgia. Johnston, who had served with Bragg earlier, was not deceived. Possibly he knew that Hood and Bragg had met secretly and that neither had commented concerning their conversation.

In previous assignments, Bragg and Johnston had worked together without serious friction. Despite the claims of the former, it was clear to Johnston that the president's personal counselor had come to make recommendations. Reportedly using a contemptuous tone of voice, Johnston was later quoted as having delivered the verdict: "Mr. Davis tried to do what God failed to do. He tried to make a soldier of Braxton Bragg."

Earlier having predicted disaster in Georgia, the president's adviser now concluded that Johnston had no more specific plans for the future than he had had in the past. Since he had not sought advice from Bragg, the official visitor from Richmond offered him none.[5]

In the Confederate capital, Davis and his advisers were convinced that the abandonment of Atlanta would lead to the fall of Mississippi. Believing a battle to be essential, they were positive that one man in the Army of Tennessee was itching for a chance to hit Sherman very hard: John Bell Hood. A native of Kentucky, Hood had hurried to Texas to enter Confederate service when his native state did not secede. Described as resembling a hunting dog or "a raw backwoodsman wearing a uniform that didn't fit," the heavily bearded Hood had been wounded at Gettysburg. With his left arm permanently disabled, he returned to the ranks in time to lose a leg at Chickamauga. While recuperating in Richmond, he was equipped with a cork leg and became an intimate of Jefferson Davis. In the capital, according to a rumor that circulated in February 1864, Hood would soon be named to command the city's defenses.

On February 1, 1864, at the age of thirty-two, he became a lieutenant general—with his promotion dated from September 20, 1863. Eager to fight once more, he was given command of the Second Corps, Army of Tennessee. As soon as he reached Georgia, he began sending a stream of secret letters and reports to Richmond. Without fail, these communications stressed the one-legged general's conviction that the Federal forces were weak and the Army of Tennessee was strong.

A recurrent phrase insisted that "we have had several chances to strike the enemy a decisive blow." As late as February 15, 1865, he continued to say that with Johnston in command, the Confederate troops had habitually fallen back "without serious resistance." He exaggerated Johnston's losses and offered a plan—called "fantastic" by analysts—for uniting all Confederate forces.

None of Hood's numerous dispatches to Bragg and Davis in the Confederate capital mentioned his own blunders and failures in Georgia. Coupled with his later disastrous leadership, this leads some analysts to give pause when assessing the Kentucky native, noting that he had "by all odds the most spectacular advance in rank of any officer in Confederate service."

Yet this usually competent brigade and division leader has been called "an unqualified disaster as the head of an army." Physical disabilities aside, he is sometimes regarded as being of "questionable emotional stability," perhaps from use of laudanum to dull his constant pain.

Bragg did not question Johnston about Hood's performance. Had he done so, he would have learned that the lieutenant general was responsible for several serious mistakes. At Resaca, men under his command were exposed to Federal fire because he found it difficult to coordinate the movements of his units with those of the other commanders. As a result, four guns of Van Den Corput's battery were abandoned; the Confederates lost no other artillery while Johnston was at their head.

At Cassville, Hood ignored an order to do battle, causing the South to give up perhaps the best defensive position it ever occupied in Georgia. Reporting about the matter to Davis, Johnston did not name Hood as the culprit; he referred only to "the officer charged with the lead." Even after Hood gave way before the enemy, Johnston wanted to hold the Confederate position. In a conference with his subordinates, he learned that Hood and Polk were eager to withdraw; Hardee alone wanted to remain and fight.[6]

Bragg may have been too concerned about the future to inquire about the recent past. Again, he may have taken at face value a letter handed to him by Hood soon after he reached Confederate headquarters. According to the document, Southern troops had repeatedly passed up good opportunities to do battle. It was imperative to attack now, Hood insisted, "even if we should have to recross the [Chattahoochee] river to do so."

After a quick look at Atlanta, Bragg mistakenly believed the city to be nearly empty and concluded that it was about to be evacuated. To

CHICAGO HISTORICAL SOCIETY

John B. Hood

Davis, he reported that Johnston did not have "any more plan for the future than he has had in the past."[7]

ALREADY HAVING decided that the situation in Georgia warranted a change in leadership, Davis replaced Johnston with Hood. Some observers, then and later, have charged that the long-simmering animosity between Davis and Johnston contributed to the decision. The two had first clashed, says tradition, when they engaged in a fistfight at West Point because both courted the same girl.

A victim of chronic neuralgia and blind in one eye, the Confederate president sometimes failed to control his temper. Very early in the war, he remained angry for days as a result of a dispute with Johnston. Yet when he drew up his first list of officers who would become full generals, Davis named Johnston as fourth of five men.

Because he was the senior U.S. Army officer to resign and offer his services to the Confederacy, Johnston felt that he had suffered an injustice. A six-page letter from him provoked Davis into a curt response concerning "insinuations" that he termed "as unfounded as they are unbecoming."

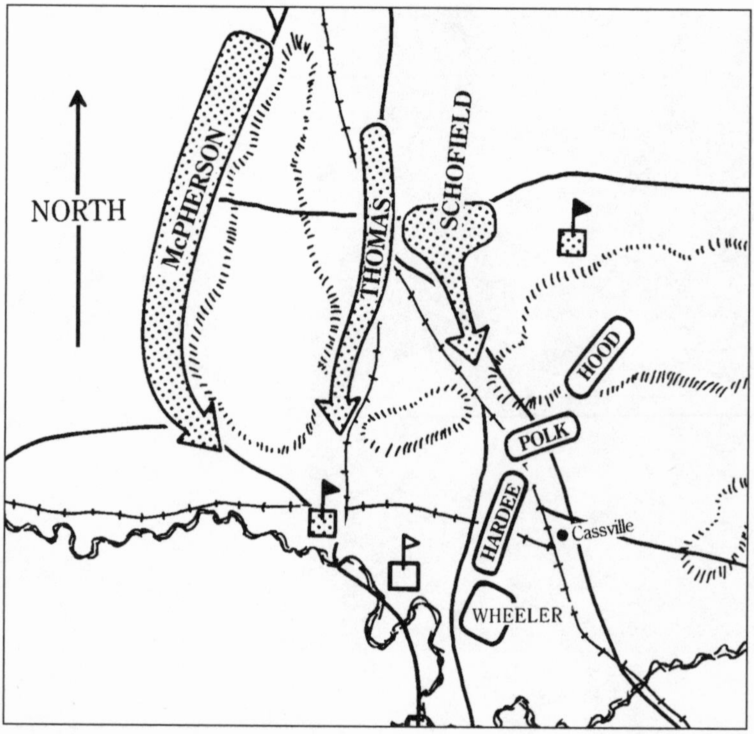

Hood ignored Johnston's order to engage the Federals at Cassville, causing the Army of Tennessee to relinquish perhaps the best defensive position it ever held in Georgia.

With the Army of Tennessee in peril, Davis clearly realized that the demotion of Johnston would infuriate the commander who had resisted Sherman so stubbornly. To complicate the matter, he could not put Hood in command without giving him an unusual promotion. In this dilemma, the president took advantage of a congressional act that permitted him to elevate the handicapped fighter to the rank of general temporarily.

News of his promotion was not yet public when Hood received a short telegram from the secretary of war: "You are charged with a great trust. You will, I know, test to the utmost your capacities to discharge it. Be wary no less than bold. It may yet be practicable to cut the communication of the enemy or find or make an opportunity of equal encounter whether he moves east or west. God be with you." Before midnight on the day Davis announced Hood's elevation, Johnston relinquished his command and prepared to move his family from Atlanta to Macon.

Hood took over immediately; yet before two hours passed he requested a conversation with his predecessor. Informing the Confederate adjutant and inspector general of his successor's actions, Johnston warned, "Confident language by a military commander is not usually regarded as evidence of competency."[8]

Hood's burst of confidence lasted only briefly. On the first full day in which he commanded the forces opposing Sherman, he waffled in a fresh communication to Richmond: "I have the honor to acknowledge the receipt of my appointment as general of the Army of Tennessee. There is now heavy skirmishing and indications of a general advance. I deem it dangerous to change the commanders of this army at this particular time." Davis replied, "The order has been executed, and I cannot suspend it." Hood therefore issued a brief statement to the men he now commanded. It reached some of them about the time that a telegram confirming the change of command was received. Hood responded to messages from the Confederate capital by requesting help from Lt. Gen. Stephen D. Lee, then at Tupelo, Mississippi. Almost as an afterthought, he said that he would "at all times be glad to receive advice or suggestions from the authorities at Richmond."

PARADOXICALLY, THE advice from Bragg and the action by Davis came just as it appeared that Johnston had finalized a plan of attack. The crossing of the Chattahoochee by Union forces meant that they had surmounted the last major natural barrier in northwestern Georgia. In doing so, however, they put themselves at great risk. Near Roswell, the river was about two hundred feet wide and usually shallow enough for easy passage by men and animals. At some points where bridges had been burned, steep bluffs towered more than fifty feet above the water.

Maj. Gen. Benjamin F. Cheatham and Brig. Gen. George E. Maney declared that Johnston was now ready to fight. With some portions of Sherman's army nearly thirty miles apart, Johnston was confident that he could successfully attack part of his foes.

Rather than confide his plans to Bragg or Davis, he asked Richmond for reinforcements. Given a substantial number, he urged, he could pin the Federals below the river and cut the railroad that was their supply line. That would place the Tombigbee River Valley in danger, Davis retorted. Sen. Benjamin H. Hill, who was informed about the exchange of ideas between Johnston and Davis, predicted that the military commander would get no help for his proposed move. "For God's sake do it," Hill urged.

Better than Hill or Davis or Cooper or Seddon or anyone else in Richmond, Hood knew that the forces he now headed were in trouble. They had withdrawn so many times that Union cavalry units appeared to be within striking distance of the prison camps. An estimated two thousand officers were being held at Macon, and Andersonville's population had soared far past its limits. On July 11, Johnston had strongly recommended the immediate "distribution of the U.S. prisoners" at Andersonville.

In contrast with his decisive actions a few days later, Davis left the Andersonville matter in the hands of Johnston and cavalry leader Joseph Wheeler. Neither Davis nor Johnston foresaw that Sherman would soon give Union cavalry leader George Stoneman permission to strike at both Macon and Andersonville.[9]

The news of the change in Confederate command first came to Sherman via an Atlanta newspaper and was received by his generals and him with mixed feelings. Describing the way in which his forces "feigned to the right but crossed the Chattahoochee by the left," Sherman noted on July 18 that "Hood was known by us to be a 'fighter.'" To his wife he confided that he must watch the new Confederate commander, "as he is reckless of the lives of his men."[10] Later admitting his pleasure upon hearing of the change, he observed, "At this critical moment, the Confederate Government rendered us most vital service."

In the opinion of the Union commander, the reputation of his new foe was tarnished. He stressed that McPherson was first in the West Point class in which Hood had graduated as forty-fourth and that Schofield was seventh in the same class. Occasional unqualified praise of Johnston by Sherman may have been voiced, however, as an alibi for his own failure to crush his foe.

Sherman's chief aide-de-camp noted, "Our enemies became dissatisfied with their old and skillful commander and selected one more bold and rash." Jacob D. Cox never wavered in his verdict that Johnston's defensive tactics were right for the time and place. To Grant, Hood's elevation meant that Atlanta would be defended "to the last extremity." Oliver O. Howard characterized the change in Confederate leaders as being "much to our comfort."[11]

Hooker took pains to interrogate recently captured Confederates to determine the sentiment in the ranks of the enemy. They reported that "the assignment of Hood gives great dissatisfaction" in an entire gray-clad corps, commanded by Lt. Gen. William J. Hardee. A correspondent who accompanied Federal forces wrote that the elevation of

Hood placed him above "a man beside whom he is a pigmy in nearly all the essentials of generalship."[12]

Confederate reactions to the substitution of Hood for Johnston came quickly. Lt. Gen. William J. Hardee, who despised both Bragg and Hood, threatened to resign immediately. Persuaded to stay, at the first opportunity he accepted a transfer to the Atlantic coast. Brig. Gen. Richard Taylor, a brother of Jefferson Davis's first wife, considered the change in leadership to be an "egregious blunder." Brig. Gen. Josiah Gorgas agreed with the widespread view, according to which "Hood has not capacity for such command."

Lt. Gen. Alexander "Old Straight" Stewart waited until the war's end to put his sentiments in writing. Earlier, during a conversation with Davis, he had told the Confederate president that the Southern troops had total confidence in Johnston. This confidence, he said, was based upon trust in "his skill and judgment" and the belief that "when he issued an order for battle, they would fight to some purpose."

Among the rank and file of men who made up the Army of Tennessee, it was reported, "Bearded men wept. Many threw away their arms and deserted." Someone later suggested that "the epitaph of the Confederacy should be: 'died of Braxton Bragg,'" and the quip was widely used.

Mrs. Fannie A. Beers, a volunteer nurse in a Confederate hospital, listened intently as news of Hood's promotion spread. Confessing that she was ignorant "of the relative merits of the two commanders," she wrote: "The whole post seemed as if stricken by some terrible calamity. Convalescents walked about with lagging steps and gloomy faces. In every ward lay men who wept bitterly or groaned aloud or, covering their faces, refused to speak, or eat. From that hour the buoyant, hopeful spirit seemed to die out. I do not think anything was ever the same again."

Civilians considered themselves to be as fully involved as were the men in the Army of Tennessee. In Richmond, rumors that Grant was dead occupied less attention than the change of command in Georgia. With Hood now facing Sherman, several editors decided that "affairs at Atlanta begin to wear a serious aspect." In Petersburg, readers were told that "the whole country is stupefied with astonishment and roused to no slight indignation at the action of the President [in ordering the change of command]."[13]

Not all reaction was negative, however. Two of Richmond's influential newspapers heartily approved of Johnston's removal. This change, said the editors, means "we are ready to fight instead of retreat." A rival journal declared, incorrectly, "The army and the people all have confidence in his ability."

Regardless of how civilians and soldiers felt, Hood was now firmly in the saddle—cork leg and all. To Sherman and his aides, the elevation of the young general meant that the nature of their long foray into Georgia was likely to change soon.

Johnston had used every possible stratagem to save lives and as a result of recent reinforcements the Army of Tennessee was relatively stronger than in April. Hood could not be expected to be guided by considerations that had dictated the actions of his predecessor. He was likely to do something rash, but precisely what course the big fellow might follow was anybody's guess.

14

Peach Tree Creek

During a period of one hundred days, the most absorbing question with which Sherman and his generals wrestled was What will Joe Johnston do now? He and his commanders discarded some answers within hours and framed new ones, but they clung tenaciously to others for day after day. Unaware of Hood's promotion, on the morning of Monday, July 18, while in the field on Peach Tree Road, the leader of the invasion tried to predict Johnston's next move.

It is hard to realize that Johnston will give up Atlanta without a fight, but it may be so, he reasoned. Meanwhile, Grenville M. Dodge was debriefing a spy just back from the town that loomed into importance as a military target once it came within sight of the invaders. General talk there, the fellow reported, assumed that "if Atlanta falls, Polk's corps will go west toward West Point, while the remainder of Johnston's army will go toward Augusta or Macon."[1]

The discovery that it was Hood rather than Johnston with whom the Federals must now reckon led to an acceleration of speculation. By 7:00 P.M. on Tuesday, Sherman knew that "the whole of the rebel army is about Atlanta." From reports of scouts and personal observation he learned that a powerful line of fortifications lay behind Peach Tree Creek. Hence he concluded that "we can approach the east with certainty of getting within cannon shot of the town, in which case it cannot be held."

During the next day, however, rumors said that part of the Confederate force lay south of Atlanta. Despite this, Sherman was "satisfied the enemy will not attempt to hold [both] Atlanta and the fort at the railroad crossing of the Chattahoochee."[2] This analysis proved to be correct—despite the fact that most of Sherman's guesses were less than accurate.

At about 1:00 A.M. on Thursday morning, he said that he would not be astonished to see Hood gone by daylight, but as yet he saw "no signs looking that way." Less than twenty-four hours later he was convinced that "Hood has let go the river and will make Atlanta his right and East Point his left, and endeavor to operate on our road with cavalry."[3]

When trying to analyze his opponent's strategy, Sherman wrestled with numerous problems within his own forces. Most of them were small in scale, but collectively they required much of his time and attention.

Readers of the *New York Times* were informed that Federal forces were across the Chattahoochee but had not "advanced much beyond the southern bank of the river." Possibly it was this report that led Sherman to storm that he'd like to boot another newspaper correspondent out of his command.

Militia promised to the Confederates by Gov. Joseph E. Brown of Georgia could not be dismissed from Sherman's mind. Though these would-be soldiers were old men and boys, five thousand of them could be a nuisance. By manning defenses with such persons, the enemy could deploy most or all of its seasoned troops against Federal forces.[4] This would substantially reduce the odds favoring the Union troops.

Worse, enlistments of many entire companies and regiments were expiring, and some men wanted nothing except to go home. A few who could have gone stayed to fight. Gen. August Mersey, a brigade leader under Dodge, was waiting for transportation. Enlistments of many of his men had also expired, but along with their general they remained south of the Chattahoochee. When spirited fighting began, they did not hesitate to join it. Dodge lauded these men in a postwar address during which he said: "They were out of service, they had written that they were coming home, and their eyes and hearts were toward the North; many an anxious eye was looking for the boy who voluntarily laid down his life that day."

A few loyal units that fought when they were not required to do so were of tremendous value to Sherman. Black troops could be used in the rear, he agreed, but even after this expedient was adopted he was forced to put many green units into combat. This made recruitment in the North a top priority in the Federal commander's mind. Yet he still objected strenuously to Northern recruitment agents who followed his trail, seeking to persuade blacks to don blue uniforms.[5]

Sherman continued to protest the presence of newspaper reporters, artists, and photographers in his line. In addition, he strenuously urged harsh treatment of those he called "dodges and make-shifts." These persons, representing the U.S. Sanitary Commission and the Christian Commission, were generally welcomed by other Federal commanders.

Because he habitually carried a pocket compass, old and faulty maps gave Sherman fewer problems than they caused his subordinates. Having established his headquarters near the only visible house—Buchanan's—one of Sherman's cavalry leaders wasn't sure of his location. There were two localities called Cross Keys, and his maps showed only one of them. Schofield was "desperate for good topographical engineers" since the only one in his command had been killed.

Maps customarily showed all old roads, which led to Decatur, but many failed to include newer ones leading to Atlanta. Once when Brig. Gen. Jeff C. Davis took the wrong road, he failed to reach his assigned position. Marietta was so important that a two-part map made early in July became standard among Union troops.[6]

Supplies were running low despite Sherman's frequent boasts about the efficiency of the railroads he now controlled. As a result, Union soldiers were ordered to take special precautions to prevent capture or destruction of wagons loaded with food and other essentials. Brig. Gen. Frank P. Blair Jr. admitted that he didn't know how many days' rations he could take along. Neither was he sure whether or not "the regimental teams should accompany the regiments."

Sherman was annoyed by fraternization between members of opposing forces. Some of them joyfully jumped into the Chattahoochee simultaneously in order to get their first bath in months. Though Sherman joined in the bathing, he tried to stop his men from swapping knives, newspapers, coffee, and canteens for tobacco. When Johnston learned what had taken place, he emphatically forbade a repetition of the frolic in the river.

FAR AND away the most pressing Federal concern not directly related to upcoming military activities centered in the person of Nathan Bedford Forrest. Although he had been rumored to be dead, he was indeed very much alive—and active.

Sherman urged Brig. Gen. A. J. Smith, stationed in Memphis, to watch the Confederate cavalry leader closely. During July alone, Forrest's dreaded name appeared a dozen times in Federal correspondence. It wasn't widely known at the time, but in Mississippi Forrest

LIBRARY OF CONGRESS

The Peach Tree Creek battlefield. Newly appointed to command the Army of Tennessee, Hood rashly ordered a direct assault against Sherman's forces here and lost more than four thousand men.

gave the Union forces one of their most humiliating defeats in June. Sherman's correspondence reveals that he seldom stopped worrying about what Forrest might do in Mississippi and Tennessee.[7]

As he approached the Chattahoochee, during the days it took his force to cross the river, Sherman was planning his next set of maneuvers. On Saturday, July 16, Blair was instructed to move toward a position between the village of Decatur and the granite hill known as Stone Mountain. Washington still feared that Grant was failing in Virginia, so the full weight of the joint East-West operation fell upon Sherman. Any day, Lee might "detach 30,000 or 40,000 men" and send them to Georgia. That made it essential for the Federals to move forward immediately. On Sunday Thomas was ordered to make a vigorous demonstration toward the new Confederate lines along Peach Tree Creek.[8]

A tributary of the Chattahoochee, the Peach Tree was described as topped on both sides by low ridges. At these points, the ground had been cleared for farming, and crops of cotton and corn were expected to be harvested soon. At frequent spots where little valleys or gullies cut into ridges, "they were left in a state of nature—wooded and full of undergrowth."[9]

Once over the Chattahoochee, Sherman decided to make "a bold push for Atlanta," which he expected to occupy within a few days. Rifle pits had been built on both sides of the river for the protection of the troops that would be left behind to guard the Chattahoochee. The Confederates appeared to be ready to offer no real resistance; they seemed to be concerned about picketing roads and arresting deserters.

On Tuesday, July 19, the time appeared likely to move directly into Atlanta, and Sherman ordered the advance for the next day, "at an early hour during the cool of the morning." By dividing his forces and making a dual thrust, Sherman hoped that Thomas could "walk into Atlanta, capturing guns and everything."[10]

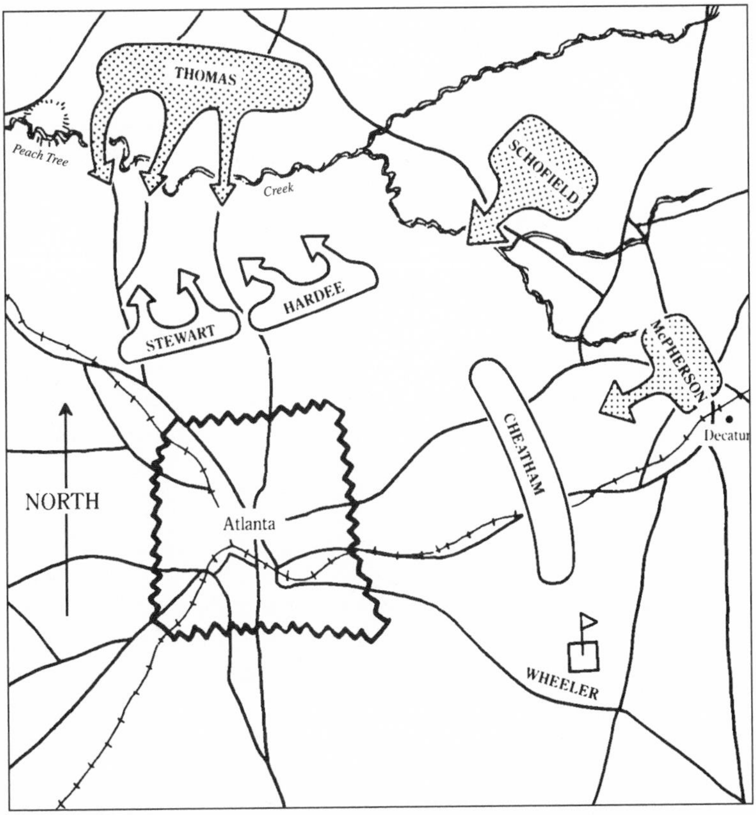

Federal forces maintained a three-pronged presence along Peach Tree Creek.

A few hours before the planned push, Sherman expected to move some of his artillery to the east of the fortified place he called a town. Once his guns were within range of Atlanta, he was sure that it would fall. Additionally, the Federal commander was confident that if Grant could "keep Lee from Reenforcing this [enemy] army for a week, I think I can dispose of it."

At 1:55 A.M. on July 20, troops began moving forward with orders to "sweep everything before them." Should soldiers or citizens fire upon them from buildings of Atlanta, they had their instructions in advance. Ignoring the fact that families of civilians might be there, Sherman ordered, "The place must be cannonaded without the formality of a demand [for surrender]."[11]

SHERMAN'S LARGEST force, the Army of the Cumberland under George H. Thomas, moved directly toward Atlanta from the north. This move seemed to have been anticipated by Johnston and communicated to his successor.

Seeing an opportunity to hit one of the three Federal armies, Hood was poised to attack. His brigades, however, proved to be far from ready to launch an offensive. Some Confederate units ordered to take the field at 1:00 P.M. dawdled or were delayed until 4:00 P.M. Wave after wave of Southern troops, described as being in a state of frenzy, soon charged the enemy for three hours.

Concurrently with the big struggle that centered about Peach Tree Creek, a smaller engagement took place to the west, or left, of the main Federal body. Following orders that directed him to turn the enemy's right flank, McPherson's relatively small Army of the Tennessee ran into trouble. Dismounted Confederate cavalry and units of the Georgia militia were in trenches dug to defend the Macon and Western Railroad. Sharp fighting erupted on Bald Hill, where Brig. Gen. Walter Q. Gresham was severely wounded by a sharpshooter in gray. Union forces, unable to complete their contemplated move, were forced to fall back.

McPherson, Schofield, and Howard had been at West Point with Hood. They were unanimous in warning Sherman that the man was "rash, erratic, headstrong," and therefore sure to attack sooner or later. At Peach Tree Creek on July 20, their judgment was shown to have been flawless.

Measured by any standard, the battle of Peach Tree Creek resulted in a significant Union victory. For the civilians in Atlanta, almost as important as the successful combat was the realization that as far as

Sherman was concerned they could expect no mercy. A report written later, but based on records of the day, said: "It was on this day, July 20, that Atlanta received her first visit from Sherman's army in the form of a shell from one of his guns, so many of which she was afterward to receive. This first shell fell at the intersection of East Ellis and Ivy streets, where it exploded and killed a little child which was with its parents at the time. The shell was seen to fall by Mr. Er Lawshe, and the fact is confirmed by Colonel Samuel Williams. . . . Two other shells fell later in the afternoon of the same day."

Within a few hours, George H. Thomas learned that Atlanta's civilians were under fire. Interviewing prisoners, he gained from them confirmation that "our shells yesterday fell into Atlanta, producing great consternation."

Approximately 40,000 men are believed to have fought, often hand-to-hand, along Peach Tree Creek on a brutally hot July day. Estimates of casualties varied wildly in July 1864, and discrepancies in counts have never been fully resolved. According to a tally once believed accurate, Confederates suffered 4,796 casualties while the Union loss was only 1,710. Sherman, who customarily multiplied the death toll by seven in his estimates, reported that 3,240 men in gray had died, while his own forces suffered only 3,521 casualties of all kinds.[12]

Still smarting from their losses to Johnston at Kenesaw Mountain, Federal troops came out on top in their first real clash with Hood. That was a source of considerable satisfaction and, they hoped, a harbinger of things to come.

Yet in addition to the redhead who directed them, officers and men in blue realized that the Confederates were a long way from being subdued. Hood was likely to take a week or so to regroup and permit his men to recover from the ordeal of July 20. Then he could be expected to strike again, perhaps at the Chattahoochee River bridge or some other vital point. While watching and waiting, many Federal artillerists improved their marksmanship and made things generally uncomfortable for the Rebels within Atlanta's fortifications.

15

The Battle of Atlanta

LATE ON the afternoon of July 20 Federal engineers discovered that a position of strategic importance was held by the Confederates. Frank P. Blair Jr. then led his men in an assault upon Bald Hill, south of the Georgia Railroad near Decatur. Driven back by the defenders of the elevated place, the men in blue vowed to make another attempt the following day.

Fearfully hot summer sun seemed to scorch the earth on Thursday, July 21. Nevertheless, soldiers not accustomed to Georgia in the summer charged up the hill and captured it, "though with heavy loss." Since the victory belonged to the men commanded by Mortimer D. Leggett, they immediately began to call the site Leggett's Hill. Though the new label commemorated a member of the invading army, the name stuck and was in general use years later.

Hours after Leggett's Hill became Federal ground, artillery units lashed and cursed their horses until they managed to get their guns to its highest point. Late that afternoon, Leggett's artillery "was given full play" upon Atlanta. Hood and his officers clearly understood that Yankee cannon were now well within range of Atlanta. Bald Hill, quickly given strong defenses by the units charged with holding it, suddenly emerged as the most vital spot within the battle lines. Unless it could be retaken quickly, Sherman's shelling of Atlanta would continue and accelerate.

The Confederates, weary and battered from the battle of Peach Tree Creek, withdrew inside the defensive line of Atlanta. Reports of

Federal pickets who observed large-scale enemy troop movements were sent directly to headquarters. There the shifts of position were interpreted to mean that Hood was leaving; if forced to fight a rear-guard action, he would be severely handicapped.

Sherman believed that Atlanta would be evacuated at once. By 7:30 P.M. aides of George H. Thomas were so supremely confident that they dispatched a buoyant promise: "We shall bounce them tomorrow." They had no idea that Hood was busy staking out and developing a new line of entrenchments.[1]

Delighted that his batteries were now in position to reach the center of Atlanta easily, Sherman summarized the fighting that had raged along Peach Tree Creek the previous day in a dispatch to Washington. He then turned to the future and acknowledged that Atlanta seemed to be heavily fortified. There appeared to be a line "all round it, at an average distance from the center of the town of one mile and a half," he acknowledged. These defenses would be of little help to secessionists, he insisted: "Our shot passing over this line will destroy the town." His confidence was such that he placed the Army of the Cumberland well apart from the armies of the Ohio and the Tennessee.[2]

Except for an occasional advanced picket, Union troops were soundly asleep by the time Hood began his preparations for July 22. Since Sherman's armies were separated into two columns with a wide gap between them, it appeared a perfect time to attack. There was also the vital matter of Bald Hill and the Federal guns now surmounting it. To Hood it seemed clear that unless he could regain the elevated position, he would have to abandon Atlanta.

He therefore chose a desperate expedient. William J. Hardee's corps, enlarged by reinforcements, was directed to make a night march around the enemy. Hood hoped he could strike before noon with forty thousand men, rout the overconfident Union soldiers, and install Confederate batteries on the strategic hill.

Sometimes termed "the premier lieutenant general of the Confederacy," William "Old Reliable" Hardee now commanded the First Corps, Army of Tennessee. His men were aware that their new commander had little use for Hood and even less for Bragg. He had wide experience, was a former commander of cadets at West Point, and was author of the standard textbook *Rifle and Light Infantry Tactics*. Hardee was generally liked as well as respected, and many of his men had volunteered a willingness to die for him; today they would have an opportunity to demonstrate what they said.

Sherman's headquarters, near the center of the Federal line, was shaded by a large tree that served to shield him and his aides from the torturous heat. About noon, during a conversation with McPherson, the two officers were startled to hear what they described as a roar.[3] It came from the general direction of McPherson's Army of the Tennessee and was the first indication of an attack.

Hardee and his veterans, determined to retake Bald Hill, were staging a series of fierce assaults after having marched for hours. The combat, now called the battle of Atlanta, was under way.

According to Grant, the struggle rapidly expanded in both directions and eventually "embraced about seven miles of ground." Watching the action, Robert Adams, a veteran observer, considered it perhaps the fiercest fighting "in the history of the Rebellion." The ferocity of the third Confederate assault led him to estimate that the Army of Tennessee must have suffered more than ten thousand casualties.[4]

Much of the fighting took place in areas Sherman tersely described as being "very hilly and stony." Muddy from the spring rains, Peach Tree Creek, "deep with very abrupt and high banks," limited the movement of perhaps thirty thousand troops seeking to hit the Federal lines from the rear. Thick woods gave the attackers protective cover until they were within three hundred yards of their objective.[5]

Partly because the terrain made it difficult for him to stay on his horse, Hood took no active part in the struggle. He found an observation point within a log redoubt and remained there much of the day. It was later said that he had a splendid view of the action when Hardee's corps—striking at the flank of blue-clad units—came into sight, "sweeping across an open valley."[6]

Sherman, however, was much more involved. He watched intently from the Howard house and sent frequent questions and commands to his subordinates. When it appeared that the Confederates were likely to overrun a position, he "personally directed an overwhelming fire of canister, which drove back the assailants."

Earlier the Union commander often had repeated assertions that Johnston's readiness to prepare fortifications foiled Sherman's attempts to trap him. Yet in his own correspondence, Sherman regularly noted that he typically began preparing defensive works as soon as his forces occupied a position. As a result, many of his men were protected by earthworks during Hardee's assault.

Between Peach Tree Creek and Atlanta, knolls were often linked by trenches that constituted a connected line. Union troops forced to fight outside this line resorted to whatever impromptu protection they could devise. Some of Leggett's men hastily threw up barricades using fence rails.[7]

Maneuvering and a series of charges caused Hardee to be lauded by Union officers, but his force was overwhelmingly defeated.[8] Near Bald Hill, the Confederates briefly enjoyed an apparent triumph that was inflated by its symbolic importance.

After firing heavily upon a Union battery commanded by Capt. Francis DeGress, men of the Forty-second Georgia Regiment charged the spot. The defenders took fright and fled, abandoning four highly prized 20-pounder Parrott guns. Two smaller cannons, 6-pounders, were abandoned by another crew. Previously the Federals had rejoiced that their artillery might successfully shell Atlanta, but the assault by the Georgians proved the guns were not invincible. Immediately turned on the retreating Federals, the heavy weapons were briefly thought to be pivotal in the struggle.

Union Brig. Gen. John A. "Blackjack" Logan shouted to his men that Washington must never hear that Union guns had been lost on the

ATLANTA CYCLORAMA

"Logan's Great Battle" is displayed at the Atlanta Cyclorama. The general commissioned the work in 1884 during an unsuccessful bid for the vice presidency.

LIBRARY OF CONGRESS

The site of Maj. Gen. James B. McPherson's death. He was the only Federal commander of an army to be killed in action during the war.

outskirts of Atlanta. His men charged against the fire of the captured Parrotts, fired so hastily that one burst immediately. Soon its wreckage and the remaining Parrotts were recaptured, but the smaller pieces remained in Confederate hands. A veteran of Gettysburg summed up the dramatic action in a single sentence: "I never seen more heroic fighting." Remembered by Sherman as having come to him in tears after three of his guns were recovered, DeGress said that no horse in his unit survived and he had only a few men left.[9]

Logan later exploited his brief period as commander of the Army of the Tennessee. An active role in the Grand Army of the Republic provided him with what he considered a strong political base. Hence he became a candidate for the vice presidency and was widely discussed as a potential occupant of the White House.

To boost his fame, Logan commissioned a group of foreign artists to depict the battle on a huge canvas. The work was called "Logan's Great Battle." After changing hands several times, it was acquired by the city of Atlanta. Restored and displayed in the Cyclorama, the canvas lauding Logan is perhaps the largest and finest work of art of its sort.

FEW CONFEDERATE officers exulted even briefly when they learned of a permanent loss by their foes. Having heard a sudden and heavy burst of gunshot while conferring with Sherman, James B. McPherson dashed toward the sound of the guns. Moving without the escort that frequently protected men of high rank, he was accompanied by only two or three aides. At least one of them warned him that the dense woods were thick with Confederates, but he brushed this information aside.

When a cry of "Halt!" came from Rebel skirmish lines, McPherson turned his horse and tried to escape. Before reaching safety, however, a heavy volley felled him.

Men of both sides generally concurred in their estimates of McPherson. At the age of thirty-five and considered handsome, McPherson was one of the ablest and best-liked Civil War generals. He was the only commander of a Union army to die in combat. While the battle of Atlanta raged, his comrades agreed that his loss was irreparable. Years later Grant praised him as having been one of the "ablest, purest and best generals" on either side.

McPherson's body was taken to Sherman's headquarters at the Howard house. News of the tragedy within the high command was relayed to Washington that night. One week after the battle of Atlanta, Lincoln was told that the youthful commander would be buried at 10:00 A.M. in his birthplace of Clyde, Ohio. A few weeks later Pvt. George J. Reynolds, D Company, Fifteenth Iowa Infantry Volunteers, was awarded a Congressional Medal of Honor for recovering McPherson's body.[10]

Sherman placed John A. Logan in temporary command of the Army of the Tennessee; after a brief leadership, he was succeeded by one-armed Oliver O. Howard. Joseph "Fighting Joe" Hooker, who claimed to have seniority over Howard, was highly offended at having been passed over. He requested to be relieved from duty in "an army in which rank and service are ignored," and was soon assigned to noncombat service as a departmental commander.[11]

Georgia native William H. T. Walker, a dozen years older than McPherson, also died that day. A West Point graduate, class of 1837, Walker had received two brevets during the Mexican War. Having been a Confederate major general more than a year at the time he was killed, he was considered inept by some of his fellow officers.

Along with Patrick R. Cleburne, also a commander in the Army of Tennessee, Walker had advocated that slaves be freed and armed to fight for the Confederacy. Numerous division and corps commanders in forces under Johnston and Hood endorsed the Cleburne-Walker proposal. In Richmond, however, this proposal was viewed with disdain and was kept secret when presented there just before Sherman's invasion.

Two facets of the Confederate defeat triggered no debate. Both sides agreed that a temporary truce was necessary to bury the dead and both said that many Confederates listed as casualties were made prisoners. In a single batch, about one thousand Southerners who were captured by their foes were reported as having been "sent North."[12]

Incomplete records make it impossible to know where all of the prisoners went, but in some cases, the disposition of men captured by Sherman's forces is documented. A member of the Third Florida Regiment, along with J. T. Derry from an unidentified unit, was sent to Camp Douglas, near Chicago. A. B. Foster's brother, who lost a leg at Peach Tree Creek, went to Johnson's Island in Ohio. Tom Bigbie was sent to Camp Chase in the same state.[13]

This trio of Northern prisons and others to which captured Confederates were sent fell well below the horror level of Andersonville. In some of them, though, the death rate was for a time almost as high as in the most notorious Civil War prisons. Had the exchange program not been ended by Grant, POWs from Peach Tree Creek and the battle of Atlanta could have facilitated the release of more than a thousand Union soldiers starving in the Georgia stockade.

Casualty estimates varied according to the viewpoint of the person making the estimate. Sherman reported a total Federal loss (killed, wounded, captured, and missing in action) of 3,521. His officers said that 3,220 Confederates had been found dead, 1,017 prisoners had been sent North, and an additional 1,000 wounded prisoners were in their hands. As a result, the Federal commander estimated total Confederate losses as being at least 10,000.

These figures were supported by Logan, but later analysts tend to challenge them. Confederates may have suffered only eight thousand casualties, while Federals may have omitted at least two hundred from the count announced by Sherman.[14]

SOME OF the summaries framed after Peach Tree Creek and the battle of Atlanta are today seen as incredible—or ludicrous. Locked in combat with Grant at Petersburg, Lee expressed delight at the news that Hood had won a glorious victory. Bragg, no longer in a position to make observations firsthand, called the three-day struggle a brilliant affair in which the enemy was badly beaten. When Hood finally admitted that his forces had suffered a major defeat, he blamed the debacle upon Hardee.

Disregarding such pronouncements, many Union officers correctly decided that "the enemy has been gloriously thrashed." Hooker concluded, "On the whole the result is most favorable to us."

At the time, few generals put into writing their views about a baffling aspect of the battle. Later some of them confessed bewilderment that their commander had held thousands of men in reserve. Sherman, whose dark side sometimes emerged quite unexpectedly, offered a bizarre explanation for the way in which he directed the conflict: "I purposely allowed the Army of the Tennessee to fight this battle almost unaided, save by demonstrations on the part of General Schofield and Thomas against the fortified lines to their immediate fronts, and by detaching one of Schofield's brigades to Decatur, because I knew that the attacking force could only be a part of Hood's army, *and that, if any assistance were rendered by either of the other armies, the Army of the Tennessee would be jealous* [emphasis added]."[15]

Grant had commanded this army for a year, beginning in October 1862. Sherman, who succeeded him, soon began proudly to refer to it as "my whiplash"[16] and led it for seventeen months. His pride in a body to which he gave a seemingly affectionate nickname may have affected his judgment as a commander. The strength of the forces under his commander was reported, perhaps optimistically, as ninety-eight thousand, or about the same number with which he launched his invasion. His battle losses had been compensated equally by the addition of new units and the return of men from furloughs and hospital stays.[17]

Despite inflated estimates of Confederate losses, Hood was far from vanquished. He still commanded forty thousand or more effectives with extensive combat experience. And they were supplemented by at least five thousand members of the Georgia militia, which was becoming more and more experienced in the ways of combat. The strength of the Confederate force was sufficient to persuade Sherman once again to alter his plans. Atlanta was so strongly defended, he decided, that he doubted that the town could be entered easily.

Again he had failed to achieve his most important objective. Though battered and bruised, the Army of Tennessee was still strong enough to resist and even to take the offensive. Under these circumstances, it was impossible to send one of his armies to Grant in Virginia as planned. Only one of the goals that had taken him into Georgia had been accomplished: he had succeeded in preventing any Confederates from leaving Georgia to reinforce Lee in Virginia.

Conscious that he had failed in his primary mission to crush the Confederate forces once stationed near Tennessee, Sherman dispatched yet another promise to Washington. Once his cavalry had rested, he proposed to "swing the Army of the Tennessee round by the right rapidly and interpose between Atlanta and Macon, the only [railroad] line open to the enemy."[18]

Forces sent to cut the last railroad leading into Atlanta should meet little opposition, the Federal commander believed. Within a few days he would accept the surrender of the town in lieu of Hood's capitulation. Though not nearly as significant as an army, a rail hub was much better than nothing. Once Atlanta was securely in his hands, Sherman could inform the North of another glorious victory.

Part 4

Too Strong to Attack,
Too Big to Invest

16

Atlanta's Defenses Were Something to See

VIEWED FROM below, Marietta—eight miles from Atlanta—seemed small and vulnerable. Sherman was sure that once his men were across the Chattahoochee River, the town would easily be captured. Though not yet regarded as a primary target, it would be foolhardy to pursue Hood past the place without seizing it. So Union scouts filed reports, and observations were made through telescopes.[1]

By the time Hood had released the pent-up fury of his forces in the battle of Peach Tree Creek, Sherman knew that Atlanta would be a difficult operation. Viewed from the north, it seemed to be completely encircled by a line of defenses whose radius was about one and one-half miles. Careful surveillance showed that one log barricade was "covered with boughs" in a crude attempt at camouflage.

Even from a distance of a mile or two, much of the construction was clearly strong; the builder had carefully utilized head-logs. To make things worse, a well-defined skirmish line was laid out in front of the permanent defensive system.[2]

Confederate withdrawals followed by Union flanking movements caused the opposing forces to inch southward. Hence four strong forts were added to the line built by Lemuel Grant. That completed the task of making Atlanta the most strongly defended Confederate city south of the capital.[3]

O. M. Poe, Sherman's chief engineer, who later supervised the production of official maps, considered Atlanta's defenses "too strong to assault, and too extensive to invest [or besiege]." He mistakenly believed that they completely encircled the city and was greatly impressed with the placement of the Confederate batteries. When fully armed, the Rebel artillery could so sweep the field in front of the twelve-foot palisades that they needed only "a very small force to hold them."[4]

Union troops didn't know it at the time, but they later discovered that plans to strengthen the line around Atlanta yet again had been formulated in the preceding month. Johnston had obtained the promise of "seven sea-coast rifles" from Brig. Gen. D. H. Maury at Mobile. He expected to mount these weapons in the existing forts to protect the railroads leading to Augusta and to Chattanooga. At the same time, the original defenses were lengthened by two miles.

Weeks after Union forces seemed to be closing in on Atlanta, one of Sherman's officers put his appraisal of the city's defenses on record: "What tremendous defenses of Atlanta the rebs had! Forts, breastworks, ditches, *chevaux-de-frise* (saw them) and stockade on flank, unapproachable by musketry, and protected by ground, etc., from artillery."

Sherman may have scoffed at Schofield's verdict, since he consistently belittled and criticized the commander of the Army of the Ohio. Yet the words of a veteran of many battles could hardly be ignored when they conveyed an unmistakable warning: "I have very little hope of being able to carry any point of the enemy's works, since I can't go beyond the strong defenses of Atlanta."

Having decided for the moment that the Confederates would not yield the city without a fight, in early July Sherman regarded Atlanta's railroads as the town's weakest points. Before the month ended he admitted—perhaps reluctantly—that defensive parapets were heavily manned and that he felt the town to be "pretty strong." He knew that any extensive line of well-manned fortifications was unlikely to be carried by assault.[5]

Hood's Confederates and many of Gov. Brown's militia units moved quickly after the battle of Atlanta. Southern troops led by Lt. Gen. Stephen D. Lee managed to join Hood's forces, adding substantially to his strength. Soon firmly entrenched behind Atlanta's fortifications, the Confederates were now impregnable despite being disheartened by two significant defeats.

Perhaps because he firmly believed in his ability to predict the future, Sherman never seemed able to resist recording his speculations about the possible actions of his enemy. During a few hopeful hours, he persuaded his generals that the Confederates were moving away.

Almost simultaneously the Federal commander decided that Grant might be right in warning him that Hood could be reinforced from Virginia. Such a move by the enemy might come too late, however; Hood's forces were likely to leave Atlanta at any hour. Union forces—especially cavalry units—must "be ready to act vigorously in case we are called upon suddenly to push a retreating army."[6]

Four days after the battle of Atlanta, Sherman reported to Washington that he was ready to move against the rail center. That action, he said, would force the enemy to choose between two alternatives. Hood could either "abandon Atlanta or allow us, at small cost, to occupy the railroad south of the town, that to the east being [already] well destroyed."

Optimism expressed at the Federal headquarters infected some of the news correspondents. W. F. G. Shanks of the *New York Herald* reported, "The [Union] army is in the most encouraging condition and it is believed that the most sanguine hopes of the capture of Atlanta will shortly be much more than realized."[7]

Every move he made against the Confederates, Sherman later said, was a blow directed against Richmond. The Southerners, however, took neither of Sherman's options. By the evening of Thursday, July 28, the Union commander reached another verdict. The next day, he confided, "The enemy will do something desperate."

When that didn't happen, a report by scout J. C. Moore took on added significance. Having been at the Atlanta depot for some hours, Moore reported that if the town should be abandoned, the enemy "would try to make their first stand at East Point."[8]

On the day that Moore's account was circulated, it was generally known that forces under Edward M. McCook had broken the railroad some thirty miles south of Atlanta. This led some of Sherman's subordinates to believe that the cavalry's relative success might evoke a desperate action by the Southerners.

By 9:00 P.M. on Friday, Schofield mirrored the view of his commander, expecting the speedy evacuation of Atlanta. Sherman took heart from Thomas's judgment that "the enemy must be very weak in Atlanta." Evidence gathered by Thomas indicated that on the right of the combat line "the enemy has withdrawn everything but his skirmish line."[9]

These and other conclusions reached by Sherman and his advisers soon proved again to be wrong. In Sherman's judgment, he was left with only one viable alternative, a move contemplated in one fashion or another for days. It was essential to gain permanent control of a segment of the railroad south of Atlanta.

LONG BEFORE he reached Marietta, the Federal commander knew that four rail lines made Atlanta an especially important transportation center. Three railroads were in Union hands or had been seriously damaged early in the conflict that raged about the town.

Sherman had held much of the state-owned Western and Atlantic Railroad virtually since leaving Chattanooga. For weeks it served as his main artery, bringing essential supplies to his armies; without it, he could not have moved so far into Georgia.

Stretching eastward to Augusta, the line had been partly dismantled through a combined operation. Troops under Schofield and McPherson helped to tear up long sections of track between Decatur and Stone Mountain. Then a raid by Garrard's cavalry destroyed important bridges and the depot at Covington.

Maj. Gen. Lovell Rousseau led Federal cavalrymen on a long and arduous raid through part of Alabama and Georgia. He rejoined the main Union forces on the day the battle of Atlanta was fought. With great satisfaction, he reported having ripped up thirty miles of railroad between Montgomery and Opelika, Alabama. This meant that the line known in Georgia as the Atlanta and West Point would be out of operation, at least briefly. Until service could be restored, there would be no more shipments of ammunition, food, or other supplies from Mobile to Atlanta.

Hood's forces and the residents of Atlanta were now wholly dependent upon a single railroad. Stretching from south of the city to Georgia's capital at Milledgeville, the Macon and Western linked Atlanta with Macon. From middle Georgia the line ran to Savannah. Another railroad connected Savannah with Richmond, completing a network vital to the Confederacy. Once this lifeline of iron was disabled, Sherman repeatedly insisted to his subordinates, the Confederates would quickly give up unless they preferred to starve.

Five days after the decisive victory in the battle of Atlanta, Sherman began moving toward the Macon and Western. Earlier, he had repeatedly given potential railroad wreckers sets of instructions much more detailed than those usually issued to commanders about to engage in battle.

A typical set of orders went out over the signature of an aide-de-camp:

> Major-General McPherson will move along the railroad toward Decatur and break the telegraph wires and the railroad. . . . [He will] keep every man of his command at work in destroying the railroad by tearing up track, burning the ties and iron, and twisting the bars when hot. Officers should be instructed that bars simply bent may be used again, but if when red hot they are twisted out of line they cannot be used again. Pile the ties into the shape for a bonfire, put the rails across, and when red hot in the middle, let a man at each end twist the bar so that its surface becomes spiral.[10]

One observer was struck by the scrupulousness with which Sherman's men obeyed his instructions. Noting that thirteen miles of track had been destroyed in a single day, he recorded how the task was accomplished:

> The operation of tearing up the road has been very interesting, and one over which the men, notwithstanding it is the hardest kind of labor, were quite enthusiastic. A regiment or brigade formed along the track; rails were loosened at their flank, whereupon the whole line seized the track and flung a stretch corresponding to the length of their line from its bed. The rails were then detached, the ties piled up and covered with fence-rails. The iron was then deposited upon the pyre, the torch applied and the thing was consummated. The men, not content with the curve made in the rails by the intense and continued heat, seized many and twisted them until they looked like members of a phonographic alphabet.[11]

Foiled in his earlier plan to capture Atlanta quickly, Sherman now expected to cut the last of its rail lines immediately. Since previous cavalry raids had been temporarily successful in this enterprise, he ordered his mounted men to render the Macon and Western useless at once. To that end he planned a grand series of raids that were launched almost simultaneously on Wednesday, July 27.

There was a good chance that the destruction of the railroads would break the stalemate and release many of Sherman's troops to go to Grant's aid. Stoneman headed toward Macon, certain that within a few days he would put the rail line out of commission for weeks or months.

Garrard had already scored spectacular success east of Atlanta. In a brief foray his forces had burned the bridges over the Yellow and Alcovy Rivers, ripped up half a dozen miles of track, and put Covington out of the railroad business.[12] Many of his animals were unshod, and most of his men were bone weary when they returned from the raid. After a few days' rest they undertook another mission, this time toward the South River.

For their targets, McCook and his riders focused on the northern end of the Macon and Western and the eastern tip of the Atlanta and West Point. Like Garrard, they set out as part of the general cavalry movement planned in detail by Sherman.[13]

Stoneman was dispatched to destroy the railroads around Macon. He accepted the assignment eagerly, then requested permission to extend its distance and scope. There was a good chance, he insisted, that after releasing Federal officers held at Macon he could proceed to Andersonville.

The capture of the infamous Confederate stockade would have little or no military impact; the enlistments of the prisoners had expired or were about to do so. Yet it would be a grand humanitarian gesture for Sherman to be able to say that he had secured the freedom of men confined to the pest hole. Apparently with some misgivings, he approved Stoneman's plan.[14]

Sherman had won a dramatic victory during his long invasion of Georgia, but his record showed one failure after another. He had not destroyed the Confederate army that was his primary target. No rein-

GEORGIA HISTORICAL SOCIETY

Prior to the bombardment, Atlanta was known as a "quietly elegant" city.

forcements had been sent to aid Grant. And Atlanta was safely nestled inside a stout line of well-manned fortifications.

Now he ruefully recorded another set of humiliations: all three carefully coordinated cavalry strikes at the enemy failed. Garrard's footsore animals and saddle-weary men accomplished nothing worth reporting. McCook was hit by Confederate cavalry near Newnan and lost perhaps one-third of his force. Stoneman failed to get across the Ocmulgee River and in a fierce battle saw his command temporarily reduced to about one thousand men. He had hoped to free the prisoners of Andersonville, but only six hundred of his riders reached the place—as prisoners of war.

By July 30, their commander was asking his aides, "Where are Garrard and Stoneman?" Through subordinates, he tried to learn something about them from the townspeople of Decatur. Consistently critical of Federal cavalry to the point of contemptuousness, Sherman's judgment of these forces seemed more than justified by the failure of the "grand movements" of three bodies of horsemen.[15]

FOR SEVERAL days the battle line along Utoy Creek had been growing in length; little or no significant progress was made by Federal infantry attempting to advance. Convinced by now that cavalry "could not, or would not, make a sufficient lodgment on the railroad below Atlanta," Sherman decided to move in force toward the city. This enterprise—essential to the success of his seizing Atlanta—he committed to Schofield. On July 28, the Army of the Cumberland went into motion charged to "be bold, even to rashness."[16]

The forward movement of Sherman's largest body of troops soon resulted in heavy fighting centered near tiny Ezra Methodist Church. Hood had been watching and waiting for another opportunity to strike; when he did so in response to Schofield's movements, his forces took out about six hundred Union troops. The cost of five hours of fierce conflict was high, however; Confederate casualties approached five thousand.[17]

Though Hood never admitted it, three sets of attacks during eight days cost the Confederates far more men than Johnston had lost during one hundred days of withdrawal. Yet Southern troops were still strong enough to halt the invasion if they could hit at the right place at the right time.[18]

The Confederates withdrew behind Atlanta's fortifications, which remained "too strong to attack, and too extensive to invest." In order to receive the surrender of the Confederate army and the town that sheltered it, Sherman had to sever the vital railroad south of Atlanta. Ruefully accepting the reality of the situation, he had every reason to hope that the end of Hood—and of Atlanta as well—would come in a very few days.

17

Iron Rain Poured During a Red Day in August

If any one day of the siege was worse than all the others it was that red day in August, when all the fires of hell, and all the thunders of the universe seemed to be blazing and roaring over Atlanta. . . . Ten Confederate and eleven Federal batteries took part in the engagement. Shot and shell rained in every direction. Great volumes of sulphurous smoke rolled over the town, trailing down to the ground, and through this stifling gloom the sun glared down like a great red eye peering through a bronze colored cloud.[1]

ATLANTA WAS under a deliberately planned, hostile bombardment whose architect was Sherman. Though the Civil War produced numerous true sieges, Atlanta was not the object of such an operation. Careful inspection of the town into which Hood's army had withdrawn convinced his Federal foe that full investment would be impractical. Engineer Lemuel P. Grant had thrown up so many miles of defensive works that there were not enough men in blue to surround them.

At Vicksburg the man who was now commander of the Division of the Mississippi had seen six separate movements against the city fail. Protected by only nine miles of breastworks, the river port held out against a full-blown siege from mid-May 1863 until July 4.

Earlier, Schofield had asserted that Atlanta would fall by August 1. Since it did not, it appeared to Sherman that he could only achieve the capture of the city and the surrender of Hood by either drawing the Confederates into a decisive battle or cutting off the railroad that was their supply line. He hoped that the latter objective would require only a few days. While it was getting under way, Union artillerists could improve their skill by using the town of Atlanta as their target.[2]

During the battle of Peach Tree Creek, Federal officers observed that field artillery could fire over defensive lines and do some damage to the town. Doubting that Hood would tolerate a prolonged bombardment, the following evening Sherman decided to use his batteries to strike Atlanta from the east and northeast and destroy as much of the town as possible.

Support for the plan came from captured Confederates. Some told him that shells fell into the city during the Peach Tree Creek conflict, "producing great consternation." A few weeks earlier the town had not been regarded as a significant target because the Federal objective was the Confederate army.[3] Once he decided to cannonade civilian rather than military targets, Sherman feared that the Army of the Tennessee might be too small to accomplish the job. Hence on July 22 he ordered the commanders of all three armies to "open a careful artillery fire on the town of Atlanta, directing their shots so as to produce the best effect." By the evening of July 23 many heavy guns were at work. The editors of an Atlanta newspaper warned readers that "there is no security from danger."[4]

Sherman believed it would take only a few days to cut the Macon Railroad, if that proved necessary. As late as July 25 he was confident that "the enemy must come out of Atlanta to fight or be invested."[5] Meanwhile, it could do no harm and might prove helpful to see how many buildings could be hit from a distance.

Unwilling to trust the destructive work to his subordinates, Sherman issued specific directives over the next few days. He ordered that two "Napoleons or 20-pounder Parrott batteries keep fire on Atlanta all night, each battery throwing a shot every fifteen minutes."

By August 1 Schofield's batteries were following instructions to "fire from ten to fifteen shots" from each cannon in a position to reach the houses of Atlanta. "Fire slowly and with deliberation between 4 p. m. and dark," Sherman ordered. By this time, he knew that ordinary 3-inch ordnance could strike the center of the city "with tolerable accuracy."[6]

But tolerable accuracy was not good enough; he was eager to knock down buildings in the heart of Atlanta. Seeking to achieve this result, Sherman requisitioned a pair of 30-pounder Parrotts and a set of fearful 4.5-inch rifled siege guns from Chattanooga.

Some of his larger Parrotts were ready for use on August 8, so he was confident that he would soon turn the heart of Atlanta into ruins. Yet he found time to select the site within an orchard from which he believed a battery of field artillery "would make sad havoc" among civilians.[7]

By then the line of battle had stretched to sixteen miles, but many details concerning skirmishing were relegated to subordinates. Some of Sherman's personal orders for August 9 went to gunners. He instructed, "All the batteries that can reach the buildings of Atlanta will fire steadily on the town, using during the day about fifty rounds per gun, shell and solid shot [a total of more than ten thousand]." It was this fearful onslaught that evoked the label, "that red day in August."[8]

Sherman could hardly wait for the arrival of the 4.5-inch rifled guns from Chattanooga. He was eager personally "to come over and watch the effect of a few of the first shots" of the four thousand shells he expected the rifles to put into "the heart of Atlanta."

Officers who witnessed the August 9 bombardment probably felt that the huge rifles were not needed; they were sure that the shells "exploded over the city and in it." According to a Confederate who had fled Atlanta, all business was suspended and the Western and Atlantic Railroad depot took at least seven direct hits.[9]

Before dusk on August 10 heavy rifles began firing at five-minute intervals. They were seen to "burst beautifully," so the speed with which they were serviced was increased. Sherman decided to have the gunners work throughout the night. "Let us destroy Atlanta and make it a desolation," he urged.[10]

Bright moonlight was welcomed by the Federal gunners that night. Though the 4.5-inch rifles were on hand and ready for use, Sherman was not pleased with the site on which they were emplaced. After they were moved and put into use, the commander of the Department of the Mississippi watched their firing rather than visit Schofield to try to heal wounds he had inflicted in a recent tongue-lashing.

Some Union gunners discovered a way to increase the sound of the detonations. At a signal they fired by battery, discharging all their guns simultaneously. When such a blast occurred, an observer said, "It was appalling to hear these fearful iron messengers as they literally tore through the air."

By August 12 all four of the huge rifles were in action and more ammunition was on the way. The following evening, Union sentries claimed that they heard women and children crying and probably praying.[11]

When Sherman learned at 10:15 P.M. on August 18 that the batteries of the Army of the Cumberland had ceased firing, he became irate. "Keep the big guns going, and damage Atlanta all that is possible," he ordered. Still personally involved in the placement of his most powerful weapons, he learned from a spy that they continued to be effective. Glass reported, "A large block of buildings near the corner of Marietta and Woodley streets was fired by our shells on Saturday night [July 16] and destroyed."

On July 19, Sherman noticed two large fires. One was very bright at daylight, and the other broke out about 3:00 P.M. Union artillery caused especially destructive fires five days later; one of which was seen to burn for twelve hours.[12]

Some of Sherman's biographers barely mention this merciless assault upon the railroad center. At intervals, officers of the opposing forces met under a flag of truce. On these occasions, the civilian survivors of the bombardment reported, "The Federals coolly declared that they were not shelling the city." They said that it could not be helped if a few shells happened to overshoot the defensive breastworks.

THOUGH A child was the first Atlanta casualty from a Union shell, there was little panic during the early weeks of the bombardment. "Many [citizens] walk about the streets as though federal shells are 100 miles away," one resident noted. Men, women, and children learned to distinguish the sounds of incoming missiles, usually in time to scurry into "bomb proofs" similar to those that were created at Vicksburg. Sherman's chief antagonist, Hood, later wrote: "It was painful, yet strange, to mark how expert grew the old men, women, and children in building their little underground forts, in which to fly for safety during the storm of shell and shot. Often 'mid the darkness of night were they constrained to seek refuge in these dungeons beneath the earth." Hood registered a formal protest and asked that cannon fire against civilians cease, but he received no satisfaction from his opponent.

Prodded by newspaper reports, numerous Atlantans blamed Jefferson Davis for their plight rather than Johnston or Hood. Most churches within the target area continued to hold services as usual, despite the fact that both First Presbyterian Church and Wesley Chapel were hit. Firemen of the town were among the most endangered residents, yet there is no record of any of them dying in the line of duty during the bombardment.[13]

Shortages of merchandise made life difficult for most merchants. Every hotel closed, and by late August only one grocery remained open.

Stationery dealer and diarist S. P. Richards found desperate Confederate soldiers to be nearly as dangerous as Union shells. A band of them, identified only as "cavalry robbers," broke into his establishment and stripped it bare. Their loot consisted of about thirty dollars in Confederate currency and Richards's entire stock of paper. Hood reportedly meted out severe punishment to the men of the Seventh Alabama Regiment who were involved in this incident.[14]

There are no reliable estimates of Atlanta's population during this period. Groups of wealthy residents, which included several hundred prosperous families, fled to what they hoped would be safer havens. Some newspaper editors apologized to readers about the exodus, but it did not stop until passenger train service was no longer possible. One Federal officer's comment that all the city residents were fleeing proved unfounded when the accuracy of his information was questioned.[15]

Many long-time residents refused to budge; they sincerely believed that Union forces would never penetrate Lemuel Grant's defenses. Until August 1864, conditions had been much worse elsewhere in the war-torn region—then called the West—than in Atlanta. Refugees poured into Atlanta from the towns and villages of the neighboring states because the city was considered safe.

Some of these newcomers broke into hastily boarded up homes and businesses; others erected tents. No one has been able to approximate the number of people who flocked into and out of Atlanta. So many came to the city that one church reserved pews for them and seated them by state.

Newspaper publishing also transferred to Atlanta. Despite the fact that its general population was less than half that of Mobile, the northwestern Georgia town had two morning and one evening dailies and several smaller papers. As Union control over Tennessee grew firmer, papers that moved to Atlanta included the *Memphis Appeal*, the *Knoxville Register*, and the *Chattanooga Rebel*.

Employees of these and other newspapers added to the population of the city. Impromptu hospitals were set up in the remaining buildings, and numerous wounded Federal soldiers spent days or weeks in them.

The Confederate withdrawal into the town and its fortifications were considered by some to be a worse evil than the Federal bombardment. Hood immediately established martial law and announced measures that made life even more difficult for the citizenry. To walk the streets without fear of arrest, every white male of age sixteen or above had to carry a pass. An adolescent of that age or a man of seventy was likely to be challenged if not in uniform. In the Confederate capital it was incorrectly reported that "Gen. Hood seems to have brought the people [of Atlanta and of Georgia] to the liveliest exultation."

Unable to leave Atlanta, some civilians entertained themselves by touring the rifle pits occupied by soldiers and the militia. One of these, near the end of Peachtree Street, was in clear view of Union sharpshooters. During the weeks in which the town was virtually closed, seventeen civilians were killed in this frequently visited "dead hole."[16]

Most Atlantans agreed that those who experienced the most trouble were known or suspected Unionists, among whom Germans and persons of northern birth were prominent. Some had come to Atlanta years before the outbreak of hostilities and were established manufacturers and merchants. James L. Dunning, who refused any Confederate contracts, was imprisoned before the cannonades began. He was still behind bars when the shelling began and there is no record of his release.

By late August, all food and other supplies for soldiers and civilians had to come from Macon by train. Federal cavalry damaged the line and interrupted traffic so often that the Macon-to-Atlanta journey typically required about seventy hours. Hood prevented starvation by ordering that rations be issued to long-time residents as well as to refugees without resources. A standard ration then consisted of bacon and corn bread—barely enough for one meager meal per day. Trains rolled into the city regularly but often brought little except ammunition and other military supplies.

During a brief visit to Macon, Braxton Bragg discovered that the Georgia militia were getting "subsistence [food] and forage [for their horses]" from the Confederate army. His angry message concerning this problem went to Jefferson Davis, who ordered that these men must enter Confederate service in order to receive supplies. Ten days later the president of the Confederacy modified his position and suggested that Hood be consulted on the matter.[17]

Georgia's conscription laws had just been revised, removing deferments from several previously exempt occupations. Most of the "train loads of reinforcements" seen by Federal signal officers carried newly conscripted soldiers. These recruits were so poorly equipped that many had no cartridge boxes. Yet their ranks inside Atlanta were estimated to have swollen to thirty thousand. All but useless in combat, these untested green troops were stationed throughout the city's defenses and freed the veterans for active duty.

During the daylight hours, when there chanced to be a momentary lull in the firing of big guns, the crackle of rifle fire could be heard throughout Atlanta. After a few weeks, most civilians became so accustomed to this background noise that they casually referred to it as "wood choppin'."

On Friday, August 26, the occasional sounds of rifle fire echoed through the streets, but many Atlantans were puzzled by the "tremendous silence." The siege guns and the artillery batteries were no longer in action. What could have happened? Was it possible that Hood had attacked during the night and won?

Until nearly noon, few civilians realized what some Confederate soldiers learned soon after they crawled out of their trenches at 3:00 A.M. Nearly all the Union force was on the move.

The bombardment had stopped because most of the heavy weaponry had been ordered to make wide sweeps toward the south. It took little imagination to conclude that the Federals hoped to cut Atlanta's lifeline, the Macon Railroad. That meant the fate of the town depended upon how well Hood's men and the militia would engage Sherman. Having suffered no decisive defeat in the past five months, the men in gray might once more thwart the invaders.

By this time, it was too late to try to preserve Atlanta; it was already in shambles. Sherman tersely described it as being "used up," an assessment which both Confederate soldiers and the town residents regarded as accurate.[18]

18

Firing Never Ceased, Day or Night

MAJ. W. H. CHAMBERLIN and his men of the Eighty-first Ohio Regiment went into Georgia under the leadership of James B. McPherson. On the first day of fighting, the Army of the Tennessee was given a dangerous assignment. As a result, four companies of Chamberlin's regiment were deployed as skirmishers on May 9.

This meant that they were expected to stay well in front of Federal battle lines in order to take Confederate pickets as their principal targets. Thomas D. Crosley of Company B was killed in front of the Confederate defenses at Resaca on the first evening of his special duty.

Some of his comrades died on the field, and others were wounded as long blue columns moved slowly southward from Chattanooga in their attempts to get behind Johnston's Confederates. It was not until they had been in hostile territory for nearly one hundred days, however, that the Buckeyes and other skirmishers learned what war was really like. Chamberlin described what happened then: "The investment of Atlanta from July 22nd until late in August, was in the main a gigantic battle of skirmishers [on both sides]. The picket firing never ceased, day nor night. Sometimes it was lazy, scattered, and weak, and again swelling into volleys like the beginning of a battle, and now and then being followed by the roar of artillery. Every day brought its lists of casualties into the hospitals."

There is no accurate data concerning the number of men killed and wounded during the five weeks of the "gigantic battle of skirmishers." Battle lines were frequently very close together, causing skirmishers to be exposed to short-range fire. Occasionally a high-ranking officer was caught in the melee.

Brig. Gen. Grenville M. Dodge, for whom Dodge City, Kansas, was later named, commanded the Federal Sixteenth Corps during this period. A Confederate ball that struck his head on August 19 took a bizarre course that left him badly wounded but a long way from dead. His was one of many unusual wounds experienced during five weeks in which men were just a step away from hand-to-hand combat.

Col. Carter Van Vleck of the Seventy-eighth Illinois Regiment was hit directly above his left eye. Surgeons probed to a depth of three inches but failed to find the ball. They admitted bewilderment as to where the Confederate missile had gone. Then they congratulated him that since he "was entire free of pain, he seemed likely to survive!"

Neither side seemed to be making appreciable gains during the skirmishing. A war correspondent summed up the situation for his readers on August 11: "Once and for all, let me tell the sensation-lovers of the North that they need not expect now, a week hence, or in a month to come any such news as 'the rebels evacuating Atlanta!' The steady day-by-day skirmishing, to which we are so well used as to scarcely notice, is picking off by degrees this large and heroic army, till our hospital lists embrace not only every regiment, but every day of the month."

Much action took place on both sides of the road between Lick Skillet and Ezra Church, west of Atlanta and slightly north. This region was of great strategic importance because it was near East Point, seven or eight miles southwest of Atlanta. A hamlet of about forty dwellings, East Point was the spot at which the Atlanta and West Point Railroad joined the Macon and Western. Running north from the village, the joint line formed by the junction of the two railroads was Atlanta's lifeline.[1]

The Federal progress was agonizingly slow. During two weeks of constant small-scale fighting, observers were unable to see that any progress had been made, but they hoped that the next day the Confederate line would give way. In spite of constant "leaden messengers," noted one reporter, "the prospects of Massachusetts and Connecticut yielding to the insolent demands of South Carolina and Mississippi were not very encouraging."

Authorities differ concerning the number of military events that occurred between the battle of Ezra Church on July 28 and the battle of Jonesborough that began on August 31. At least twenty-four separate sets of actions were involved; one authority claimed the total was an

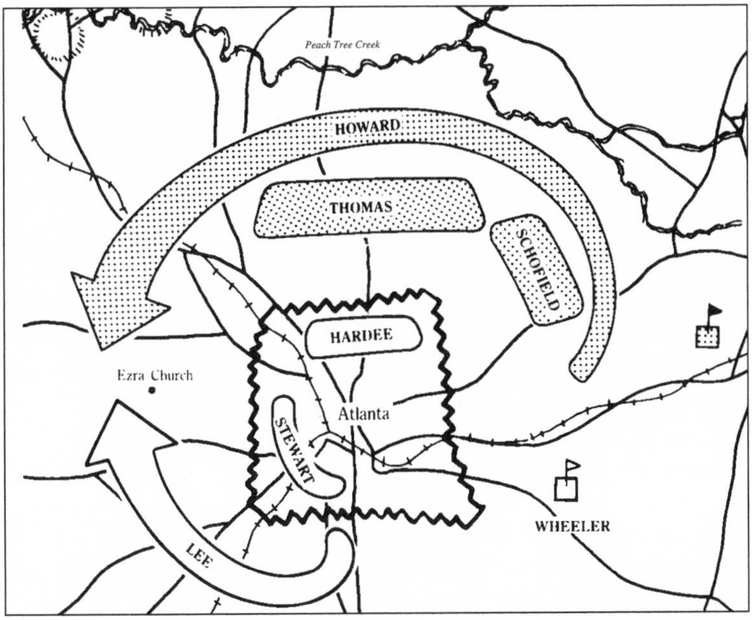

Howard's attempt to outflank Hood's force was foiled at Ezra Church.

even fifty. A cavalry engagement at Jug Tavern on August 3 involved four Federal regiments whose members charged against twelve hundred yards of rifle pits. Like the actions taken in August, there were numerous casualties but the outcome was less than decisive.

Combat at Utoy Creek on the Sandtown road erupted two days later on a larger but still indecisive scale. Union troops from Indiana, Kentucky, Michigan, Missouri, Ohio, Pennsylvania, Tennessee, and Wisconsin fought desperately for hours. Along with members of four U.S. Army regiments and two batteries of artillery, they kept up the struggle until August 7.

The Confederates wavered several times but never gave up enough ground to justify a struggle of such proportions. Albert Castel, describing the action in detail, called the battle of Utoy Creek "Union Fizzle at Atlanta."

At least once an entire Federal regiment was taken prisoner. Soon afterward, on July 29, the combat was hailed as a complete Federal victory. About two thousand Northerners were listed as casualties, but the Southern total was believed to be five times as many. On August 6, Schofield unsuccessfully tried to break through the Confederate defenses. Sherman estimated his casualties from this combat to be about five hundred; others said only that they were heavy.[2]

It had long been a point of honor for both sides to keep the dead from falling into enemy hands. Now the Federals were repeatedly ordered to "secure, count, and bury the enemy dead." No other procedure afforded Sherman even an approximately correct base from which he could estimate total casualties.[3]

Regardless of how many or how few had fallen on both sides, Sherman's second major effort to cut Hood's supply line failed. Bickering between his generals was a major contributing factor to the way in which Federal troops stalled before East Point. Maj. Gen. John M. Palmer refused to take orders from Schofield, insisting that he had seniority over the commander of the Army of the Ohio. This was only one of numerous squabbles among generals in both blue and gray. It was of special importance, however, because it contributed heavily to Sherman's burden of command.[4]

Confederate cavalry seemed to pose little or no danger to a push by the Union troops, but their defensive works were another matter. Described by Sherman as fifteen miles in length, for most of that distance the Confederate works were formidable. Atlanta's fortifications were far from being encircled so that the town could be besieged. The Federal earthworks opposite those of the enemy were estimated to be only about ten miles in length.[5]

Having decided that he would have to cut the railroad that led into Atlanta from the south, Sherman originally believed his infantry and artillery could easily do the job. Utoy Creek, considered to be a weak spot in the enemy's line, persuaded him otherwise.

Thereafter the internal dissension and the Confederate strength made immediate flanking movements difficult for the Federals. Instead of quickly sweeping through East Point to a strategic site, perhaps Jonesborough, Union troops spent day after day going nowhere. In this situation Sherman turned to one group he inherently distrusted—his cavalry.

Sherman had earlier requested Washington to send him the only cavalry leader in whom he had confidence. Brig. Gen. Hugh Hudson "Kill Cavalry" (or "Kil Cavalry") Kilpatrick was a fighter, if nothing else. His long red nose seemed pale in comparison to his sideburns, which were much redder than Sherman's. Kilpatrick was eccentric, if not downright peculiar. He spent many evenings giving lessons to a fourteen-year-old nephew he took with him. Sherman allegedly said of

Kilpatrick, "I know he is a hell of a damned fool, but I want just that sort of man to command my cavalry."

Approximately half of all Union cavalry had been lost during raids well to the south of Atlanta. Enough remained, Sherman decided, to bypass the enemy fortifications and hit the railroad he had to cripple. Therefore, at 7:10 P.M. on August 18, Kilpatrick led about forty-five hundred men from Sandtown on the Chattahoochee toward Jonesborough. No ordinary cavalry raid, this was a carefully planned attack designed to make it impossible for Hood to supply his army.

The riders made a wide swing around the enemy, then headed for their target more than twenty miles south of Atlanta. When they reached their objective, they met only token resistance, so they spent six hours tearing up the tracks of the Macon and Western Railroad. Not fully satisfied, Kilpatrick hit the rail line again at Lovejoy's Station, but this time he was almost trapped by Confederate forces.

Leading his men in what some called "maybe the grandest cavalry charge of the entire war," Kilpatrick managed to extricate his troops. They then rode miles out of the way in order to pass the rear of the Confederate forces around Atlanta. Reaching Sherman's headquarters, Kilpatrick summarized his exploits and claimed that it would take the enemy ten days or more to repair the damage his men had done.

Delighted, Sherman congratulated his subordinate warmly and began poring over his maps. With food, clothing, and ammunition no longer flowing smoothly into Atlanta, Hood had to either come out and fight or surrender. In a very few days Sherman believed he would have the satisfaction of accomplishing his primary goal: the destruction of the Army of Tennessee.

Kilpatrick and his riders seemed to have accomplished too much to be true. To Sherman's consternation, that turned out to be the case. Within a day after the return of the triumphant riders, Union signal officers ruefully reported that railway traffic continued to move into Atlanta from the south. The Confederates were rapidly learning what the Federals already knew: it sometimes was easier to repair a railroad than to tear it up.

Since Kilpatrick had failed in his mission, Sherman reluctantly turned to Garrard. Although he had disparaged the Kentuckian earlier, he now needed him as part of the reorganization of his mounted forces. There was, however, a stipulation attached to the new leadership role: Garrard was under strict orders to report daily to Sherman. Less than a week after their relationship was reestablished,

Sherman joyfully concluded that his cavalry was now superior to that of the enemy.[6]

At the same time, he regretfully concluded that cavalry alone could not disable the railroads. Days earlier he had realized that the bombardment of Atlanta would never bring about the victory over Hood for which he yearned. This meant he'd have to revert to his original plan and move toward the south of Atlanta with his principal force.

Heading just one corps, the Twentieth, Slocum was sent to guard the vital railroad bridge over the Chattahoochee River. Virtually all Federal offensive works around Atlanta were evacuated, and by 4:00 P.M. on August 28 the three Union armies were on the move.

Carefully coordinated plans called for the three columns to march well west of the Confederate fortifications, then turn toward the south. Once more, Sherman was leaving the vital Western and Atlantic Railroad behind and resorting to horse-drawn wagons. More than three thousand wagons, loaded only with ammunition and essential supplies, constituted a train about thirty miles long.[7]

Willing to risk everything, the Union commander ordered his men to "march light." That meant they could not casually toss their tools and utensils into the wagons; hence most of them trudged along encumbered with odds and ends.

Kettles and coffee pots dangled from many belts, while spades and picks were carried over the shoulders of many men. As a result, observed a newspaper correspondent, the column seemed to have a "tinkerish aspect." That quality was perhaps enhanced by the fact that music from at least one brass band could be heard in the distance.[8]

Before making the long-contemplated and dangerous move, Sherman had pondered the possibility of being cut off from his supply line. Should that happen, he notified Washington, he'd head straight for the coast. That meant his destination would be either Saint Mark's, Florida, or Savannah, Georgia. Clearly, an Atlantic port would be his only route of escape if he had to leave Georgia hurriedly.[9]

For the moment he had no intention of ending his invasion. Disappointed in his expectations after Kilpatrick's raid, he now expected to preside personally over the destruction of the Macon Railroad. Such an accomplishment was worth a pitched battle, he concluded, although another all-out attack by Hood was unlikely. As a symbol of his willingness to risk everything in order to wreck the rail line, he had his telegraph line cut when he left his headquarters.

LIBRARY OF CONGRESS

Joseph Wheeler, Hood's chief of cavalry

SOUTHERN SPIES reported to Hood that Sherman seemed about to move, taking along meager supplies. This led to the logical but incorrect conclusion that the Federals had abandoned their attempt to take Atlanta. Hood presumed that Wheeler's cavalry must have cut the Atlantic and Western and throttled Sherman's supplies.

Exultant, Hood informed Richmond that a great victory had been won in Georgia. His aides helped to plan a victory ball, which would be enhanced by the presence of many ladies from Macon.

This hasty and erroneous conclusion was based upon the discovery that the Federal trenches were empty. Southern cavalry constituted "the eyes and ears of the army." With half of this force in other parts of the region—an estimated forty-five hundred men—those who remained near Atlanta couldn't monitor every move the enemy made. Had Wheeler's riders been able to conduct their usual patrols, they would have discovered Sherman's intentions within hours of his grand movement. Despite the glowing newspaper headlines about Confederate cavalry action near Chattanooga, the absence of his riders left Hood "blind and deaf."[10]

Hood's responsibilities were enlarged by the recommendation of Bragg and with the approval of Davis. Once he was sure that his control extended 120 miles to the east, all the way to Augusta, the Confederate leader slightly relaxed the normal routine of the men in the trenches.

It had been customary for the Atlanta defenders to be aroused at 3:00 A.M., prepared to meet new assaults. Now Hood's hand had been strengthened, and it was plainly evident that Federal artillery could not force him out of Atlanta. Hence he felt confident enough to allow half of his men to sleep until 3:45 A.M. Others wouldn't have to get up even then "unless movements of the enemy make it necessary to awaken them."[11]

Hood's growing confidence and relaxation, combined with the absence of Wheeler's cavalry, led to the commander's most catastrophic error in judgment. From the beginning of his leadership, his comrades had known him to be a risk-taker who hoped for the best. Now he thought he had reason to believe that Sherman had given up the siege.

THE FEDERAL withdrawal was cause for celebration, as Hood had no idea that his foe was headed toward the Macon Railroad. "We don't care about Jonesborough," Sherman said, "but we want to destroy our

LESLIE'S

Federal cavalry destroyed the Macon and Western Railroad at Jonesborough.

enemy." That could be accomplished only by rendering the railroad inoperable.[12]

"Marching light," sixty thousand or more men were headed toward Jonesborough in precisely coordinated columns. Thomas led the Army of the Cumberland, and Schofield headed the Army of the Ohio. Succeeding McPherson, O. O. Howard now commanded the Army of the Tennessee. These generals expected to move so far to the west that little opposition would be met. They were troubled, however, by the lack of easily identified landmarks. Maps showing Jonesborough and its surroundings were dotted with entries such as J. Stovey, Dr. Powell, Kemp, Cotton Gin, McCord, and E. Hutchinson.[13]

Along with their commander, most of the Confederate units were still within Atlanta's fortifications. Aside from the Georgia militia, Hood commanded about thirty thousand veterans. That number of Confederates couldn't have stopped the Union troops, but this time they didn't even try.

The audacious Hood did not know what was taking place west of his position, but the clock was running down for him. When the trains ceased to puff into Atlanta, there would be no more supplies for either soldiers or civilians. Within hours, the Confederate commander would be forced to choose between two unpalatable alternatives. He could abandon his defensive position and engage the enemy in the open, or he could evacuate his position and find another haven. It would be infernally hard to take the latter course. That would require him to adopt Johnston's strategy, which he had long and vocally criticized earlier.

19

Atlanta Is Ours, and Fairly Won!

A WOMAN WHOSE name was not recorded is believed to have played a major role in setting the stage for the fall of Atlanta. Pleading hunger, she went to soldiers commanded by William J. Hardee and said Union troops had refused to give her food.

Once she had eaten, she was questioned. For some days she had been among men whose leader was named Schofield, she said. His soldiers didn't seem like the well-fed Yankees she had heard about; they were lean and hungry. The supply wagons had fallen behind, so they didn't have enough for themselves—to say nothing of a secesh woman.

Keenly interested in what her story seemed to mean, Hardee personally took her to Hood, at whose headquarters she insisted that the Yankees must be "powerful" hungry. Delighted, the Confederate commander seized upon her account as sufficient evidence for his theory that the Federals were turning back toward the Chattahoochee to replenish their supplies. Once there, he theorized, they'd continue northward and soon abandon their invasion of Georgia.

Sherman had resorted to wagons, but for a different reason: his men might be away from their supply line for two weeks while operating against Hood. This meant each wagon had to carry a heavy load of rations and one hundred rounds of ammunition per man. Many of the vehicles moved with more than ordinary clumsiness because their drivers had only four mules instead of the normal six.

Having decided that it was futile to assault Hood's fortifications, Sherman turned toward what he termed "the communications of

Atlanta." To sever them, his men had to make long marches with wagon trains serving as supply lines.

Thousands of heavy wagons raised a great deal of dust, and Confederate lookouts had no difficulty in monitoring Sherman's movement. Yet the Confederates failed to realize that the Union force had again decided to leave their steel supply line. Instead of heading north, the Federal convoy would soon move southward, traveling between two armies for safety's sake.

During the third week of July, most crucial decisions concerning the push toward the Macon Railroad had been finalized. All three Federal armies would have to cross the Flint River, which had its headwaters between the two rail lines Sherman hoped to render useless. Perhaps a bridge or two might even be standing in this area that had as yet seen little combat.[1]

Considered to be the least effective of Sherman's forces, Schofield's Army of the Ohio moved along a comparatively narrow arc whose terminus was Rough and Ready. Not deserving to be termed even a hamlet, this railroad station lay about a dozen miles from Atlanta, halfway to the village of Jonesborough.

Thomas was expected to make a considerably wider swing in order to reach the Macon line between Rough and Ready and Jonesborough. Howard's Army of the Tennessee, admittedly Sherman's favorite, would curve far to the west and south in order to strike Jonesborough. If all three armies proceeded as planned, the Atlanta and West Point Railroad would be demolished at three separate points; so would the Macon and Western.

Sherman had found East Point, where the two railroads became one, to be heavily defended. During more than a month of constant skirmishing he had made little progress. Now he hoped to move suddenly and silently at such a distance that his objective would not be discerned by his enemy.

Officers were instructed, "Commands will not be given except in a very low tone of voice." Troops were told to move "without sound of bugle or drum." Skirmishers were ordered to "be bold, even to rashness" so that their actions would help to cover the planned three-part movement. Men of the Twenty-third Corps, who began marching at 7:00 A.M. on August 28, would make a strong demonstration, hoping to divert attention from the massive movements on the Federal right. Should his finely tuned and lengthy march not be successful, Sherman reasoned, it would at least serve "to draw the enemy out of Atlanta."[2]

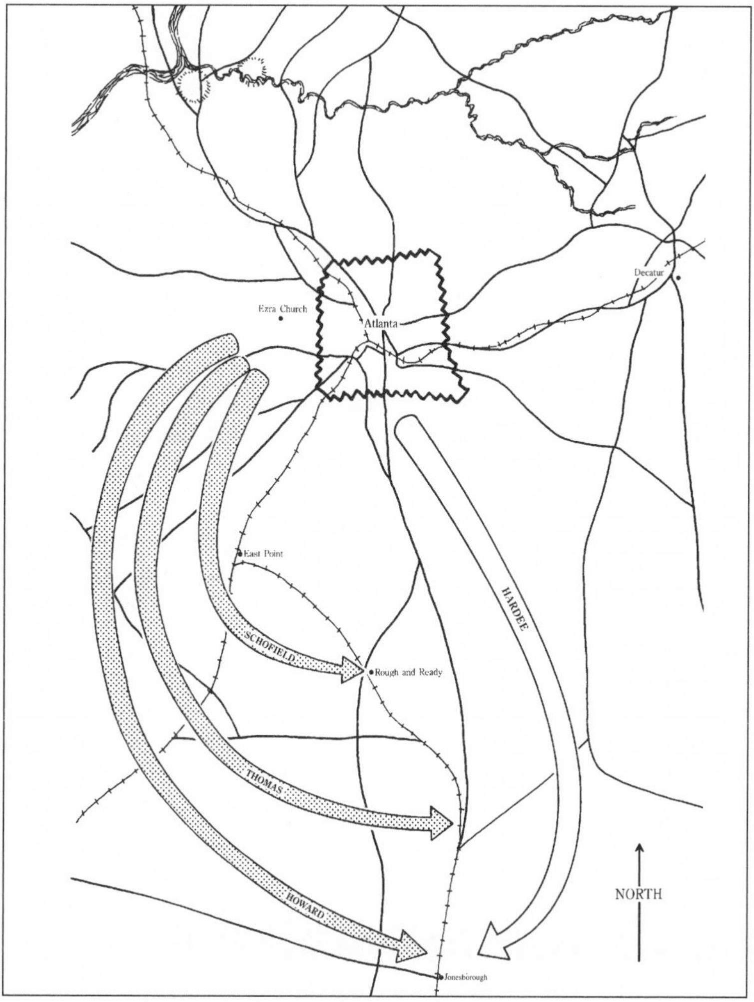

Sherman sent all three of his armies toward Jonesborough.

At the Flint River an undamaged bridge provided a quick crossing for the Army of the Tennessee. About 3:00 P.M., on August 31, however, sentries reported that Confederates thought to be led by Hardee were rapidly approaching. Believing Jonesborough to be threatened by a Union detachment, Hood sent a small force to defend the region. To their surprise, they found a large body of Union troops entrenched near the railroad. They made a futile attack and left an estimated four hundred dead on the field.

This was a foretaste of things to come, called by an exultant newspaper correspondent "big with history." With Howard already having demolished the West Point railroad for miles, Hood and Atlanta were totally dependent upon the track that stretched from Macon.

Frequently pushing through dense underbrush and swamps, long lines of men in blue began to converge on Jonesborough. Word of their movement had reached Hood earlier, but he misinterpreted the information. When a train brought word that the Federals were moving along the Macon Railroad, he concluded that Atlanta would be attacked from the south.

This misreading of Sherman's goal led Hood to believe that only Hardee's forces could be spared for railroad defense. Most of his men were desperately needed in Atlanta, the Confederate commander decided, to meet the expected onslaught against its weakest defenses.

Near Jonesborough, Hardee interrogated his prisoners and concluded that only the Union Twentieth Corps remained close to Atlanta. This meant that Atlanta's defenders would have been outnumbered nearly two to one had every Confederate in Hood's command been on the way to Jonesborough.

For two deadly hours on the afternoon of August 31, Hardee's men did their best against overwhelming odds to stave off the attack. Much of the fighting was hand-to-hand, resulting in carnage labeled by veterans as "simply dreadful." The collapse of a crucial Confederate salient meant that the end was near. A survivor tersely commented that Union troops "ran over us like a drove of Texas beeves."

Often classified as an engagement, the combat at Jonesborough was small in scale when compared with major battles in the East. Yet in the Western theater it was of tremendous importance. During more than sixteen weeks following May 5, only five of Sherman's men were awarded Congressional Medals of Honor. Three were earned at Jonesborough in a few hours.

Weeks afterward, readers of the London *Times* were offered a reasoned verdict. "Compared with the great battles of the [American Civil] war," the editors said, "the action at Jonesborough is little more than a skirmish. Yet it has been more decisive in effect than all the fighting and bloodshed of Grant's campaign [in the eastern theater]."[3]

Hood recognized the long-range significance of the combat at Jonesborough. He was being flushed out. Now he would find it impossible to take refuge in another haven as strong as Atlanta.

As soon as he learned of the defeat, the Confederate commander laid the blame upon Hardee. Though Hood made significant errors in judgment, he never wavered in his assertion that his subordinate caused the surrender of Atlanta.

WITH HARDEE certain to retreat, Sherman hoped soon to finish him off. Instead of turning toward Atlanta to claim victory, he pursued Hardee for six miles. Late that afternoon, a probe revealed that the Confederate defensive works were stronger than they appeared from a distance. Hence Sherman decided not to make an assault; instead, he waited for news from Atlanta.

Early on the morning of September 1, Hood learned the dreadful truth. Federal forces were firmly astride the Macon Railroad; he was no longer safe inside Atlanta's fortifications. Army rations were hastily distributed to civilians, and Lovejoy's Station was selected as the assembly point for all units.

LIBRARY OF CONGRESS

When Federal troops entered Atlanta, all that remained of Hood's ordnance train were its wheels. At least twenty-eight boxcars of ammunition exploded during a five-hour period. Every building within a quarter mile of the site was demolished.

A few storekeepers packed what merchandise they had and prepared to follow the army. Soldiers set fire to an estimated one thousand bales of cotton that the Federals would have liked to seize.

Late that afternoon, columns of Confederate soldiers began to file out of the town in concert with the Georgia militia. Special units remained in Atlanta, preparing for what they knew would be a difficult task. Locomotives and boxcars within the town would aid Sherman if his forces captured them; therefore they must be destroyed.

It was easier to arrive at this decision than to implement it. Cavalrymen, some with special skills, were detailed for the complex job. Seven locomotives, eighty-one freight cars, and thirteen siege guns were herded together. The locomotives were then "dashed into each other at the highest speed."

When the rolling stock was set afire, car after car loaded with ammunition exploded over a five-hour period. At the Chattahoochee River, Slocum believed that Hood might be attacking Sherman. More than twenty miles to the south, Sherman was torn with anxiety over the possibility that Hood might be seizing the railroad bridge Slocum was guarding.

Sherman's uncertainty continued until a courier arrived before dawn on September 3. Slocum was not only safe, he had taken possession of Atlanta. At 6:00 A.M. Sherman sent a dispatch to Washington from a point about twenty-six miles below Atlanta.

Since downed lines forced the telegram to travel through Cumberland Gap, it did not reach the capital until 5:30 P.M. on September 4. Lincoln and his advisers then received the famous message: "Atlanta is ours, and fairly won."

Two days earlier Slocum had sent Secretary of War Stanton the first word of the surrender. When that telegram was dispatched, Slocum did not know where his commander was.

Sherman was too busy trying to do away with Confederate soldiers to bother about being on hand for the surrender. A newspaper correspondent who had followed the army for weeks had watched the Federal commander closely. Positive that he knew the achievement for which the Federal commander really yearned, he told readers: "The city of Atlanta merely is clearly of little importance in the eyes of the Commanding general as a desirable military position. . . . Sherman does not want Atlanta unless he can also receive Hood's whole army within his lines as prisoners of war."[4]

That observation is supported by the later actions of the Federal commander. Sherman personally led the pursuit of Hardee until

September 5, and only then turned toward the surrendered rail hub. His first telegram dispatched from Atlanta was sent at 6:00 A.M. on September 8, six days after the surrender. His quick and well-executed movement, he said, brought these results: "27 guns, over 3,000 prisoners; have buried over 400 rebel dead, and left as many wounded." According to him, the Southerners lost "Atlanta, immense stores, at least 500 dead, 2,500 wounded, and 3,000 prisoners." The aggregate loss of Union forces he estimated at less than 1,500, so he concluded triumphantly: "If that is not success, I don't know what it is."[5]

ATLANTA WAS in Federal hands. Capt. Henry M. Scott of the Seventieth Ohio Regiment led a small band of soldiers inside the fortifications about 9:00 A.M. on September 2. Col. John Coburn, from the command of Brig. Gen. William T. Ward, followed closely behind. Soon Union troops spotted a small group of civilians approaching them under a flag of truce. These men introduced themselves as representatives of the town's government and offered a surrender paper. The Federal officers refused to accept it but went with the civilians to the courthouse and dictated the terms of a new document. When completed it read:

> *Brigadier-General Ward, commanding Third Division, Twentieth Corps:*
> Sir: The fortunes of war have placed the city of Atlanta in your hands, and as Mayor of the city, I ask protection to non-combatants and private property.
>
> JAMES M. CALHOUN,
> Mayor of Atlanta
>
> Attest—H. M. Scott, Captain and A.A.G.
> A. W. Tibbetts, Captain and A.D.C.
> J. P. Thomson, Lieutenant and Provost-Marshal.[6]

Shortly after the formal surrender ceremony was concluded, Slocum selected the Trent House Hotel as his headquarters. With bands playing lustily, the men of the Army of the Ohio began selecting camp sites.

Writing in retrospect, the Union commander, who was miles away from the surrender of Atlanta, said of it, "The glad tidings flew on the wings of electricity to all parts of the North."[7] When the news reached Grant at City Point, Virginia, he sent a 9:00 P.M. telegram to Sherman: "I have just received your dispatch announcing the capture of Atlanta. In honor of your great victory, I have ordered a salute to be fired with *shotted* guns from every battery bearing upon the enemy. The salute will be fired within an hour, amid great rejoicing."[8]

Washington echoed with exultation that was even more profound than among the men of Grant's forces, who were bogged down before Petersburg. Lincoln sent a telegram on September 3 expressing "national thanks" to "Major-General W. T. Sherman and the gallant officers and soldiers of his command before Atlanta."[9]

Almost simultaneously, the chief executive framed an "Order for Celebration of Victories." Like Grant, he ordered a formal salute and stipulated that it must consist of one hundred guns. They were to be fired in Washington at the U.S. Arsenal and Navy Yard and at every other arsenal and navy yard within Union territory.[10]

INFLUENTIAL CONFEDERATE newspapers minimized the importance of the Federal victory in Georgia by devoting little space to it. In contrast, prominent newspapers in Union territory urged readers to rejoice at "Sherman's Glorious Victory." Throughout the North, sermons were preached extolling his accomplishments. Noted orators, among whom Edward Everett was especially zealous, rejoiced at the capture of the faraway railroad center.[11]

Experienced officeholders and political leaders throughout the North and the South were united upon one aspect of the events in Georgia. Virtually without exception, they agreed that the Union desperately needed something to celebrate.

Grant seemed powerless to crush Lee, and casualty lists from battles in the East seemed to grow longer with each passing week. That made the surrender of Atlanta tremendously important, although the Confederate army that held it so long was still far from being destroyed. Although supporters of the Lincoln administration indulged in an orgy of wild rejoicing at Sherman's victory over Atlanta, any victory anywhere would have evoked similar celebrations.

Some of Sherman's officers vividly remembered that their commander expected to take Atlanta in July, but they remained silent about the five-week delay. Thousands of men, inspired by the commander's optimism, had expected to go home within ninety days after their invasion was launched. Some were able to do so when their enlistments expired; others swore, grumbled, and continued to fight.[12]

If Lincoln ever offered aloud prayers of thanksgiving, he must have uttered powerful ones on September 3. Atlanta's fall was a plum already picked, ripe for exploitation. Although Hood's army remained in the field and continued to be a target, the conquest of a strongly fortified town could be made into a potent symbol. Voters everywhere would be awed by guns thundering salutes throughout the North.

Atlanta was little known outside its immediate area until it became a haven for the Southern army. Yet its evacuation might boost to victory the president who faced an uphill fight in his bid for reelection.

Part 5

New Gibraltar of the West

20

You Must All Leave

"Here's your *New York Herald!* Here's your *Harper's Weekly!*" News vendors began shouting on the streets of Atlanta about 3:00 P.M. on Friday, September 2. Companies and regiments of men in blue dominated the town by that time. Wagons and troops continued to move in until long after dark, so that the place was crowded on Saturday. Among the newcomers were stragglers and deserters plus "negroes delirious over their strange sense of freedom."

Residents who remained were keenly aware that they were in danger. "Lean and haggard men and women of the lowest class were going through the stores, picking up such odds and ends as had been left behind by their owners."

Military orders were precise and detailed. Men making up the Army of the Cumberland occupied much of the town and guarded communication lines with Chattanooga. East Point, too small to hold the entire Army of the Tennessee, saw blue-clad units spill past its borders. Decatur was occupied by the Army of the Ohio. Roswell, Sandtown, and "other points on the flanks and along our line of communication" overflowed with cavalry.

Orders issued from "In the Field, near Lovejoy's [Station]," ended with a cluster of promises. To his men Sherman promised "an opportunity to have a full month's rest, with every chance to organize, receive pay, replenish clothing, and prepare for a fine winter's campaign."[1] Officers and privates alike were ready for cash; they had not been paid for months. All were bone-tired, and many were hungry.

Since so large a body of troops was involved, it took several days for these orders to be implemented. Their commander, meanwhile, was occupied with other matters. He hoped that Hood's main force would be found and smashed. If that should prove to be impossible, Sherman wanted to put Hardee's troops out of action. As a result, his movement toward Atlanta was described as "exceedingly slow." In his absence, Henry W. Slocum was named as commander of "the town of Atlanta."[2]

By September 7 Sherman was within ten miles of the town. Mildly alarmed at learning that Confederate cavalry were striking far to the north, he offered to send infantry to Chattanooga or Cleveland, Tennessee, "to head Wheeler off."[3] In Atlanta, bristling with "pride and pleasure," Thomas dictated a lengthy tribute to his men and praise for the Army of the Cumberland.

Sherman's pursuit of the defeated forces was briefly interrupted by a visit to Jonesborough's "rebel hospital, full of wounded officers and men." From that point he moved northward about ten miles to spend a night at Rough and Ready. Six days after Mayor Calhoun had formally surrendered Atlanta, the conqueror of the town finally rode into it. For his headquarters he selected the residence of Judge Lyons, partly because it was adjacent to the courthouse.[4]

For the present it would be futile to send his weary men to seek out and engage the still-substantial army he had entered Georgia to destroy. Hence Sherman turned his attention to the prize he had seized and gave orders concerning the future of Atlanta. His plans were so momentous that he had earlier hinted of them to Washington to see how they would be received there.

On September 4, after outlining a proposed winter campaign, he confided to Halleck, now chief of staff in Washington: "I propose to remove all the inhabitants of Atlanta, sending those committed to our cause to the rear, and the rebel families to the front. . . . If the people raise a howl against my barbarity and cruelty, I will answer that war is war and not popularity seeking."[5]

A lengthy letter written the same day was devoted largely to the importance of the upcoming Federal draft and the November election. Though addressed to Halleck, these communications were clearly intended for the War Department and the White House.

Halleck did not reply to the telegram that hinted of things to come. His detailed communication of September 16 responded only to Sherman's "very interesting letter of the 4th." Chatty to the point of being informal, Halleck passed along speculation and gossip. He wrote about his "annual attack of 'coryza,' or hay cold," and castigated Joseph Hooker.

Concerning Atlanta's past and future he said nothing but offered his congratulations on its capture. Secretary of War Stanton carefully acknowledged numerous dispatches from Sherman: one on August 31, three on September 6, one on September 7, and two on September 8. The all-important telegram of September 4 was not mentioned, however.[6] Washington knew what was planned and remained silent. One axiom of law is that silence gives assent.

Headquarters of the Military Division of the Mississippi were still "In the Field" four days after Washington was warned of what Sherman planned to do. Using civilians James M. Ball and James R. Crew as messengers, he had his September 7 statement of intentions hand-delivered to Hood.

A truce could be established in the vicinity of Rough and Ready to allow for the evacuation to the south, he suggested. Hood, who had no choice, agreed to a two-day truce that was later extended to ten days. He concluded his reply of September 9 by denouncing the upcoming deportation as transcending "in studied and ingenious cruelty, all acts ever brought to my attention in the dark history of war."[7]

Meanwhile, Sherman framed one of the controversial orders of the Civil War. Transmitted before he had received Hood's reply, it was addressed to the mayor of Atlanta. Section 1 conveyed the heart of the matter: "The city of Atlanta, being exclusively required for warlike purposes, will at once be vacated by all except the armies of the United States and such civilian employes as may be retained by the proper departments of the government."[8] As soon as it was made public, this directive had the effect its author anticipated; it raised a very loud "howl" against his barbarity and cruelty.

Calhoun immediately went to Sherman's headquarters and registered an oral protest. Rebuffed, he received detailed instructions not included in the written order. Before the day ended, the mayor had placards posted throughout the town. Addressed simply "To the Citizens of Atlanta," they read in part:

> Major-General Sherman instructs me to say to you that you must all leave Atlanta; that as many of you as want to go North can do so, and that as many as want to go South can do so, and that all can take with them their movable property, servants included, if they want to go, but that no force is to be used, and that he will

> furnish transportation as far as Rough and Ready, from thence it is expected that General Hood will assist in carrying it on. . . .
>
> All persons are requested to leave their names and number in their families with the undersigned as early as possible, that estimates may be made of the quantity of transportation required.[9]

JOINED BY councilmen E. E. Rawson and S. C. Wells, Calhoun spent two days drafting a formal appeal.

Sherman's directive, they told him, "would involve extraordinary hardship and loss," whose consequences would be "appalling and heart-rendering." They insisted that words were inadequate to depict "the woe, the horrors, and the suffering" sure to follow implementation of the order. Atlanta's population included pregnant women, young children, and the very sick, they pointed out. The southward advance of Union forces had driven many people from their homes north of Atlanta. As a result, "the country south of this is already crowded, and without houses enough to accommodate the people."[10]

This plaintive "howl" was precisely what Sherman wished to hear, since he took care that it reached Washington. There it was released to the press, along with the Sherman-Hood exchange over the deportation order, and was reprinted in part or in full throughout the North. Sherman's September 12 reply to Calhoun was blunt and unequivocal. His orders, he said, "were not designed to meet the humanities of the case." He knew "the vindictive nature of our enemy," he continued, and had to be prepared for an attack since he anticipated "many years of military operations from this quarter."[11]

HOOD WAS not intellectually agile enough to spar successfully with Sherman. Had he been Sherman's equal, he probably would have pointed out that the United States had not declared war upon the Confederacy. Federal armies, Lincoln repeatedly insisted, were engaged in putting down an insurrection rather than in making war. This line of reasoning logically meant that Atlanta's civilians were protected by the U.S. Constitution, which had made no provision for the deportation of citizens without trial.

Not qualified to debate the constitutional rights of civilians, Hood was also far from accurate in labeling the Atlanta order as without parallel. He could hardly have not known that Sherman had deported hundreds of women and children from Roswell a few weeks earlier.

Before joining the Army of Tennessee, while he was recuperating in Richmond from wounds received at Chickamauga, Hood also must have heard of a similar order issued in Kansas by Sherman's foster brother, Thomas Ewing Jr. Ewing entered the service as a colonel of cavalry. He was made a brigadier general on March 13, 1863, and took command of the Military District of the Border. Here he issued his General Order Number 11, which specified that the residents of Jackson, Cass, Vernon, and Bates Counties, Missouri, would have to evacuate.

Some civilians in this region were staunch Unionists; others supported William C. Quantrill's guerrillas. Although Lincoln objected to the "indiscriminate slaughter on the Missouri border," he supported Ewing's directive, including its threat of execution against any who refused to leave.[12]

It is not known how many people were affected by Ewing's deportation order, and his foster brother did not report how many of the Atlanta evacuees elected to go to the North. In the case of those who chose to go south, however, meticulous records were kept. They show that 446 family units of one to thirteen persons were transported to Rough and Ready. Collectively, they numbered more than 1,600 men, women, and children.

Despite the care with which the counts were made and preserved, the story of the deportation includes a mystery. Corresponding with Hood on the possible exchange of prisoners, Sherman almost casually acknowledged that he held many Atlanta civilians as prisoners. When the town was taken, his troops found about one thousand workers in the railroads and shops being treated as "detailed soldiers." His offer included exchanging these workmen for Hood's prisoners.[13]

Sherman presumed that all of these people were actively engaged in work for the Confederacy. Otherwise, he argued, they would not have been exempt from military service. Yet the Federal list of persons who moved to Rough and Ready for transportation to points south includes only 143 men presumed to be adults.

Since the proposed prisoner exchange was never implemented, the approximately eight hundred males to whom the Union commander referred seem to have dropped from the record.[14] What happened to these men is an even more obscure riddle than that of the fate of the factory workers and their children transported to the North from Roswell.

HOOD AND Sherman exchanged a series of long and acrimonious letters concerning the deportation of Atlanta's civilians. From the perspective

LIBRARY OF CONGRESS

LIBRARY OF CONGRESS

of later years, it is clear that both military commanders made extravagant charges or claims. Hood protested "in the name of God and humanity"; Sherman responded "in the name of common sense."

Sherman insisted that his shelling of Atlanta was accidental. His gunners occasionally overshot the Confederate defenses, he claimed. This preposterous claim was counterbalanced by Hood's assertions concerning early actions of secessionists.

Of the Confederate men and women, Hood declared that they: "by force of arms, drove out insolent intruders and took possession of our own forts and arsenals, to resist your claims to dominion over masters, slaves, and Indians, all of whom are to this day, with a unanimity unexampled in the history of the world, warring against your attempts to become their masters."[15]

While the generals bickered, Atlanta's residents stuffed their portable belongings into 8,842 packages.[16] They knew it would be futile to protest or attempt to evade Sherman's order.

During the truce, Georgia officials hurriedly purchased a forty-seven-acre tract of land in Terrell County. It came to be known as the "Exile Camp" when tents were erected as temporary shelter to about three hundred of the deportees. Eventually the tents were replaced with about sixty houses. Little else is known about the people who were made to leave Atlanta against their will.

PAINFUL AND clumsy as the evacuation of Atlanta and the resettlement of 1,650 civilians proved to be, the attempt to exchange prisoners was far worse. While discussing details for the planned mass deportation, Hood raised the issue of an exchange. He wanted it to be "man for man" in keeping with "the stipulations of the cartel" that had been suspended by Grant.[17]

Sherman agreed to base the negotiations upon "the old cartel" but quickly began adding conditions. Reporting to Washington, he claimed to hold about two thousand prisoners and ended his telegram, uncharacteristically, with a statement about the weather. Frequently pessimistic and even despondent, this time he rejoiced, "Weather beautiful and all things seem bright."[18]

The extent of Lemuel Grant's fortifications can be appreciated in the photo at the top of the facing page. Rows of chevaux-de-frise stood in front of the trenches that surrounded the city. These fortifications were erected in northwest Atlanta. The house above is seen in detail below. Known as the Potter house, it was occupied by Southern sharpshooters, making it a special target for Federal artillery. Almost a ton of shot and shell was found in the house after the fall of the city.

In an unusual move, Sherman proposed that Atlanta become a Federal fortress and ordered the evacuation of all civilians from the town.

A count showed that Union forces held in or near Atlanta 128 officers and 782 enlisted men. An additional 93 officers and 907 men were en route to Chattanooga. In addition to these 1,810 soldiers, Sherman offered to exchange the estimated 1,000 Confederate workmen alluded to earlier. He suggested that the exchange be made near Rough and Ready, promising that he could recall from Chattanooga Brig. Gen. Daniel C. Govan, who had been captured at Jonesborough. In exchange, he requested Brig. Gen. George Stoneman and Capt. George P. Buell.

Like the Confederates, Sherman was keenly aware that Andersonville was badly overcrowded. Sumter County, which housed the stockade, couldn't produce sufficient food to feed the prisoners. Now holding an estimated thirty-two thousand Union soldiers, any reduction in its population would reduce its horrors somewhat.

Though Hood repeatedly urged Richmond to take the prison more seriously, his concerns centered, not in the welfare of the inmates, but in the danger that Sherman might be strengthened. Unlike most members of the Northern press, he knew that the prisoners usually received the same food and medical care given to Confederate soldiers in the field.[19]

His government, Sherman informed Hood, wished "to release from prolonged confinement the large numbers of prisoners held by both parties." He insisted that he was personally eager to gain the release of some of "our poor fellows at Anderson."

After seeming to cooperate in the planning for the exchange, Sherman balked and began to add other conditions and stipulations. In exchange for Confederates whom he held as prisoners of war, he'd take only men from his own regiments. Any prisoner who had served in an army not under his command would not be accepted for exchange. Neither would those "who belong to other regiments whose times are out and who have been discharged."

Jefferson Davis approved of the exchange in advance and gave Hood a free hand to negotiate, but he preferred not to exchange able-bodied prisoners. Suddenly the fresh stipulations added by Sherman effectively ruled out most of the men held at Andersonville. Identification of units in which prisoners had fought would be difficult and time consuming, if not impossible. Confronted by demands he could not meet, Hood indignantly rejected Sherman's revisions and the proposed prisoner exchange never took place.[20]

ATLANTA'S EVACUATION was denounced in the handful of Southern journals still being published. Northern reaction to the news of the mass deportation was generally cautious and guarded. Officially, Washington informed Sherman only that "the course you have pursued in removing rebel families from Atlanta, and in the exchange of prisoners, is fully approved."

Many military reports and newspaper stories about the invasion of Georgia and eyewitness accounts of battles were published in an 1868 book. Yet the thick volume includes neither "deportation" nor "evacuation" in the index. Nearly two decades later, compilers of the *Official Record* released correspondence from Sherman, Calhoun, and Hood. Yet its immense index gives no hint that a city was evacuated or that its civilians were deported. Many accounts of Federal actions during more than one hundred days after entering Georgia bypass the deportation issue entirely. So do early biographies of the president who did not protest Sherman's actions and contemporary biographies of Sherman.

In the town whose remaining civilians were forced to choose between traveling either to the North or farther south, hundreds of soldiers soon erected tents and prepared camps. Some managed to build rough cabins with lumber ripped from "Judge Erskine's residence and other fine houses."

Members of a few units began sporadic work on a new and much smaller line of fortifications. At East Point and Decatur, as well as in Atlanta, scores of officers began to prepare all-too-terse summaries of their activities since leaving Chattanooga.

With the town effectively cleared of civilians, Sherman's announced plan to turn it into a long-term Union bastion seemed to face no insurmountable problems. Given six months or a year, the Federal commander could memorialize himself by creating a new Gibraltar of the West.

21

An Empty Town, Barely Occupied

> Now, I know the vindictive nature of our enemies, and that *we may have many years of military operations from this quarter,* and therefore deem it wise and prudent to prepare in time. The use of Atlanta for warlike purposes is inconsistent with its character as a home for families. There will no manufactures, commerce, or agriculture here for the maintenance of families, and sooner or later want will compel the inhabitants to go. Why not go now, when all the arrangements have been completed for the transfer, instead of waiting till the plunging shot of contending armies will renew the scenes of the past month? . . . *I assert that my military plans make it necessary for the inhabitants to go away.*[1]

PRIOR TO drafting his lengthy statement that went to the mayor and councilmen of Atlanta, Sherman notified Washington of his plans. "I am not willing to have Atlanta encumbered by the families of our enemies," he said. "I want it a pure Gibraltar, and will have it so by October 1."

Sherman sent a brief summary of his actions to his wife. Yes, he had exchanged "sharp correspondence with Hood about expelling the poor families of a brave people." No, the action could not be construed as vindictive or cruel. To Ellen he wrote: "I take the ground that Atlanta is a conquered place and I propose to use it *purely for our own military purposes* which are inconsistent with its habitation by the families of a brave people. I am shipping them *all,* and by next Wednesday [September 21] *the town will be a real military town.*"[2]

It is highly unlikely that Sherman contemplated using the conquered town in the fashion he indicated. The deportation was an act of calculated savagery, designed to make a few residents of Georgia learn a lasting lesson:

> War is cruelty and you cannot refine it, and those who brought war into our country deserve all the curses and maledictions a people can pour out. . . . You might as well appeal against a thunder-storm as against these terrible hardships of war. They are inevitable, and the only way the people of Atlanta can hope once more to live in peace and quiet at home is to stop the war, which can alone be done by admitting that it began in error and is perpetuated in pride.[3]

LIBRARY OF CONGRESS

The Rebel entrenchments around Atlanta were later occupied by Federal troops and posed a significant impediment to Hood's efforts to regain the city.

In the "Federal fortress" he pretended to be creating, Sherman issued no detailed orders concerning its defense. Instead, he instructed Maj. Gen. Henry W. Slocum's Twentieth Corps to guard the Chattahoochee River bridge and to occupy Atlanta.

During the first ten days in which the town was empty of civilians, Sherman fired one verbal volley after another. Directed to his subordinates, they dealt with Hood, Confederate cavalry leaders Joseph Wheeler and Nathan B. Forrest, the destruction of the enemy's railroads, and the actions he wished taken at distant points within the District of the Mississippi.

Unwilling to give his subordinates a free hand, by October 4 Sherman was out of Atlanta and briefly established at Smyrna Camp Ground. On Wednesday, October 5, he went to Kenesaw Mountain and then Marietta before returning to Kenesaw. From that camp he visited Pine Hill on Friday, came back to Kenesaw on Saturday, and then went to Allatoona on Sunday. On Monday, October 10—not quite three weeks after the evacuation—Sherman was at Cartersville, where he remained only briefly before proceeding to Kingston, Rome, and Resaca.

On Saturday, October 15, he visited Snake Creek Gap, where some of the first fierce fighting of the invasion had erupted, and then went to Ship's Gap and Villanow on Sunday. Part of Wednesday was spent at Summerville, after which he shook the red dust of Georgia off his feet and spent a week at Gaylesville, Alabama.

Headquarters of the District of the Mississippi were established at Rome, Georgia, on October 29. Four days later Sherman was back at Kingston, where he remained until November 12. During the five weeks he was away from Atlanta, the Union commander directed operations in the field, planned future operations, and supervised the destruction of rail lines.

In addition to revealing where he was every day, his communications raise a question that cannot be answered. With rare exceptions his messages are headed "In the Field," with place and date following—often accompanied by a notation of the time at which the dispatch was sent. Why do typical communications from subordinates show only the approximate place of origin and date; that is, "Rome, Ga., Oct. 13, 1864"?

Sherman displayed unbounded zeal in personally supervising the work of rendering Southern railroads useless. Weeks earlier, he had found that it seemed to take less time for the Confederates to repair track than for his men to rip it up. Now he was grimly determined to effect permanent damage. Planning to start back toward Atlanta, he ordered the bridges of the Western and Atlantic Railroad to be burned behind him. He ordered his troops to "take up all the iron back to Dalton or even to Chattanooga [from the Chattahoochee]."[4]

Led by Hood, the Confederates executed numerous raids. Many were directed against Sherman's line of communications, the vital one-track railroad he had ordered destroyed as he withdrew from Kingston in mid-October. Against the specific instructions of Jefferson Davis, Hood pursued this course instead of putting the Army of Tennessee between Atlanta and the seacoast.

During weeks of constant skirmishing, it began to look as though the Confederates intended to move into middle Tennessee. Sherman's railroad, his supply life, ran through a region stripped of food for humans and forage for animals. Moving to stave off disaster, Sherman sent George H. Thomas to Nashville. In addition to the troops he took with him, Thomas soon received reinforcements from the North and hundreds of men from Sherman's forces.

Confederate and Federal commanders tested one another's strength for two months but had only one engagement of any size. A railroad pass at Allatoona, held by Union troops under the command of Brig. Gen. John M. Corse, was initially considered to be safe. Because it contained an estimated seven thousand head of cattle needed to feed the Federal army, it was judged a likely target for Confederate forces. On October 7 Sherman decided it was so vulnerable and important that he made it the subject of a general order.[5]

Less than twenty-four hours later he commanded the Armies of the Ohio and the Cumberland to converge on the spot in the mountains. Sherman himself headed for the obscure site and surveyed its surroundings. Satisfied that it was safe, he then turned back toward Marietta.

By the time he reached his field headquarters, his aides knew that a Confederate force under Maj. Gen. S. G. French was determined to take Allatoona. Helpless to intervene, Sherman watched from a distance of about eighteen miles as wave after wave of Southerners stormed toward the Federal lines.[6]

Although the telegraph lines had been cut, Union signal officers managed to transmit an urgent plea for help. General Corse reputedly received Sherman's challenge to "hold on," coupled with his promise, "We are coming!" Under Corse's urging, the two thousand defenders held Allatoona against an almost equal body of attackers. Losses were also nearly equal—more than seven hundred from each force, or 35 percent of the men engaged.

Inspired by news of the engagement, evangelist P. P. Bliss wrote a commemorative hymn entitled "Hold the Fort, For We Are Coming!" Long after Allatoona was forgotten, the song continued to be sung widely in both the North and the South.[7]

At least as early as the first week of September, Hood invited Davis to visit the Army of Tennessee in person. Recognizing the crucial importance of Georgia, but unwilling or unable to send reinforcements, the Confederate president came to Macon by way of Savannah.

In a lengthy oration delivered on September 23 Davis urged his soldiers to look to the future rather than the past. Barely acknowledging the loss of Atlanta, he challenged his listeners:

> It does not become us to revert to disaster. Let the dead bury the dead. Let us, with one army and one effort, endeavor to crush Sherman. . . .
>
> It has been said that I abandoned Georgia to her fate. Shame upon such falsehood. . . . The man who uttered this was a scoundrel. He was not a man to save our country. . . .
>
> You have not many men between eighteen and forty-five left. The boys—God bless the boys—are, as rapidly as they become old enough, going to the field [of battle].

At Montgomery, Alabama, Davis lauded Hood's gallant conduct and his strategy. Confederate soldiers, insisted the Southern chief executive, would soon have a firm hold upon the Federal lines of communications. Once this objective was achieved, Davis insisted, "I see no chance for Sherman to escape from a defeat or a disgraceful retreat. I therefore hope, in view of all the contingencies of the war, that within thirty days that army which has so boastfully taken up its winter quarters in the heart of the Confederacy will be in search of a crossing of the Tennessee River."

Again with the Army of Tennessee at Palmetto Station, Georgia, on September 21, Davis delivered peroration after peroration. Sherman, he promised, would soon begin a retreat that would prove more disastrous to Federal forces "than Napoleon's retreat from Moscow had proved to the French armies."

Listeners, described as apathetic, watched Davis go into a meeting with his generals when his speech was concluded. If he had doubts about how most of these officers felt, they were soon dispelled. Learning first-hand that there was a general clamor to relieve Hood, he seems to have spoken vaguely about possibly replacing him with P. G. T. Beauregard.[8]

While in Georgia, Davis apparently learned nothing about a political move that might have brought the war to an end. Gov. Joseph E. Brown, a fervent advocate of states' rights, had little more use for Richmond than for Washington. He consistently played an obstructionist role when asked to support the programs of the central government. Earlier he went on record as holding that Atlanta was "to the Confederacy as important as the heart is to the body." Blaming Davis for having caused "loss of the heart," he dropped hints that he might be willing to bargain with the Federal leaders.[9]

Sherman may have learned of Brown's threats from his spies. It is equally possible that overtures came directly to him, with or without the knowledge of Brown. Whatever the case, the Federal leader considered it of utmost importance to participate in an exchange of messages with the Georgia governor.

He hoped that Brown might be persuaded to negotiate a treaty of peace involving only the state. Should this be done, Sherman informed Lincoln, Georgians could join him in driving the Army of Tennessee out of the state. His optimism concerning a potential visit to Atlanta by Brown was so great that he confided about it to Washington and found Lincoln to be keenly interested.[10]

The Confederate vice president, Alexander H. Stephens of Georgia, was known to be at odds with Davis. Hoping for his support in the projected political coup, the Federal leader used William King as an intermediary to approach him. To Sherman's chagrin, Stephens refused the invitation. Neither he nor Sherman was empowered to negotiate for peace, wrote the Confederate leader, yet stressing his eagerness to have any just proposal "submitted to the action of our respective Governments."[11]

Stephens, Brown, and Sherman knew that their presidents took firm but opposite stands. Davis was eager to bring the war to an end and to gain recognition of the Confederacy as an independent nation. Lincoln was unyielding in his insistence that peace would come only as a result of the unconditional surrender of the Confederacy. Stephens was unwilling to have any part in an agreement between the state of Georgia and the United States. His stance seems to have put an end to Sherman's clumsy attempts to win new glory by leading Georgia out of the Confederacy.

LIBRARY OF CONGRESS

Hardly secure within the environs of Atlanta, Sherman dabbled with securing a separate peace between the United States and Georgia and nervously inspected his many outposts along his invasion path through Georgia. Here he posed, leaning on a cannon like the old artillery officer he was, with his staff at Federal Fort Number 2 in Atlanta.

Political issues aside, Sherman's hands were more than full with military matters. He was making little progress toward implementing what he often called the "grand plan," drawn up between Grant and him months earlier. Hood's forces were still formidable; in mid-October he was estimated to have at least ten thousand cavalry and thirty thousand infantry at his command. Sherman's armies were much larger, but they were shrinking because many enlistments had expired.[12]

QUERULOUS EMPHASES often surfaced in Sherman's letters to his wife. Having reached a point he estimated to be four miles from Atlanta, he told her: "This army is much reduced in strength by deaths, sickness, and the expiration of service. It looks hard to see regiments march away when their time is up. On the other side they have everybody, old and young, and for indefinite periods. . . . No recruits are coming, for the draft is not until September, and then suppose it will consist mostly of [blacks] and bought recruits that must be kept well to the rear. I sometimes think our people do not deserve to succeed in war; they are so apathetic."[13]

Still despondent a week later, Sherman confided his apprehension for the future:

> The time of the three year men is expiring all the time, and daily regiments are leaving for home, diminishing my fighting force by its best material; and the draft has been so long deferred, and the foolish law allowing [blacks] and the refuse of the South to be bought up and substituted on paper (for they never come to the front) will delay my reinforcements until my army on the offensive, so far from its base, will fall below my opponent's, who increases as I lose. I rather think to-day Hood's army is larger than mine, and he is strongly fortified. I have no faith in the people of the North. They ever lose their interest when they should act.[14]

In August, his hopes centered upon the upcoming lottery scheduled to be held throughout Union territory. Provided that the law was scrupulously obeyed everywhere, thousands of conscripts would be chosen in a few weeks. In a telegram to Grant he urged him to "tell Mr. Lincoln that he must not make the least concession in the matter of the September draft."[15]

By October, Sherman had ceased to wheedle and began to make demands. He must have at least five thousand to six thousand men from among the recruits gained as a result of the Federal draft and sent to Nashville. To minimize the risks involved in using green troops, he planned for all recruits to "go to the regiments in due proportion." Half of these men he wished to put into the Army of the Cumberland, with the Armies of the Ohio and the Tennessee getting one-fourth of them each.[16]

Plenty of men were available in a special fast-growing pool, but Sherman wanted nothing to do with them. John A. Sooner came to Chattanooga as a recruiting agent for Massachusetts, seeking to enlist black soldiers. Under pressure from Washington, Sherman reluctantly issued a pass. Recruitment depots could be established, he suggested, at Macon and Columbus in Mississippi, Mobile and Montgomery in Alabama, and Columbus, Milledgeville, and Savannah in Georgia. For practical purposes, that meant any major center with which Sherman was not personally involved could be used.

To Sooner he admitted his opposition to the congressional action aimed at recruiting black soldiers. As he saw the racial situation, "The negro is in a transition state, and is not the equal of the white man." He was glad to have the service of blacks, he added, "as pioneers, teamsters, cooks, and servants." Branding his racial ideas as "peculiar," he stressed that "they are shared by a large proportion of our fighting men."[17]

As a long-time master of framing explanations and excuses, Sherman ended his detailed communication with a note of sympathy for freed slaves. "I would not draw on the poor race for too large a proportion of its active, athletic young men," he told Sooner, "for some must remain to seek new homes and provide for the old and young—the feeble and helpless."

Sherman's lengthy letter opposing "state negro recruiting-agents" was made public in Washington. Late in August, Lincoln had twice paid tribute to black soldiers serving with Union forces. Halleck, however, privately sympathized with Sherman. "You must have been very considerably annoyed," he wrote on September 16.[18]

The adjutant general, Lorenzo Thomas, was furious at the continued opposition to one of his favorite projects. To the secretary of war he stressed awareness "that General Sherman has been and is opposed to the organization of colored troops." Sherman should, wrote Thomas, "bear in mind that they guard along lines of his communications, and that on the Mississippi they are greatly relied on for holding the important points."[19]

More than a year earlier, in 1863, Sherman confided his feelings to his wife. Bemoaning the poor quality of all soldiers not in the regular army, he said, "It may be the whole war will be turned over to the negroes, and I begin to believe they do as well as Lincoln and his advisers."

That verdict represents one of his frequent reversals of judgment. A few days earlier he had written Ellen, "With my opinions of negroes and my experience, yea prejudice, I cannot trust them yet. Time may change this but I cannot bring myself to trust negroes with arms in positions of danger and trust."[20]

If in 1863 he really believed that he might modify his views concerning black soldiers before war's end, he was deceiving himself. One of his postwar boasts concerning his exploits in Georgia was based upon his claim that he didn't use a single black soldier in the state.

A substantial number of freed slaves remained at least briefly in Atlanta after the fall of the town. There is no indication that even one of them was used in any capacity other than that of laborer.

Probably not considering blacks to be civilians, Sherman took drastic steps to buttress his claim that he was creating a permanent Federal base for soldiers only. His deportation order, which included six separate provisions, banned all business in the occupied town. Traders, manufacturers, and sutlers were ordered to stay away. If they failed to do so, "the quartermaster will seize their stores and appropriate them to the use of the troops."

Officers and men of Slocum's Twentieth Corps, many of whom were busy guarding the Chattahoochee River railroad bridge and its approaches, were spread very thin around Atlanta. Some of them supervised the makeshift construction of what they called an "interior fort" near the city hall. But no other military work of consequence was erected, despite Sherman's grandiose announcements. By October he admitted to Washington that it was easier to take Atlanta than to defend it.[21]

Staying briefly at Ship's Gap, the Union commander told Slocum he would leave him in Atlanta "and swing round in the country for forage and adventure." Almost simultaneously he directed Slocum to strip the region of food and forage. By October 23 he was gratified to know that this expedition was highly successful. Slocum brought in four hundred wagon loads after one foray, seven hundred as a result of another, and had men on six hundred more wagons busy stripping the countryside.[22]

Conquered Atlanta was empty of civilians and occupied by only a token force of Federal troops. It would take many months, perhaps even years, to transform the railroad center into the "new Gibraltar" promised by Sherman.

22

Saltwater!

SHERMAN'S IDEAS were as diverse as his names; the Indian warrior for whom he was first named—Tecumseh—took second place to "a proper Christian name"—William. His motives ranged as widely as did his affectionate forms of address—from Cumpy to Uncle Billy. Most of his 1864 official communications are signed simply, "W. T. Sherman, Major-General."[1] Yet no other commanding general was more ambivalent in his goals and emotions than was Sherman.

Sherman's life was marked by dichotomies in emotions, loyalties, ambitions, and self-esteem. Because of his complexities and diversities, it is often impossible to determine if he said and wrote what he really meant. Despite this dilemma, it is clear that he never planned to use Atlanta as a long-term military base. Long before the town was abandoned to his troops, he realized that he could not maintain an extended sojourn in the heart of Georgia. Hence he must have asked himself over and over, If we pursue the Army of Tennessee a great distance, where do we go from there?

Bvt. Brig. Gen. Willard Warner later claimed that his commander had an answer to that question before he left Resaca. Lieutenant Colonel Warner of the Seventy-sixth Ohio Regiment was brought from Nashville early in May. He soon became an inspector general on Sherman's staff, which required him to be with his commander several times a day. Warner later stated that Sherman in May 1864 confided that he was eager to smell saltwater soon.[2]

Lt. Col. Horace Porter, Grant's aide-de-camp, was present at a luncheon meeting of Grant and Sherman. Having agreed to strike simultaneously in the East and in the West, Sherman became more specific. According to Porter, before setting foot in Georgia he said, "I want to strike out for the sea."[3]

These second-hand recollections cannot be taken at face value; memories may have been tainted by subsequent events. It is clear, however, that once he achieved his primary goal of crushing the Army of Tennessee, Sherman had no intention of remaining in Georgia for long. On August 12 he was encamped near the Chattahoochee River, frustrated by the strength of the Confederate defenses. Reporting to Washington, he said, "If I should ever be cut off from my base, look out for me about Saint Mark's, Fla. or Savannah, Ga."[4]

Sherman had at least a general idea of where he would go once the Army of Tennessee surrendered. His choice of what Warner remembered as "saltwater" was based on military considerations. Hundreds of miles away from Louisville, he would find himself dependent upon single-track railroads for the entire distance.

It had taken ten thousand men an entire week to repair a single seven-mile section. Their work required thirty-five thousand ties and huge quantities of spikes sent from Chattanooga. Hood, Wheeler, Forrest, "and the whole batch of devils" were after him. Without moving from Atlanta he could lose one thousand men a month trying to protect the railroads.[5] Small wonder that this astute strategist decided that it was impossible to secure his line of communications permanently. Once that verdict was reached, he had only one alternative: Wagons south!

His primary motive for undertaking the March to the Sea was strategic: he wanted to get his armies out of Georgia before it was too late to move them. Besides, this man who was so often affected by intuition and hunches had a long-established personal rule of conduct. To his wife, he referred to it as "my old rule never to return by the road I had come."[6]

He had promised Grant to come to him with fifty thousand or sixty thousand infantry as soon as possible. It would take months for his men to march nearly one thousand miles to Virginia. How would they and their animals subsist if that route were to be taken? Middle Tennessee was already bare of food and forage; civilians there were in desperate straits.

To reach Grant as soon as possible, Sherman believed the most feasible plan would involve a relatively short overland march by his troops. When he reached navigable water at any of several points, he was confident that he could make contact with Adm. John A. Dahlgren's blockade fleet. Guarded by warships, transports would then make a quick trip up the coast so he could keep his promise to reinforce Grant's armies.[7]

A third motive for marching through Georgia stemmed from the realization that it would demonstrate the strength of the North and "the vulnerability of the South."[8] Not incidentally, this would make a household word of his own name. A former soldier who was a guilt-ridden failure only a few years earlier would become a modern Caesar.

Though it was never given first priority in his communications, Sherman had a fourth reason for undertaking the "great raid." Almost from the day he first stepped into the state, he was fervently eager to "make Georgia howl." Hence he confessed that the movement he hoped to undertake would not be "purely military or strategic" in nature.[9]

THERE IS a widespread impression that the March to the Sea was launched as a result of a sudden inspiration by a master strategist devoted to the concept of total warfare. T. Harry Williams has pointed out that Sherman's plan evolved quite slowly. Far from being an exaggeration, that is a calculated understatement. Having had saltwater in mind for weeks before his troops began to move toward the Atlantic, Sherman vacillated between several destinations. Both Grant and officials at the War Department hesitated to approve any route he proposed. Many telegrams were exchanged before his radical and daring plan won tentative and then final approval.

By September 10 Sherman was openly worried about his dependency upon the Western and Atlantic Railroad. Atlanta was close at hand, but he calculated that he was 175 miles from navigable water at Augusta. Grant no longer toyed with the idea of asking him to move his armies toward Mobile to help capture that vital port. Instead, he suggested sending Edward R. Canby's troops to Savannah by water. Sherman, he said, could simultaneously "move on Augusta."[10]

Caught on the horns of a strategic dilemma, Sherman made a counteroffer for a joint operation:

> If I could be sure of finding provisions at Augusta or Columbus, Ga., I can march to Milledgeville and compel Hood to give up Augusta or Macon and could then turn on the other. The country will afford forage and many supplies, but not enough in any one

> place to admit of a delay. . . . If you can manage to take the Savannah River as high as Augusta, or the Chattahoochee as far up as Columbus, I can sweep the whole state of Georgia. Otherwise I would risk our whole army by going too far from Atlanta.[11]

Grant described his own line of battle as being "necessarily very long." Still, he hoped to send six thousand to ten thousand men against Wilmington, North Carolina. "What you are to do with the forces at your command, I do not see," he told his friend and subordinate. Perhaps it would be well for Sherman to divide his force, "sending one-half to Mobile and the other half to Savannah."

Within twenty-four hours Sherman had revised his thinking. His forces could not remain in Atlanta and on the defensive for any length of time. Hood's army was still strong enough to "constantly break my [rail]road," he pointed out. That being the case, he reasoned:

> I would infinitely prefer to make a wreck of the [Western and Atlantic] road and of the country from Chattanooga to Atlanta, including the latter city, send back all my wounded and worthless, and, with my effective army move through Georgia, smashing things to the sea.

HARPER'S

Federal foraging parties stripped the Atlanta countryside bare.

> Hood may turn into Tennessee and Kentucky, but I believe he will be forced to follow me. Instead of being on the defensive, I would be on the offensive; instead of guessing at which he means to do, he would have to guess at my plans. The difference in war is full 25 per cent. I can make Savannah, Charleston, or the mouth of the Chattahoochee.[12]

Grant had just received a telegram briefly outlining a plan under which Sherman would split his forces and leave men at Nashville to hold Tennessee. Earlier, he had pondered a hand-delivered letter brought to him from Georgia.

In his detailed outline, Sherman said that he hoped gunboats could be sent to Savannah. Once the port was in Federal hands he would proceed "to cross the State of Georgia with some 60,000 men, hauling some stores and depending on the country for the balance." After having carefully studied what he called "the game," he concluded, "It would be wrong for us to penetrate farther into Georgia without an objective beyond."[13]

Still extremely wary of Sherman's central idea, Grant warned that Sherman's troops might find themselves "bushwhacked by all the old men, little boys, and such railroad guards as are still left at home." He preferred that Sherman should move against Hood's army rather than strike out for the coast.[14]

In 1864 and for many years afterward, some admirers of Grant insisted that he formulated the plan for the March to the Sea. He later denied having done so but mistakenly remembered that he had been "in favor of Sherman's plan from the time it was first submitted to me."[15]

At 7:55 A.M. on October 12, Sherman received the long-desired permission to act as he wished. Dispatched at 11:30 the previous evening, it informed him, "If you are satisfied the trip to the sea-coast can be made, holding the line of the Tennessee firmly, you may make it, destroying all the railroad south of Dalton or Chattanooga, as you think best."[16]

HOOD HAD pondered his options and made his decision. It was impossible for him to guess what Sherman might do, he admitted. When all variables were taken into account, it seemed to him that Sherman's forces would move in a body "on Columbus or Montgomery to open communication with Mobile."[17]

Acting on this assumption, Confederates moved to Gadsden, Alabama, a town about 50 miles below Rome on the Coosa River. From that site, Hood believed he could throw his forces between the Union armies and their supply bases in the North. Sherman followed Hood as far as Gaylesville, Alabama, on the Coosa River. The Southern troops responded by marching to Tuscumbia, Alabama, about 150 miles west of Chattanooga.

Sometimes described as a "backward movement," the route chosen by the Confederates had a decisive impact upon Sherman's plans. He was no longer torn between moving southwest, south, or southeast. Hood's actions, the Union commander later said, had the effect of "stepping aside and opening wide the door for us to enter Central Georgia."

Despite having hesitantly approved of Sherman's plan to head for the sea, Grant still wanted his subordinate to drive Nathan B. Forrest's cavalry from middle Tennessee. Since there was no way to strike at both objectives simultaneously, Grant sent more troops to Nashville. To Washington, Sherman confided that he preferred to move on "Milledgeville, Millen, and Savannah River." Believing Hood to be at the moment about twenty-four miles away, he said, "I can whip his infantry, but his cavalry is to be feared."[18]

Still not settled on a precise destination, Sherman made plans to destroy Atlanta and march to either Savannah or Charleston, "doing irreparable damage" on the way. To counter the threat posed by Forrest, he ordered the seizure of all horses in middle Tennessee. "If Forrest be prevented getting supplies," he reasoned, "he cannot stay long north of the Tennessee [River]." Forrest must not be permitted to alter or to delay Sherman's plan "to march and punish."[19]

By October 11 some of Sherman's officers were sure that he intended to make a large scale move soon. Far away in Virginia, Grant still wanted Sherman to strike at Hood. But since he had turned Sherman loose to act upon his own best judgment, there was nothing for Grant to do but wait and listen.

In Georgia, most traces of uncertainty vanished. Sick, wounded, and inexperienced men in Sherman's army were sent to the rear. Withdrawing from near Chattanooga where he had been poised for a possibly decisive meeting with Hood, Sherman moved toward Atlanta as rapidly as possible. Wrecking the Western and Atlantic behind him, he decided to "move through Georgia, smashing things to the sea."

Finally convinced that "Sherman's proposition is the best that can be adopted," Grant took the necessary steps to have supplies waiting for him at the coast. He requested that vessels be loaded with two hundred thousand rations of grain, five hundred thousand rations of provisions, and three million rounds of ammunition. Once word was received that "Sherman has struck south," he said, this flotilla should set sail for Ossabaw Sound near Savannah. Earlier, Hilton Head, South Carolina, had been tentatively selected as the point at which the supplies would be waiting.[20]

Grant knew that his suggestion concerning the arming of blacks by Sherman had been ignored. He had succeeded in quieting some of the concerns and fears expressed by Lincoln. It was now up to his subordinate to show that he could act as vigorously as he had spoken. Hence he gave the nod that prompted Stanton to send formal War Department approval of the projected "grand move into Georgia."[21]

While at Gaylesville, Alabama, still ostensibly hoping to fight it out with Hood, Sherman pored over his maps. Soon he concluded that if it proved impossible to reach Savannah, he could "open communication with the sea somewhere in that direction." If the recollections of a staff officer are accurate, Sherman abandoned the idea of transporting his men by sea to reinforce Grant. Instead, he'd march north—perhaps making Goldsborough, North Carolina, his objective.

No one in Washington had the remotest idea that Sherman's march might continue through both Carolinas. A coded telegram was initially so puzzling that Sherman didn't know where he was expected to go. "Horse-i-bar" did not appear on his maps, so he wondered if he should head toward Mobile. When finally deciphered, the scrambled message cleared the way for him to head toward Ossabaw Sound, close to Savannah.[22]

Mobile and the mouth of the Apalachicola River continued to be alternative destinations. By October 20, however, a firm decision had been reached concerning the size of the raiding force. Sherman wanted at least sixty thousand men, but not more than sixty-five thousand. He demanded that his generals maintain "a large amount of secrecy," partly because of a top-level change by Confederates. P. G. T. Beauregard was now head of the Military Division of the West. Hood's position as commander of the armies was nominal.

Writing to his wife, Sherman warned her to "get used to being without letters."[23] Ten days later the Union commander recognized that it would be impossible to start on November 1; it might take five more days "to get everything [not needed] back" to Nashville. Schofield's twelve-thousand-man Twenty-third Corps was dispatched there to bolster Thomas's strength.[24]

At his City Point command post directing the siege of Petersburg, Grant continued to put top priority upon the destruction of Hood's army. Sherman's "other move" he labeled as secondary.

Sherman strongly disagreed with this assessment. In order to field a force equal to that of the Confederates, he argued, he'd have to abandon Atlanta. Somehow he ignored the fact that his projected march toward the sea would take every Federal from the captured town.[25]

Grant gave his second assent to the plan, this time without reservation. Once more delaying his start, on Monday, November 3, Sherman was confident that it would be made before the beginning of another week. Again he proved to be wrong. Severe weather set in, and he was told that three hundred to four hundred railroad cars would be required for a single trip from Atlanta to Nashville. That meant he'd be lucky to turn his back upon Atlanta by November 10.[26]

By this time a factor beyond his control acted to delay the start of the march again. The voters would go to the polls on Tuesday, November 8. In both North and South it was seen as a momentous day. Lincoln might be returned to the White House and his war policy would be validated. But it looked as though the electorate might reject his administration—and his conduct of the war. Coupled with uncertainty about his political fate, the president was "anxious, if not fearful" about Sherman's high-risk plans.

Under these circumstances it was not possible for Sherman's troops to start toward Savannah before November 10 or 11. In a lengthy report to Grant, Sherman attempted to justify his decision to make the hazardous journey. "If we can march a well-appointed army right through his territory, it is a demonstration to the world, foreign and domestic, that we have a power which [Jefferson] Davis cannot resist."[27]

At 10:30 P.M. on the day before the election, Grant dispatched a brief telegram wishing for his colleague "great good fortune." At the worst, he said, the projected raid could only be "less fruitful of results than is hoped for." Having earlier conceded that it would be impossible for him to capture Savannah as initially planned, Grant had no more to say for the present. In Georgia, Sherman had already made it clear that of three possible routes, he would take the shortest. That would enable him to send help to Grant at the earliest possible moment.[28]

Four days after Lincoln's reelection, Sherman notified his cavalry leader, Kilpatrick: "Be all ready to start tomorrow." Still at Kingston, he then set out for Atlanta, with the jump-off scheduled for November 15 or 16. Soon after the Union commander and his aides started south for the last time on the Western and Atlantic, their telegraph line was severed behind them, almost certainly ordered by Sherman. This meant that he could no longer receive advice, instructions, or orders from Grant, Halleck, Stanton, or Lincoln.

SHERMAN CONTINUED to tell his officers as little as possible and no more news went from him to Washington. Early into his long March to the Sea, however, Northern newspapers gave detailed accounts of the "grand raid" and its objectives. Grant was both puzzled and angry that the *New York Times* reported Sherman's plans and strength accurately.

Stanton blamed the officers of the invading forces and concluded that Sherman may not have been "very guarded in his own talk." Grant soon learned that an Indianapolis newspaper made public the plans for the march. Furious, he planned to investigate, identify army officers who talked too much, and "send them to the Dry Tortugas."[29]

Who was responsible for the publication of Sherman's plans? Firm answers are lacking, but a substantial body of evidence raises some intriguing questions. Had Sherman undergone a radical transformation in his views concerning the press? Or was he uncontrollably ambivalent?

Sherman had been embarrassed early in the war by news stories that questioned his sanity while he served in Kentucky under Robert Anderson, the heroic commander of Fort Sumter. As a result, Sherman began to lash out at newspapers, editors, and reporters in general. Especially in his personal letters he reveled in vituperation. A few fragments from his many verbal assaults reveal the depth of his animosity:

> The newspapers will tell ten thousand things, none of which are true. . . . The press caused the war, the press gives it point and bitterness, and as long as the press, both North and South, is allowed to fan the flames of discord and hostility, so long must the war last. . . . Our camps are full of newspaper spies revealing each move, exaggerating our trouble and difficulties and giving grounds for discontent. . . . Buzzards of the press hang in scent about our camps. . . . Corrupt editors . . . are the chief cause of this unhappy war. . . . The press . . . is the base means of building up spurious fame and pulling down honest merit. . . . Freedom of the press has been the chief cause of this horrid war.[30]

He raged that any editor who voiced opinions concerning the terms of enlistments should get "a good horse-whipping." Braxton

Bragg or P. G. T. Beauregard would make a better ruler than the public press, he stormed.[31]

The incident with Thomas W. Knox of the *New York Herald* has been discussed earlier in chapter 6. Sherman accused Knox of spying and had him court-martialed. Though not found guilty of the crime, Knox was removed from Sherman's jurisdiction. Of course, a long-range result of this celebrated case was to make Sherman's name familiar throughout the North.

Following his successes in Mississippi, notably the Meridian campaign, it was a new experience for Sherman to read glowing accounts of his actions in the *New York Times,* the *Mobile Advertiser,* and other papers.[32] In the aftermath of having been lauded in print, Sherman may have reached a turning point of sorts. About to be charged with leading the Federal invasion of Georgia, he set out to use the press for his own purposes when possible—despite his conviction that "newspaper correspondents, encouraged by the political generals and even President Lincoln," virtually did as they pleased.[33]

If Sherman did not know it earlier, in July he learned that his dispatches to Washington were being made public. As late as September, he pretended not to know that this was the case.[34]

Soon he had an opportunity to see if the press could be manipulated. Portions of his exchange with Hood concerning the Atlantans' deportation were published in several Southern newspapers. Blaming his enemy for this publicity, he informed Washington, "This could have had no other object than to create a feeling on the part of the people, but if he expects to resort to such artifices I think I can meet him there too." In that spirit, he saw to it that the entire Sherman-Calhoun-Hood correspondence was accessible to many newspapers.

Shortly afterward he prepared a summary of his achievements since entering Georgia. In his cover letter he suggested that it be amended slightly before being made public. Though his report does not indicate that he expected the information to affect the attitudes of general readers, his request to Halleck makes that objective clear.[35]

In late September, Sherman took the time to scold Associated Press correspondent George W. Tyler of Louisville. Dispatches concerning the Atlantans' exodus were full of errors, he charged. He would have paid no attention, he claimed, had he not wanted "the people of the North" to have a correct version of what took place.[36]

Col. Willard Warner was dismissed in October 1864 "for premature publication of news." Given Sherman's entrenched opinions concerning the press, it seems that he would have heartily supported this action. But he asked his Washington superiors to overturn the dismissal. Warner's being an active agent in Sherman's own leaks to the press is a possibility.[37]

Sometimes the man who labeled reporters as "buzzards of the press" failed to cover his tracks. On August 23 a brief telegram conveyed a carefully considered request: "All well. Give currency to the idea that I am to remain quiet till events transpire in other quarters, and let the idea be printed, so as to reach Richmond in three days. You understand the effect."

Communicating with the assistant secretary of war a bit later, he offered another suggestion: "If indiscreet newspaper men publish information too near the truth [concerning the ongoing March to the Sea], counteract its effect by publishing other paragraphs calculated to mislead the enemy."[38]

After the march was well under way, another news leak occurred. From an unknown source the *Chicago Times* reported that Sherman didn't intend to sail his troops up to Grant once they reached Savannah. Instead, the newspaper reported, Sherman planned to sweep through South Carolina after leaving Georgia.[39]

Sherman knew how to manipulate the news media of his day and was often eager to do so, especially since he had experienced such grief early in the war at the hands of newspaper editors who had speculated on his dim future while he served in Kentucky. His plans for the raid through Georgia and the Carolinas were not divulged to his generals, but they somehow found the headlines and propelled a man of many failures into lasting national prominence.

23

Atlanta Tipped the Scales for a Despondent Lincoln

CONGRESSIONAL ELECTIONS at the midpoint of Lincoln's first term dealt a serious setback to his administration. In states ranging westward from New York, Republicans lost twenty-one representatives. As a result, the party's majority in the House of Representatives dropped to just twenty-four. Of these, many were Radical Republicans who consistently opposed the president. Democrats and anti-Lincoln members of his own party would have taken control had they gained about a dozen more seats.[1]

State elections presaged an even more dismal future for the Lincoln administration that many saw as refusing to seek peace. Office seekers at odds with the fledgling Republicans were elected in such crucial states as Pennsylvania, Ohio, Illinois, and Indiana. Republican control of Michigan, Iowa, Wisconsin, and Minnesota was reduced. With some key seats in the U.S. Senate scheduled to be filled by state legislatures, Lincoln's bid for reelection was in serious trouble.[2]

It is widely believed that the president turned to Grant and placed him over the Union army because he viewed him as "a general who will fight." While that characterization is accurate, it does not convey the entire story. With hope for a second term fading, Lincoln could no longer devote his time to sending lengthy "suggestions" to his commanders.

Correspondence of this nature fell off sharply even before Congress recreated the rank of lieutenant general. After Grant's promotion in February 1864, the president's frequent and voluminous directives to his commanders dwindled to a trickle.

After giving up the role of actual rather than nominal commander in chief of U.S. forces, Lincoln's hands were still very full. Throughout the Union states there was wide and articulate opposition to many of his policies and their effects. Forced enlistment in the army, or the draft, and the fast-growing migration of former slaves into the North resulted in riots and rage. Still, the greatest internal danger the administration faced was the fast-growing peace movement.

The first national conscription act, enacted in March 1863, was soon labeled unconstitutional and void by Chief Justice Roger B. Taney of the U.S. Supreme Court. Four months later the New York City draft riot left scores of persons dead. Draftees were permitted to purchase their deferments if they also hired a substitute. (For reasons he never explained, Lincoln hired a substitute despite the fact that the president was not susceptible to the draft.) Most Union states and many counties and cities offered bounties to anyone who would voluntarily enroll rather than wait for his name to be picked in the draft lottery.

Bounty brokers profited from persuading others to enlist, often more than once, and became anathema to ordinary folk. Elaborate rules for the payment of bounties were drawn up at the War Department but had little effect.

Lincoln called for a second draft in February 1864, this time for five hundred thousand men for three years. Sherman repeatedly urged Washington to adopt stringent policies concerning this draft, initially projected for March 10. He could expect to replenish his forces, reduced by expired enrollments, only if draft regulations were enforced effectively. In many states they were delayed or evaded.

Even in rock-solid Unionist Maine there were complaints that this draft call in 1864 was for political rather than military reasons. From Ohio to Iowa, plaintive requests went to Federal officials. In Lincoln's home state of Illinois, the governor begged that the draft quota of 28,058 men had to be reduced. Failure to take this action, he warned, "will not only endanger the peace of the state but will hopelessly defeat us in the coming Elections." Pennsylvania Gov. A. G. Curtin warned, "the whole remaining population of able-bodied men" could be taken from the state by the draft.[3]

Illinois had serious racial problems. An 1862 statute prohibiting the immigration of blacks into the state was approved by the voters. Whether free or enslaved, any black who entered Illinois was subject to a heavy fine. To make matters worse, the chief architect of antiblack legislation was Gen. John A. Logan, soon to become a brigadier general. Few Union commanders were so outspoken in support of white supremacy as were Logan and Sherman, but many agreed with their views.[4]

Illinois, Ohio, Indiana, and Pennsylvania each shared a border with a state in which slavery was legal—Kentucky and Virginia. Widespread fear of mass immigration by runaways contributed largely to Republican losses in all four states.[5]

Adding to Lincoln's worries was the fact that he knew that Southern sympathizers, known as Copperheads, were seeking to block his reelection. New York City was the haven for many of them, and ten thousand soldiers were sent there to prevent violence during the election of 1864.

In addition, the Confederates planned an operation from Canada aimed at releasing prisoners of war held at Camp Douglas, near Chicago. In 1864 this "Northwest Conspiracy" was seen as threatening the future of the Union. Its importance is generally considered to have been magnified by the imminent election. The leaders of the plot were arrested just two days before the general election.

Yet several factors could be counted upon to boost Lincoln's reelection effort: new states, "reconstructed" Confederate states, votes cast by soldiers in the field, enforced "campaign contributions" by Federal employees, and a vigorous public relations program stressing the significance of the Union.

Everyone in the North and in the South knew that the Lincoln administration was waging war to save the Union. But the president's denial that secession had taken place did not deter him from taking a step of questionable legality. In 1863, supported by Washington, Unionists in western Virginia had seceded from the state. The resultant state of West Virginia banned blacks from entering it, but it could be counted upon to support the chief executive. So could Nevada, a territory until October 1864.

For those Confederate states with numerous Unionists within their borders, Lincoln devised a novel plan. Electoral college votes from such regions could be decisive. Hence presidential directives authorized the formation of new, loyal governments within the Confederate states. Under the terms of a December 8, 1863 proclamation, this could be done rapidly. Only 10 percent of adult white males who had voted in 1860 had to swear allegiance to the U.S. Constitution to gain recognition and power. Arkansas and Tennessee were judged likely to take this course; Louisiana was also almost certain to do so.[6]

Often termed "Lincoln's plan for reconstruction," this political ploy was calculated to boost his strength substantially on November 8, 1864. Especially in Louisiana, Tennessee, and Arkansas it was all but guaranteed to do so, until the congressional foes of the administration took a hand. Under the leadership of several Radical Republicans, the lawmakers prohibited representatives of the ten Confederate states from being seated in the electoral college. This action occurred just as Johnston's Confederates withdrew from Kenesaw Mountain.

It took little political skill to bar former secessionists from the presidential election process. Union troops were another matter; most political and military leaders wanted the wishes of the fighting men to be registered at the polls. Again, Sherman was a conspicuous exception. From his headquarters near Atlanta he refused to give leaves to his troops from Indiana so they could return home and cast their ballots in the state elections.

Several key figures in the Lincoln administration were furious. Secretary of War Stanton bypassed Sherman and ordered Col. Benjamin Harrison and six other Hoosier officers to Indiana. Lincoln, afraid that this action was not enough to win the state, offered what he called "in no sense an order." Since men from Indiana could not vote in the field, he suggested, it would be nice to let many of them go home so they could cast ballots.[7]

Had Sherman responded promptly, he probably would have denied his commander in chief. Aggressive action on Hood's part provided him with an excuse to act as though he had not received the presidential plea. This meant that twenty-nine regiments of Hoosiers were barred from taking part in the state election on October 11 and the national election on November 8.

Eager to get the backing of the soldiers for the administration, several states asked to send commissioners to Georgia and other battlefields. When Grant reluctantly consented, these officials collected the ballots and then conveyed or shipped them to their respective states. One soldier not in Sherman's forces who voted in the field was future president William McKinley.[8]

Contributions provided part of the money needed to fund an unprecedented effort to win an election. Substantial financial support of the campaign came from a novel source. Five percent of the annual pay of government employees was deducted and funneled into the Republican Party treasury.[9]

By the time some of this money reached the party leaders, their party had a new name. In a bold bid for enlarged popular support, at its convention of 1864, Lincoln's followers called themselves the National Union Party. Seeking support wherever it could be found, the delegates chose as their vice presidential nominee a Southerner, Andrew Johnson of Tennessee.

In 1864 Lincoln and the Civil War were inextricably linked; hence his reelection was regarded as dependent upon battlefield victories. Grant was entrusted with command early in 1864; soon afterward he and Sherman devised their joint operation. For months after they had conferred in Cincinnati prior to the invasion of Georgia, the North was plunged into gloom. Battles grew fiercer and longer; casualty lists often filled pages of newspapers rather than columns.

Grant sent Nathaniel P. Banks into Louisiana's Red River country early in April. Driven back before reaching Shreveport, Union forces lost nine ships, fifty-one cannon, and about eight thousand men. In the Wilderness area of Virginia, Union forces suffered seventeen thousand casualties during a forty-eight-hour period.

A few days later, Grant again took the offensive at Spotsylvania Court House, where his ranks were thinned by eighteen thousand men. A Federal assault at Cold Harbor on June 3 lasted only about half an hour, but added eight thousand more names to the casualty lists. With his forces bogged down in the brutal ten-month siege of Petersburg, Grant came to be widely known as "the Butcher."

As a result of these and other factors, outwardly exuberant members of the National Union Party were less than gleeful when they nominated Lincoln for a second term. Their June convention in Baltimore was followed by an effort to put Secretary of the Treasury Salmon P. Chase into the White House. Confederate Maj. Gen. Jubal A. Early threw Washington into a panic when he reached its suburbs on July 12. Democrats rejoiced that war veteran George B. McClellan had accepted the nomination as their candidate for the presidency.

Despair became the prevailing mood within the Lincoln administration and among its supporters. Shortly before McClellan was nominated, the president drafted a poignant message: "This morning [August 23], as for some days past, it seems exceedingly probable that this Administration will not be re-elected. Then it will be my duty to so co-operate with the President elect, as to save the Union between the election and the inauguration; as he will have secured his election on such ground that he can not possibly save it afterward."[10]

Folding the paper so that the text could not be read, Lincoln required every member of his cabinet to sign the reverse side. Not knowing what pledge they had taken, the officials remained in the dark until November 11.

Veteran politicians had already told the president that his reelection bid was doomed. Noted editor Horace Greeley informed his readers, "Mr. Lincoln is already beaten. . . . And we must have another ticket to save us from utter overthrow."[11]

WHEN THE telegraph brought word that "Atlanta is ours and fairly won," the news seemed to have come from heaven rather than Georgia. Small wonder that Grant and Lincoln ordered the firing of massive salutes and that their supporters danced in the streets.

Measured by the standards of the massive battles in the East, Sherman's victory in Georgia was insignificant. Viewed from the perspective of Republicans in early September 1864, however, it was stupendous, incredible, gigantic, and transforming. Atlanta, the symbol of Southern resistance for week after week, had fallen!

Elation throughout much of the North was so great that a handful of political leaders considered nominating Sherman for the presidency. Their plan failed to take into account the general's outspoken disdain for government and politics. In his personal correspondence, he voiced his feelings so frequently and so vigorously that his expressions of loathing became almost monotonous.[12]

Instead of being pleased or flattered, Sherman was furious that his capture of Atlanta might make him a political figure. Few men who found their names bantered about nationally would have gone on record with sentiments such as he then expressed: "Some fool seems to have used my name. If forced to choose between the penitentiary and White House for four years, like old Professor Molinard, I would say the penitentiary, thank you, sir. If any committee would approach me for political preferment, I doubt if I could have patience or prudence enough to preserve a decent restraint on myself, but would insult the nation in my reply."[13]

Sherman was scornful of the political process and had little good to say about any elected official except his brother, John. Busy making plans for his next military operation, he had a ready explanation for failing to vote. "I was not qualified," he said.

Because of Sherman, the national mood changed almost overnight. Lincoln's reelection and the war to save the Union had been hanging in the balance. The Union victory in Georgia was of sufficient military weight to tip the scales toward a second term for Lincoln.[14]

Once the surrender of Atlanta began to affect the mood of Northern voters, Lincoln's momentum increased. The war would continue until the Confederates yielded to the demand for unconditional surrender.[15]

When the results were tabulated in Washington, McClellan trailed Lincoln by 400,000 votes. The soldiers supported the president by a majority of nearly 100,000. In the electoral college, Lincoln stood to take 212 votes against 21 for his Democratic opponent.

News of the Lincoln victory at the polls reached Federal forces in and around Atlanta on November 10, two days before the telegraph line to the North was cut. The troops had little time to celebrate. Already, it was generally known that sixty-two thousand men would be divided into two columns with O. O. Howard and Henry W. Slocum at their heads. The Federals would abandon Atlanta. Living off the land, they'd push through hostile country toward an unknown destination.

Little else remained for the troops to do. Special details under Col. Orlando M. Poe had their hands more than full, however. It was not enough to demolish the 360-foot railroad bridge over the Chattahoochee River; Sherman wanted its timbers burned or destroyed to prevent easy rebuilding.

In Atlanta, Adjutant Henry Hitchcock made careful notes to preserve orders concerning the city. According to him, pioneers under Poe were told to destroy the large central railroad depot and the machine shops and warehouses. All buildings of potential use to the enemy were to be leveled or burned, Hitchcock noted. He was emphatic, however, in recording that "no *dwellings* were to be injured."

It is impossible to square that account with earlier reports that Atlanta was about to be transformed into a long-term Federal fortress. Exuberant soldiers, carousing on the night of November 11, set about twenty houses on fire for the fun of seeing them go up in flames. Slocum, still in command of Atlanta, had designated November 12 as the day on which the destruction was to begin, with the fire being delayed "until the last moment."

Perhaps in obedience to the restraining order concerning fire, Poe rigged a crude battering ram. Moving slowly from block to block, it demolished small stone and brick buildings. Federal pioneers used explosives with some of the larger buildings, then resorted to kerosene-soaked canvases. During a period of four days, there was no hour at which flames or smoke or both could not be seen above the doomed railroad center.

Maj. Ward Nichols of Sherman's staff noted in his journal that "the heart was burning out of beautiful Atlanta." A Confederate description, written on the spot after the Federals had left, insisted: "The work was done with terrible completeness; buildings covering 200 acres were in flames at one time; the heavens were an expanse of lurid fire; and amid the wild and terrific scene Federal bands played 'John Brown's soul goes marching on.'"

Private homes, theoretically protected, were treated as though they were manufacturing plants or business houses. A survey of the ruins indicated that forty-five hundred dwellings in and around Atlanta had been destroyed. About four hundred were left standing, but many of these had suffered serious damage from Federal artillery.

SOME OF the awesome destruction was captured by pioneer photographer George N. Barnard. Matthew Brady's name does not appear in the *Official Record.* No mention of Alexander Gardner is to be found in this immense collection. Barnard is unique among Civil War photographers because his name was listed in the military records. By April 1864 he was the cameraman of the Division of the Mississippi.[16]

Although calling himself a foe of the press, Sherman included a photographer in his entourage to make sure that his invasion of Georgia would be captured on film. As a result, images from Barnard's postwar book, *Photographic Views of Sherman's Campaign,* are very familiar today.

Busy with last-minute preparations for his next move, Sherman must have paused long enough for reflection. In the North, devastated Atlanta would be viewed with delight in that the war was soon to be over. He had no need for the prestige of the White House. For generation after generation to come, neither the South nor the North would forget the orphan boy whose father had named him for an Indian warrior.

24

Up from the Ashes

Barely two weeks after the fires that leveled Atlanta ceased to burn, a handful of Confederates returned to the desolate site. A detachment of soldiers implemented a system of street patrols, and a new Confederate command center on December 2 began to issue directives.

Veteran politician James M. Calhoun and Connecticut-born William Markham were among the first refugees to return. Calhoun urged obedience to martial law but wanted an immediate return to government as usual. Hence an election was held on December 7, and Calhoun was reelected as mayor for the year about to begin. During the following week three election managers certified that five councilmen had been chosen. On January 6, 1865, all six officials were on hand for the first meeting of the town council since July 18, and the city began to rebuild.

Three weeks after the Confederate surrender at Appomattox Court House, Col. E. B. Eggleston led the First Ohio Cavalry into Atlanta and established Union control for the area. At the same time, volunteers began to devise ways to feed and clothe the Southern veterans who were arriving home in increasing numbers.

Sherman's invasion had brought disaster to the railroads. After May 1864 his forces had been in control of the Western and Atlantic. When they abandoned it in November, it was a trail of wreckage stretching from Atlanta to Chattanooga. Other railroads between

Upon leaving Atlanta, Sherman ordered the town torched and the city's railroad station demolished.

Atlanta and the coast suffered almost as much damage; at least 265 miles of track were destroyed.

To make matters worse for the railroad companies, in the last year of the war the Confederate government was unable to pay its bills. At war's end Richmond owed the Georgia Railroad $674,245 in freight charges. This sum was never paid, and the rail line suffered $500,000 in war damages plus the loss of nearly $1.5 million from worthless Confederate and state notes and bonds.

LIBRARY OF CONGRESS

Atlanta's roundhouse was devastated but functional. Knowing his railroad lines were tenuous, Sherman used the Western and Atlantic tracks to stockpile supplies for the forthcoming March to the Sea.

Rebuilding the railroads proceeded as rapidly as iron could be secured. Atlanta's spacious central depot was gone, but locomotives again puffed toward the town late in the winter of 1865. Every train brought refugees as well as newcomers who had only heard of Atlanta in newspaper headlines since August and September 1864.

Rail lines taken over by the U.S. War Department were returned to their owners in August 1865. A section foreman of the Macon and Western learned that many twisted and bent rails could be straightened; by December, he had restored twenty-seven miles of track to some sort of usefulness. There was no way to salvage iron that lay along the right of way of the Western and Atlantic, so in September 1865 the company's directors voted to spend the necessary funds for the renovation.

By that time, trains were moving from Augusta to Atlanta over the repaired rails at about ten miles an hour. Passenger fares ranged from four to eight cents per mile, and the lines leading to Atlanta seemed to have all the business they could handle. Cotton resumed a fraction of its former importance after the 1866 crop was gathered and ginned. In that season, the railroads received about two cents per mile to transport a bale from farm to market.

CONFEDERATE VETERANS saw great hope for the future of the city made famous by Sherman's siege. Their zeal and enthusiasm contributed largely to the adoption of the mythical phoenix as a symbol for Atlanta.

Northerners flocked to Atlanta. In only a few years they greatly outnumbered the native-born residents. Some early newcomers were officers of the army of occupation; others were carpetbaggers hoping to take advantage of opportunities created by Reconstruction.

Entrepreneurs swarmed to Atlanta. Many of them had never heard of the Georgia town until cannonades had been fired to celebrate its fall. Any place whose capture warranted a salute of one hundred guns must be fertile soil in which to plant new business enterprises.

That line of reasoning brought to the city a population destined to help make it become more northern than southern. By 1880 the population of Atlanta was thirty-seven thousand, more than twelve times that of 1850. No other U.S. city enjoyed a comparable rate of growth during this period.

Barely completed buildings were being occupied as rapidly as they could be erected. New industries depended heavily upon farming. The Southern Agricultural Works was designed to produce cast- and wrought-iron plows and cotton gins. Raw materials for the Atlanta Cotton Seed Oil Mills came by rail, and finished products went out in boxcars. That was also the case with the Exposition Cotton Mills, the Atlanta Cotton Mills, and the Atlanta Steam Dye Works. Industrial expansion in Atlanta helped the railroad companies remain solvent during a period when many went under.

A TIME of trouble quite different from Sherman's siege began in August 1866. At the National Union Convention meeting in Philadelphia, the delegates called for harsh retaliatory measures toward the defeated South. Congress responded with a Reconstruction bill, one of whose principal authors was Sen. John Sherman, brother of William Tecumseh Sherman.

Atlantans held a series of public meetings in which they protested and framed futile attempts to modify the "Sherman law."

LIBRARY OF CONGRESS

The vagaries of war are no more apparent than in this photo of the ruins of a bank next to a saloon.

Almost simultaneously, Maj. Gen. John Pope assumed command of the Third Military District, made up of Alabama, Georgia, and Florida. From his Birmingham headquarters he announced that most office holders would be allowed to complete their terms. New elections, however, would be held soon.

Traveling from Montgomery, Pope reached Atlanta on April 11, 1867, and on the following evening was the guest of honor at a civic banquet. Quite early, toasts were offered to Pope and to President Andrew Johnson. Later in the evening similar tributes were paid to the Thirty-ninth Congress, to "our country's flag," to Reconstruction, and "our Army and Navy."

When news of the evening's events was broadcast throughout the villages and towns of the South, hordes of former Confederates reacted indignantly. The actions in Atlanta, they said, offended the former leaders of the Confederacy and all those who had fought for the cause. The city came to be regarded as a haven for renegades and carpetbaggers.

With Georgia under military rule, Pope called for a convention to write a new constitution. Simultaneously, he took steps to make Atlanta the state capital. The constitutional convention, which met intermittently for weeks, chose Rufus B. Bullock as the next governor of Georgia.

Bullock's election was a harbinger of things to come, for Bullock was a native of Albany County, New York. After serving as a Confederate lieutenant colonel, he became president of the Macon and Augusta Railroad Company. Pushing to build the state's first new postwar line, Bullock completed forty miles of track-laying in record time. He then solicited the future underwriting of the railroad from New York to complete the line. Since Georgia had initially rejected congressional plans for reconstruction, no northern money was forthcoming. Bulloch returned to the state, helped to organize the Republican Party there, and then defeated war hero John B. Gordon for governor.

During less than four years in office, the New York native made repeated trips to the North and found funds with which to build six hundred miles of railroads. Though despised by the opponents of Reconstruction, Bulloch's career was a symbol of things to come. For decades, Atlanta's growth would be more closely tied to the North than to the South. Largely because of this, Atlanta attracted the capital and willing entrepreneurs badly needed in the Cotton Belt.

BY 1880 the Atlanta Chamber of Commerce entertained a proposal for an exposition. Several notable international expositions had been held in Europe, but thus far no American city had ventured to host such a gigantic undertaking.

Edward Atkinson of Boston had suggested that the time had come to plan an international festival in honor of cotton. Naturally, it should take place in the South, said the Massachusetts citizen in a letter to a New York newspaper. Henry W. Grady, editor of the *Atlanta Constitution,* reprinted the Atkinson letter and became the leading proponent for the proposal.

Opposition proved far less formidable than it would have been in older and larger centers such as New York, Cleveland, or Baltimore. Atlanta accepted the challenge and hosted the 1881 International Cotton Exposition.

The venture's success was on a scale that none had anticipated. Hordes of visitors came to the Atlanta exposition. One American visitor, a native of Ohio, was an army officer planning to retire soon. He took a keen personal interest in the event because he had accepted an invitation to make a substantial investment in the enterprise. Though he never regarded himself as an able public speaker, he was persuaded by Grady and his colleagues to take the platform.

On Mexican Veteran's Day, November 15, Gen. William Tecumseh Sherman strode to the podium and delivered a few brief remarks. Listeners responded with far more applause than followed the oratory of the one-time Confederate general and former governor Alfred H. Colquitt. Alone among the cities of the United States, Atlanta transformed its conqueror into a lauded public figure, then welcomed him as though he were a native son.

THE BREASTWORKS and redoubts that once protected the small rail center disappeared as Atlanta grew. Little evidence remains in the city that points to its role in the deadliest of America's wars. Only the Cyclorama and nearby Stone Mountain allude to the war between the Americans.

Notes

In citing works in the notes and bibliography, short references have generally been used. Works frequently cited have been identified by the following abbreviations:

B&L	Buel, Clarence C., and Robert U. Johnson, eds. *Battles and Leaders of the Civil War*
CMH	Evans, Clement A., ed. *Confederate Military History*
CV	*The Confederate Veteran* magazine
CWT	*Civil War Times* and *Civil War Times Illustrated*
DAB	Johnson, Allen, and Dumas Malone, eds. *Dictionary of American Biography*
DAH	*Dictionary of American History*
EC	Current, Richard N., ed. *Encyclopedia of the Confederacy*
JSHS	*Journal of the Southern Historical Society* (1876–1944)
MOLLUS	Publications of the Military Order of the Loyal Legion of the United States. Various cities and dates.
OA	Davis, George B., et al. *The Official Military Atlas of the Civil War*
OR	*The War of the Rebellion: A Compilation of the Official Records of the Union and Confederate Armies*
RR	Moore, Frank, ed. *The Rebellion Record*

Chapter 2 • Hit Hard on Both Fronts at Once!

1. "Closing Days of the Siege," 11:274b.
2. Warner, *Generals in Blue,* 442.
3. Lewis, *Sherman,* 161; Dupuy et al., *Encyclopedia of Military Biography,* 681a.
4. Grant, *Memoirs,* 1:239–40.
5. Dupuy et al., *Encyclopedia of Military Biography,* 291a; Grant, *Memoirs,* 1:242.
6. Lewis, *Sherman,* 159–61; Grant, *Memoirs,* 1:243.
7. Grant, *Memoirs,* 1:244–47.
8. Faust, *Encyclopedia of the Civil War,* 320b.
9. Boatner, *Civil War Dictionary,* 876–77.
10. As early as September 1863 Dana had suggested that if a new chief commander were selected, he should be "some Western general of high rank and great prestige, like Grant"; Dana to Edward M. Stanton, *OR,* 1, 30 (Serial #50), 201–3.
11. Grant, *Memoirs,* 2:114.
12. Nevins, *War for the Union,* 4:8–9; Grant to Sherman, *OR,* 1, 32, iii (Serial #59), 245–46.
13. Nevins, *War for the Union,* 4:6–7.
14. Catton, *Grant Takes Command,* 118–23.

15. Quoted in the *Charleston Mercury,* April 13, 1864.
16. Miers, *Lincoln Day by Day,* 3:245–46.
17. Nevins, *War for the Union,* 4:9.
18. Catton, *Grant Takes Command,* 118–22; Stepp and Hill, *Mirror of War,* 243–45.
19. Badeau, *Grant,* 2:8.
20. H. Nicolay, "Lincoln's Cabinet," 5:282.
21. Sherman, *Memoirs* (reprint), 1:428–29, but not in Grant's memoirs.
22. For the full text of this summary, see *OR* 1, 52, i (Serial #109), 561–64.
23. Dupuy, *Encyclopedia of Military Biography,* 681.
24. Boatner, *Civil War Dictionary,* 836, 794, 726, 538.
25. Sherman, Report of September 15, 1864 (*OR* 1, 38, i [Serial #72], 61–85), 61.

Chapter 3 • Far Too Strong for a Frontal Assault

1. Shavin, *The Atlanta Century,* December 20, 1863 (pages are dated rather than numbered).
2. Johnston, "Opposing Sherman's Advance," *B&L,* 4:260ff.
3. Sifakis, *Who Was Who,* 316–17; Hood, *Advance and Retreat,* 94.
4. Cole to William H. Gibbons, *OR,* 1, 32, iii (Serial #59), 772–74.
5. "Re-enlisting at Dalton," *CV,* 13:500; "Re-enlistment in Army of Tennessee," *CV,* 10:351; "Concerning Re-enlistment at Dalton," *CV,* 9:13.
6. Ridley, "Camp Scenes Around Dalton," *CV,* 10:67f.
7. Johnston to Bragg, *OR,* 1, 32, iii (Serial #59), 714.
8. Johnston, "Opposing Sherman's Advance," 260ff.
9. Longstreet to Samuel Cooper, *OR,* 1, 32, iii (Serial #59), 655.
10. Grant, *Memoirs,* 2:163.
11. "Sherman in Georgia," *RR,* 11, 24–39.
12. Sherman to George H. Thomas, *OR,* 1, 38, iv (Serial #75), 112.
13. *CMH,* 7:299.
14. James Wilson, Special Field Orders, no. 1, ibid., 55.
15. Glumer, map, *OA,* plate 47, sec. 1.
16. Robert H. Ramsey to Joseph Hooker, *OR,* 1, 38, iv (Serial #75), 45.
17. R. R. Townes, Special Field Orders, No. 1, ibid., 69.

Chapter 4 • Ready to Destroy Joe Johnston

1. Sherman, *Memoirs,* 2:11, 24, 29.
2. Sherman to Grant, *OR,* 1, 32, iii (Serial #59), 220.
3. F. M. Davidson to E. E. Potter, ibid., 16f.
4. Sherman, *Memoirs,* 2:312, 314.
5. Sherman to Halleck, ibid., 521.
6. Robert Allen to Sherman, ibid., 425, 494, 498.
7. Montgomery C. Meigs to Thomas, ibid., 423.
8. Grant to Thomas and Sherman, ibid., 11, 46
9. Sturgis to E. E. Potter, ibid., 31.
10. Sherman to Allen, ibid., 141–42.
11. Allen to Meigs, ibid., 311.

12. Sherman to Grant, ibid., 465–66.
13. Allen to Meigs, *OR,* 1, 38 (Serial #75), 4.
14. Sherman to Thomas J. Haines, *OR,* 1, 32, iii (Serial #59), 398.
15. Sherman to Kilburn, ibid., 385.
16. A. R. Lawton to James Longstreet, ibid., 598f.
17. Longstreet to Cooper, *OR,* 1, 32, i (Serial #57), 94.
18. H. L. Clay to Johnston, *OR,* 1, 32, iii (Serial #59), 597.
19. Sherman to Halleck, *OR,* 1, 31, iii (Serial #56), 497f.
20. Lawton to Longstreet, *OR,* 1, 32, iii (Serial #59), 598f.
21. J. G. Parkhurst, *OR,* 1, 32, i (Serial #57), 13.
22. Sherman to Allen, ibid., 240f.
23. General Order No. 8, *OR,* 1, 32, iii, (Serial #59), 420.
24. Lincoln to Sherman, *OR,* 1, 38, iv (Serial #75), 25.
25. Sherman to Lincoln, ibid., 33f.
26. Sherman to Bramlette, *OR,* 1, 32, iii (Serial #56), 263.
27. Sherman to McPherson, *OR,* 1, 32, iii (Serial #59), 733f.
28. Sherman to Roswell M. Sawyer, ibid., 542; Sherman to McPherson, ibid., 325f.
29. Sherman to McPherson, ibid., 459; Sherman to Schofield, ibid., 474.
30. Some newspaper correspondents believed Sherman was deliberately slow to move, refraining "on Grant's account, from pushing Johnston to the wall" (see "The Situation," *RR,* 11:222).
31. Grant to Sherman, *OR,* 1, 32, iii (Serial #59), 409.
32. Sherman to R. M. Sawyer, *OR,* 1, 32, ii (Serial #58), 278–81.
33. Some suggest that Sherman had his eye on Atlanta before he left Chattanooga but didn't mention it because he did not want to inform Grant of his plans. Nothing in the record supports this conclusion.

Chapter 5 • Orderly Withdrawal in Lieu of All-out Combat

1. Grant to Sherman and Sherman to Grant, *OR,* 1, 32, iii (Serial #59), 11.
2. Sherman, *Home Letters,* 289.
3. Grant to Sherman, *OR,* 1, 32, iii (Serial #59), 521.
4. Sherman to Grant, ibid., 312.
5. Sherman to Halleck, *OR,* 1, 38, iv (Serial #75), 70.
6. J. S. Fullerton to David S. Stanley, ibid., 35.
7. Sherman to Meigs, ibid., 20.
8. J. A. Campbell, Special Field Orders, No. 1, ibid., 55.
9. McPherson, Circular, ibid., 41–42.
10. Sherman to Schofield, ibid., 84.
11. "Sherman in Georgia," 11:29a.
12. Schofield to Sherman, ibid., 83.
13. Sea, "Rocky Face Ridge," 6:318a.
14. Grant, General Report, *OR,* 1, 38, 1 (Serial #72), 2.
15. Sherman to McPherson, *OR,* 1, 39, iv (Serial #75), 138.
16. Sherman, "War of the Rebellion," *Century* (July 1887 and February 1888).
17. Sherman to McPherson, *OR,* 1, 38, iv (Serial #75), 8, 9; Smith to Sherman, ibid., 155.

18. Sherman to Webster, ibid., 146.
19. McPherson to Blair, ibid., 68.
20. Grant, General Report, *OR,* 1, 38, 1 (Serial #72), 5.
21. McPherson to Hooker and Garrard, *OR,* 1, 38, iv (Serial #75), 152.
22. Sherman to Thomas, ibid., 161.

Chapter 6 • Over the Oostenaula

1. Sherman to J. D. Webster, *OR,* 1, 38, iv (Serial #75), 3.
2. Sherman to Morgan et al., *OR,* 1, 17, i (Serial #24), 616–17.
3. General Orders, No. 13, *OR,* 17, ii (Serial #25), 889–92.
4. Harris, "Military Relations with the Press," 29–34.
5. Van Horne, *George H. Thomas,* 210–21; Sherman to McPherson, *OR,* 1, 38, iv (Serial #75), 39–40; Sherman to Halleck, ibid., 88, 111.
6. Lewis, *Sherman,* 357; S. Foote, *Civil War,* 3:325.
7. Johnston, "Opposing Sherman," 4:266.
8. *CMH,* 7:304; *RR,* 16:302.
9. Sherman to Halleck, *OR,* 1, 38, iv (Serial #75), 111.
10. Sherman, *Home Letters,* 296.
11. Sherman to Halleck, *OR,* 1, 38, iv (Serial #75), 133.
12. L. M. Dayton to Thomas, ibid., 147; J. A. Campbell, Circular, No. 2, ibid., 159; William T. Clark, Special Field Orders, No. 7., ibid., 160; W. L. Elliott to Joseph Hooker, ibid., 179f.
13. Thomas to Sherman, ibid., 160f; Sherman to Thomas, ibid., 161f.
14. Stevens, *Georgia,* 150, 658f, 687, 771.
15. Daniel E. Sickles to Lincoln, *OR,* 1, 38, iv (Serial #75), 215f; Sherman to Howard, ibid., 163.
16. Willis Blanch, Report, *OR,* 1, 38, i (Serial #72), 345; Luther P. Bradley, Report, ibid., 352; Robert H. Higgins, Report, ibid., 480.
17. Overley, "What 'Marching Through Georgia' Means," *CV,* 18:444.
18. Robert P. Barry, Report, *OR,* 1, 38, i (Serial #72), 575.
19. Daugherty, "Another Account," 11:37b.
20. Fullerton, "Journal," 855.
21. Sherman to Halleck, *OR,* 1, 38, iv (Serial #75), 189, 202; J. C. Van Duzer to T. T. Eckert, ibid., 215; Craig L. Symonds, "Atlanta Campaign," *EC,* 1:113a.
22. Daugherty, "Another Account," 39a; "The Campaign for Atlanta," 37.

Chapter 7 • Three or Four Miles a Day

1. Sherman, "Grand Strategy," 4:247.
2. Sherman, *Home Letters,* 300.
3. Dayton, Special Field Orders, No. 8, *OR,* 1, 38, iv (Serial #75), 215; secs. 1, 2, and 3.
4. Sherman to Howard, ibid., 163; Sherman to Halleck, ibid., 189, 201.
5. Ruger, map, *OA,* plate 48, sec. 1.
6. Hooker to William D. Whipple, *OR,* 1, 38, iv (Serial #75), 220.
7. Schofield to Sherman, ibid., 222.
8. Sherman to McPherson, ibid., 227.

9. D. S. Stanley, Report of Operations May 3–July 26, ibid., 72, 226.
10. C. L. Matthies to Lt. Col. Sawyer, ibid., 229; Matthies to J. E. Smith, ibid., 259.
11. For a summary of the elaborate U.S. conscription law of 1863, see E. D. Townsend to Sen. H. S. Lane, *OR,* 3, iii (Serial #124), 1177–78.
12. Sherman to Thomas, *OR,* 3, iv (Serial #125), 454f.
13. Sherman to Halleck, ibid., 260.

Chapter 8 • The Rubicon of Georgia

1. Johnston, General Orders, *OR,* 1, 38, iv (Serial #75), 728.
2. Stevens, *Georgia,* 539, 590, 622, 658f, 664, 743, 785f.
3. Fullerton, "Journal," 858; Ruger, map, *OA,* plate 48, sec. 1.
4. Sherman to Thomas, *OR,* 1, 38, iv (Serial # 75), 233.
5. Sherman to Schofield, ibid., 242.
6. Sherman to governors of Indiana, Illinois, Iowa, and Wisconsin; ibid., 294f.
7. Dayton, Special Field Orders No. 9, ibid., 271.
8. Montgomery C. Meigs to Thomas, *OR,* 1, 32, iii (Serial #59), 423.
9. William T. Clark, Special Field Orders, No. 15, *OR,* 1, 38, iv (Serial #75), 273f.
10. Schofield to George Stoneman, ibid., 303.
11. Robert Allen to J. L. Donaldson, ibid., 299.
12. Sherman to Halleck, ibid., 274.
13. L. H. Rousseau to Gov. Oliver P. Morton of Indiana, ibid., 265.
14. Garrard to Sherman, ibid., 268.
15. Sherman to Stoneman, ibid., 224.
16. Sherman to Thomas, ibid., 56.
17. Sherman to McPherson, ibid., 322.
18. Sherman to Halleck, ibid., 260.
19. Sherman to Stoneman and Stoneman to McCook, ibid., 319f.
20. Sherman to governors of Indiana, Illinois, Iowa, and Wisconsin; ibid., 294f.
21. Sherman to Blair, ibid., 298.

Chapter 9 • Into the Hell Hole

1. Sherman to Halleck, *OR,* 1, 38, iv (Serial #75), 385.
2. Sherman, "Grand Strategy," 4:250.
3. McPherson to Sherman, *OR,* 1, 38, iv (Serial #75), 211.
4. Special Field Orders, No. 15, ibid., 371.
5. Stoneman to Sherman, ibid., 379.
6. McPherson to Sherman, ibid., 327; McPherson to Garrard, ibid., 328; Sherman to McPherson, ibid., 389.
7. J. W. Barnes, Special Field Orders, No. 8, ibid., 330.
8. Helmle, map, *OA,* plate 57, sec. 3.
9. Stoneman to Sherman, *OR,* 1, 38, iv (Serial #75), 379.
10. McPherson to Dodge, ibid., 397f; A. J. Alexander to W. Q. Gresham, ibid., 399.
11. Order of March for June 6, ibid., 415f.
12. Sherman, Report of September 15, 1864, 314.
13. Sherman to Joseph D. Webster, *OR,* 1, 38, iv (Serial #75), 418.

14. Sherman to E. K. Owen, *OR*, i, 31, I (Serial #57), 184f.
15. Milo S. Hascall to John A. Campbell, *OR*, 1, 38, iv (Serial #75), 297–98.
16. Dayton, Special Field Orders, No. 17, ibid., 406.
17. Dayton, Special Field Orders, No. 20, ibid., 427.
18. McPherson to Garrard, ibid., 329; Stanton to Sherman, ibid., 331f; Halleck to Sherman, ibid., 418.

Chapter 10 • The Enemy Must Be in a Bad Condition

1. Because the struggle is being viewed from the perspective of the spring and summer of 1864, throughout this work in both text and quotations, numerous usages of the period are followed. E.g., "Kenesaw" rather than modern "Kennesaw" appears throughout.
2. *OR*, 1, 38, iv (Serial #75), 448f.
3. Van Duzer to Eckert, ibid., 479; Sherman to Schofield, ibid., 486f.
4. McPherson to Dodge, ibid., 490; Van Duzer to Eckert, ibid., 507; *CMH*, 7:314–15.
5. Sherman to Grant, ibid., 507–8.
6. Sherman to Halleck, ibid., 544.
7. Phisterer, *Statistical Report*, 1:668, 1:690, 1:710.
8. Sherman to Halleck, ibid., *OR*, 1, 38, iv (Serial #75), 481; Sherman, Report of September 15, 1864, 68.
9. Sherman to Stoneman, *OR*, 1, 38, v (Serial #76), 61; Sherman to E. R. S. Canby, ibid., 84.
10. Dayton, Special Field Orders, No. 16, *OR*, 1, 38, iv (Serial #75), 400.
11. Thomas to Sherman, ibid., 542, 571.
12. Sherman to Halleck, *OR*, 1, 38, v (Serial #76), 236.
13. Both the Fourteenth and Sixteenth U.S. Colored Troops, 1,170 infantry and 1,119 men in artillery units, remained in Tennessee; ibid., 256, 258, 635.
14. C. W. Foster, Annual Report, Bureau for Colored Troops, *OR*, 3, 4 (Serial #125), 789.
15. Basler, *Lincoln*, 4:157, 175f, 232, 240, 252–59, 264f, 267–70, 432–37; 7:6–7, 55, 132.
16. For the text of the cartel, see H. Thompson, "Exchange of Prisoners," 7:345ff.
17. Moore, *RR*, 8:37.
18. H. Thompson, "Exchange of Prisoners," 7:118.
19. Shavin, *Atlanta Century*, February 28, 1864; March 17, 1864.
20. Persons to Cooper, *OR*, 2, 7 (Serial #120), 63f.
21. Cooper, General Orders, No. 45, ibid., 103.
22. McElroy, *Andersonville*, 21.

Chapter 11 • Judgment Day at Kenesaw

1. Sherman to Thomas, *OR*, 1, 38, iv (Serial #75), 607; Sherman to Schofield, ibid., 616; Sherman to McPherson, ibid., 622.
2. "Assault on Kenesaw," 11:225b.
3. Sherman to Schofield, *OR*, 1, 38, iv (Serial #75), 598.
4. L. S. Ross to William H. Jackson, ibid., 792, 793, 799, 800.

5. Cox to J. W. Reilly, ibid., 600.
6. Sherman, *Memoirs,* 2:61.
7. Howard, "Struggle," 4:310.
8. Dawes, "Confederate Strength," 283.
9. Sherman to Halleck, *OR,* l, 38, iv (Serial #75), 635; Van Duzer to Eckert, ibid., 639f.
10. Sherman, *Memoirs,* 2:61.
11. Howard, "Struggle," 4:322; *CMH,* 7:321; Johnston, "Opposing Sherman," 272.
12. Schofield to Sherman, *OR,* 1, 38, iv (Serial #75), 618.
13. Sherman to Thomas, 1:30 P.M., ibid., 509; Thomas to Sherman, 1:40 P.M., ibid., 609; Sherman to Thomas, ibid., 610; Thomas to Sherman, ibid., 610.
14. Sherman to Joseph D. Webster, ibid., 629.
15. Sherman, *Memoirs,* 2:64.
16. Sherman to Halleck, June 27, 8:00 P.M., *OR,* 1, 38, iv (Serial #75), 607.
17. George C. Tichenor to T. W. Sweeny, ibid., 632; William T. Clark to Blair, ibid., 632; J. P. Willard to Sherman, ibid., 636.
18. Sherman to Thomas, ibid., 611; Sherman to Schofield, ibid., 616; Schofield to Cox, ibid., 620; Schofield to Stoneman, ibid., 622; Sherman to McPherson, ibid., 622; Van Duzer to Eckert, ibid., 633–34.; Sherman, *Memoirs,* 2:61.
19. Sherman to Halleck, *OR,* 1, 38, iv (Serial #75), 635.

Chapter 12 • Joe Johnston Can Withdraw; Atlanta Cannot

1. Johnston, "Opposing Sherman," 273; Sherman, *Memoirs,* 2:31.
2. Bailey, *Sherman Moves East,* 76.
3. Sherman, *Memoirs,* 2:66–67, 69; Bowman and Irwin, *Campaigns,* 196; Sherman to Rousseau, *OR,* 1, 38, v (Serial #76), 19, 82; Sherman to Schofield, ibid., 89; Sherman to Steedman, ibid., 112.
4. Sherman, *Home Letters,* 252, 272, 287, 321.
5. Sherman to Halleck, *OR,* 1, 38, v (Serial #76), 108.
6. Sherman to Thomas, ibid., 114; Dodge to McPherson, ibid., 118; Dodge to Sherman, ibid., 119; Van Duzer to Eckert, ibid., 122; Grant to Halleck, ibid., 143.
7. Johnston to Jefferson Davis, ibid., 883; Sherman to McPherson, ibid., 147; "Campaign for Atlanta," 39.
8. Sherman to Thomas, ibid., 637; Sherman to Halleck, *OR,* 1, 38, v (Serial #76), 73; A. P. Mason, Circular, ibid., 791; Andrews, *South Reports,* 161.
9. Sherman to Garrard, *OR,* 1, 38, v (Serial #76), 42, Sherman to Garrard, ibid., 48.
10. Sherman, Report of September 15, 1865, 306a; Garrard to Sherman, *OR,* 1, 38, v (Serial #76), 68; Garrard to Lewis M. Dayton, ibid., 60; Garrard to Sherman, ibid., 69; Cox, *Atlanta,* 137; "Another Account," 11:245a; "General Sherman's Method of Making War," 444.
11. Sherman to Halleck, *OR,* 1, 38, v (Serial #76), 73.
12. Basler, *Lincoln,* 4:252–53, 264–65.
13. Sherman to Garrard, *OR,* 1, 38, v (Serial #76), 76.
14. Sherman to Halleck, ibid., 92.
15. Sherman to Webster, ibid., 192.
16. Thomas to Sherman, ibid., 104; Sherman to Thomas, ibid., 104.
17. Dodge to William T. Clark, ibid., 129; Grant to Sherman, ibid., 149; Halleck to Sher-

man, ibid., 150–51; letter of July 5, Grant to Russell Jones (Chicago Historical Society collection).
18. Viewed in retrospect, by September 3 it seemed that the capture of Atlanta had been "the object of the four months' campaign" (Fullerton, "Journal," 934). There are occasional brief references to Atlanta in earlier correspondence (see, e.g., Sherman to Halleck, *OR,* 1, 38, i [Serial #72], 3). Atlanta, however, grew in importance only after having come into view.

Chapter 13 • John B. Hood Takes Command

1. Cooper to Johnston, *OR,* 1, 38, v (Serial #76), 885.
2. Davis to Johnston, ibid., 867; Johnston to Davis, ibid., 869.
3. Davis to Johnston, ibid., 882.
4. Seitz, *Bragg,* 445–51; Bragg to Davis, *OR,* 1, 39, ii (Serial #78), 712–14.
5. Whitney, *Bragg,* 385; "Interesting Batch of Telegrams," 2:111.
6. Johnston, *Narrative,* 322–23, 351; Johnston, "Opposing Sherman," 268; *CMH,* 11:306–7; Robinson, "Johnston," 358.
7. Hood to Bragg, *OR,* 1, 38, v (Serial #76), 879–80; McMurry, *Hood,* 118–19.
8. Johnston, General Orders, No. 4, *OR,* 1, 38, v (Serial #76) 887.
9. Johnston to Bragg, ibid., 876; Davis to Johnston, ibid., 877; Sherman to Halleck, ibid., 260–61; Stoneman to Sherman, ibid., 264; Sherman to Stoneman, ibid., 265.
10. Sherman, *Home Letters,* 304.
11. Sherman, "Grand Strategy," 4:253; Sherman, *Memoirs,* 2:72; Sherman to Stoneman, *OR,* 1, 38, v (Serial #76), 61–62; Grant to Sherman, ibid., 211; Dayton, Special Field Orders, No. 68, *OR,* 1, 38, i (Serial #72), 88; Cox, *Atlanta,* 186; Dyer, *Hood,* 251.
12. Hooker to Whipple, *OR,* 1, 38, v (Serial #76), 190.
13. *Richmond Examiner,* July 20, 1864; *Petersburg Daily Express,* July 23, 1864.

Chapter 14 • Peach Tree Creek

1. Sherman to Thomas, *OR,* 1, 38, v (Serial #76), 170; Dodge to McPherson, ibid., 177.
2. Sherman to Thomas, ibid., 185; Stoneman to Thomas, ibid., 206.
3. Sherman to McPherson, ibid., 219 (Sherman, *Memoirs,* 2:75); Sherman to Thomas, ibid., 223.
4. Cooper to Marcus J. Wright, *OR,* 1, 38, v (Serial #76), 878.
5. Sherman to Halleck, ibid., 137; Sherman to John A. Spooner, ibid., 305–6; Lincoln to Sherman, ibid., 169; Sherman to Lincoln, ibid., 210.
6. Sherman, *Memoirs,* 2:76; Garrard to Logan, *OR,* 1, 38, v (Serial #76), 165; Sherman, memo to Special Field Orders, No. 36, ibid., 167.
7. Sherman to Grant, ibid., 350; Sherman to R. S. Granger, ibid., 377; Sherman to Webster, ibid., 329.
8. Sherman to Halleck, ibid., 150.
9. Sherman, *Memoirs,* 2:78–79.
10. Sherman to Thomas, *OR,* 1, 38, v (Serial #76), 170; Sherman, *Memoirs,* 2:72–73.
11. Sherman to Thomas, *OR,* 1, 38, v (Serial #76), 195–96.
12. Sherman to Halleck, ibid., 248.

Chapter 15 • The Battle of Atlanta

1. Sherman, *Memoirs,* 2:75; Van Duzer to Eckert, *OR,* 1, 38, v (Serial #76), 222.
2. Sherman to Halleck, ibid., 211; Hood, "Defense of Atlanta," 338.
3. Sherman, Report of September 15, 1865, 307.
4. Grant, *Memoirs,* 12:168–69; Adams, "Battle and Capture of Atlanta," 153; Woodworth, *Davis and His Generals,* 287.
5. Hood, "Defense of Atlanta," 339; Sherman, Special Field Orders, No. 36, *OR,* 1, 38, v (Serial #76), 166–67; R. W. Johnson to A. C. McClurg, ibid., 172; Johnston, *Narrative,* 347; Adams, "Battle and Capture of Atlanta," 150; Sherman, *Memoirs,* 2:79.
6. Cox, *Atlanta,* 171; Woodworth, *Davis and His Generals,* 288.
7. *Washington National Republican,* July 21, 1864; Cox, *Atlanta,* 167; Tuthill, "Recollections," 303.
8. Tuthill, "Recollections," 297–99; Higbee, "Personal Recollections," 325.
9. Cox, *Atlanta,* 173; Adams, "Battle and Capture of Atlanta," 149, 157; Sherman, *Memoirs,* 2:81; DeGress, Report, *OR,* 1, 38, iii (Serial #74), 263–66.
10. Sherman, *Memoirs,* 2:78; Van Duzer to Eckert, *OR,* 1, 38, v (Serial #76), 232; C. W. Page and R. W. Foster to Lincoln, ibid., 288; A. J. Alexander, General Orders, No. 8, *OR,* 1, 38, iii (Serial #74), 556; Rowland Cox, General Orders, No. 13, ibid., 556–57.
11. Sherman to Halleck, *OR,* 1, 38, v (Serial #76), 271–72; Thomas to Adjutant-General U.S. Army, ibid., 272; Whipple, Special Field Orders, No. 205, ibid., 273–74.
12. Sherman to Halleck, *OR,* 1, 38, v (Serial #76), 248; Dayton to Thomas, ibid., 249; Munson, "Battle of Atlanta," 228–29; Chamberlin, "Recollections," 285. Sherman (*Memoirs,* 2:84) wrote, "We have sent to the rear one thousand prisoners, including thirty-three commissioned officers of high rank."
13. Kellum, "Third Florida Regiment," 554; Foster, untitled letter, *CV,* 6:585.
14. Sherman, *Memoirs,* 2:83–84; Grant, *Memoirs,* 2:168.
15. Sherman, *Memoirs,* 2:82.
16. F. Dyer, *Compendium,* 486; Bailey, *Sherman Moves East,* 33.
17. Sherman, Report of September 15, 1865, 301.
18. Sherman to Halleck, *OR,* 1, 38, v (Serial #76), 240.

Chapter 16 • Atlanta's Defenses Were Something to See

1. Sherman, Report of September 15, 1865, 70. If he realized in July 1864 that "it was full of arsenals, foundries, and machine-shops" whose capture would mean "the death-knell of the Southern Confederacy," he was strangely silent about matters that he later treated as important (*Memoirs,* 2:99).
2. Sherman to Halleck, *OR,* 1, 38, v (Serial #76), 211; Howard to Whipple, ibid., 171; John Newton to Whipple, ibid., 214–15.
3. O. M. Poe, Report No. 6, *OR,* 1, 38, i (Serial #72), 138–39; Thomas J. Wood to Fullerton, *OR,* 1, 38, v (Serial #76), 138.
4. Grant, "Atlanta's Defenses," *OA,* plate 51, sec. 2; Grant, *Memoirs,* 2:167.
5. Schofield to Thomas, *OR,* 1, 38, v (Serial #76), 284, 114; Sherman to Halleck, ibid., 92, 289; Sherman to Thomas, ibid., 291; Roy, "Hardee and Atlanta," 349.
6. H. W. Perkins to Alpheus S. Williams, ibid., 249–50; Sherman to Garrard, ibid., 251; Stoneman to Garrard, ibid., 251–52.
7. *New York Herald,* July 18, 1864.

8. Sherman to Halleck, *OR,* 1, 38, v (Serial #76), 260–62; Sherman to Thomas, ibid., 280; Thomas J. Wood to Fullerton, ibid., 281–82.
9. S. E. Pittman to W. T. Ward, ibid., 282; Schofield to Sherman, ibid., 285; Sherman to Schofield, ibid., 293; J. A. Campbell to M. S. Hascall, ibid., 294; Shavin, *Atlanta Century,* July 24, 1864.
10. Dayton, Special Field Orders, No. 37, *OR,* 1, 38, v (Serial #76), 179–80.
11. "Closing Days of the Siege," 275.
12. Cox, *Atlanta,* 174; Garrard to Sherman, *OR,* 1, 38, v (Serial #76), 221; Sherman to Garrard, ibid., 245; Garrard to Sherman, ibid., 250; Sherman to Garrard, 251; Hood to G. W. Rains, ibid., 906.
13. McCook to Dayton, *OR,* 1, 38, v (Serial #76), 274; Sherman to Thomas, ibid., 309.
14. Grant, *Memoirs,* 2:170; Sherman to Garrard, *OR,* 1, 38, v (Serial #76), 251; Stoneman to Garrard, ibid., 251–52; Stoneman to Sherman, ibid., 264; Sherman to Stoneman, ibid., 265; Sherman, *Memoirs,* 2:88, 98.
15. Grant, *Memoirs,* 2:171; Sherman, Report of September 15, 1865, 309; J. A. Campbell to Israel Garrard *OR,* 1, 38, v (Serial #76), 304; T. J. Harrison to Sherman, ibid., 396; F. A. Shoup to Hardee, ibid., 937; Sherman to Halleck, ibid., 339–40.
16. Sherman, *Memoirs,* 2:98; Sherman to Schofield, *OR,* 1, 38, v (Serial #76), 275; communications of Schofield and Sherman, ibid., 283–85.
17. Shavin, *Atlanta Century,* July 31, 1864; Sherman to Halleck, *OR,* 1, 38, v (Serial #76), 279; F. A. Shoup to Hardee, ibid., 925; Shoup to Joseph Wheeler, ibid., 927; Shoup to Joseph E. Brown, ibid., 930.
18. Hood, Report of Operations July 18–September 6, *OR,* 1, 38, iii (Serial #74), 636–37. In his report, submitted on February 15, 1865, Hood declared that his effective total on July 31—after Peach Tree Creek, Atlanta, and Ezra Church—was 44,495 out of the 47,250 of whom he took command.

Chapter 17 • Iron Rain Poured During a Red Day in August

1. Reed, *History of Atlanta,* 191–92.
2. Using a variety of expressions to convey the same idea, Sherman several times stressed that Atlanta "was not . . . and could not be completely invested" (McDonough and Jones, *War So Terrible,* 31a).
3. Sherman to Thomas, *OR,* 1, 38, v (Serial #76), 196–97, 212–13; Sherman to Halleck, ibid., 211; J. M. Palmer, report of 7:30 P.M., July 21, ibid., 217.
4. Dayton, Special Field Orders, No. 40, ibid., Sherman to Thomas, ibid., 223; Fullerton to David S. Stanley, ibid., 225; *Atlanta Appeal,* July 29, 1864.
5. Sherman to Cadwallader C. Washburn, *OR,* 1, 39, ii (Serial #78), 205.
6. Sherman to Thomas, *OR,* 1, 38, v (Serial #76), 280; Sherman to Schofield, ibid., 285, 324; Sherman to Howard, ibid., 325; John M. Corse to John W. Barnes, ibid., 326.
7. Sherman to Thomas, ibid., 412, 419; Sherman to Halleck, ibid., 408–9; Sherman to Schofield, ibid., 421–22; Sherman to Howard, ibid., 428–29.
8. Van Duzer to Eckert, ibid., 431. Sherman reported to Washington that he threw "about 3,000 solid shot and shell" into Atlanta that day (Sherman to Halleck, ibid., 434).
9. Sherman to Thomas and Howard, ibid., 435; Sherman to Grant, ibid., 447.
10. Thomas to Sherman, ibid., 448; Sherman to Thomas, ibid., 449; Sherman to

Schofield, ibid., 450; Sherman to Howard, ibid., 452, 453.
11. Sherman to Howard, ibid., 453, 454.
12. Sherman to Thomas, ibid., 572–73, 573–74; Sherman to Schofield, ibid., 602; Sherman to Halleck, 649.
13. *Atlanta Intelligencer,* July 7, 1864; Shavin, *Atlanta Century,* July 31, 1864.
14. *Columbus (Georgia) Daily Sun,* August 9, 1864.
15. Sherman to Thomas, *OR,* 1, 38, v (Serial #76), 86, 114; Thomas J. Wood to Fullerton, ibid., 115–16; Dodge to McPherson, ibid., 117–18.
16. *Richmond Dispatch,* August 15, 1864.
17. Bragg to John B. Sale, *OR,* 1, 38, v (Serial #76), 944; Davis endorsement, ibid., 945; Bragg to Davis, ibid., 955; Davis to his secretary of war, ibid., 955.
18. Sherman to Halleck, ibid., 409–10.

Chapter 18 • Firing Never Ceased, Day or Night

1. Ruger, map, *OA,* plate 48, sec. 1; C. Evans, *CMH,* 7;342.
2. Thomas to Sherman, *OR,* 1, 38, v (Serial #76), 291; Sherman to Howard, ibid., 403.
3. Cox to J. S. Casement, ibid., 401.
4. Schofield to Sherman, ibid., 333–34; Howard to Sherman, ibid., 335; Sherman to Thomas, ibid., 341, 342.
5. Sherman to Schofield, ibid., 414–15, 462–63; Sherman to Halleck, ibid., 391–92; Sherman to Thomas and Howard, ibid., 435.
6. Sherman to Thomas, ibid., 526; J. A. Campbell, Special Field Orders, No. 79, ibid., 470; Garrard to W. D. Whipple, ibid., 714.
7. Sherman to Halleck, ibid., 688; Sherman to Slocum, ibid., 691; "Diary of Events," 272b; Ruger, map, *OA,* plate 48, sec. 1.
8. Sherman to Thomas, *OR,* 1, 38, v (Serial #76), 721.
9. Sherman to Halleck, ibid., 482.
10. *New Orleans Picayune,* August 28, 1864; Sherman, Report of September 15, 1865, 311b.
11. Bragg to John B. Sale, *OR,* 1, 38, v (Serial #76), 942; Samuel W. Melton, Special Orders, No. 192, ibid., 965; J. W. Ratchford, Circular of August 12, ibid., 961.
12. Sherman to Schofield, ibid., 754.
13. Cox, *Atlanta,* 205.

Chapter 19 • Atlanta Is Ours, and Fairly Won

1. Ruger, map, *OA,* plate 48, sec. 1.
2. R. R. Townes, Special Field Orders, No. 62, *OR,* 1, 38, v (Serial #76), 269.
3. Rowland Cox, General Orders, No. 13, *OR,* 1, 38, iii (Serial #74), 556–58; Medals of Honor Awarded for Distinguished Services, ibid., 612.
4. Sherman to Halleck, *OR,* 1, 38, v (Serial #76), 777.
5. McMurry, *Hood,* 149; Sherman to Stanton, ibid., 829–30.
6. Cox, *Atlanta,* 207; Sherman to George W. Tyler, *OR,* 1, 38, v (Serial #76), 821–22.
7. Report of H. M. Scott, *OR,* 1, 38, ii (Serial #73), 333; report of John Coburn, ibid., 393; report of Henry W. Slocum, ibid., 21.
8. Sherman, *Memoirs,* 2:109.

9. Ibid., 2:110.
10. Ibid.
11. Basler, *Lincoln,* 7:532.
12. On July 20 Sherman reported that he was "closing in upon Atlanta." Five weeks before he succeeded in driving Hood from his fortifications, he was confident that "a few more days will bring matters to a crisis" (Sherman to C. C. Washburn, *OR,* 1, 39, ii [Serial #78], 184)

Chapter 20 • You Must All Leave

1. Dayton, Special Field Orders, No. 64, *OR,* 1, 38, v (Serial #76), 801.
2. Whipple, Special Field Orders, No. 245, ibid., 805.
3. Sherman to commanding officers, Nashville and Chattanooga, ibid., 824.
4. Sherman, *Memoirs,* 2:110–11.
5. Sherman to Halleck, *OR,* 1, 38, v (Serial #76), 794.
6. Halleck to Sherman, ibid., 856–57; Stanton to Sherman, ibid., 839.
7. Sherman to Hood, ibid., 822; Hood to Sherman, *OR,* 1, 39, ii (Serial #78), 415.
8. Dayton, Special Field Orders, No. 67, *OR,* 1, 38, v (Serial #76) 837–38.
9. Ibid., 838.
10. Sherman sent the Calhoun letter, plus his exchanges with Hood, as "inclosures" in a September 20 communication (Sherman to Halleck, *OR,* 1, 39, ii [Serial #78, 414–22], 417–18).
11. Sherman, *Memoirs,* 2:124–25.
12. Basler, *Lincoln,* 6:423.
13. Sherman to Hood, *OR,* 2, 7, (Serial #120), 791–92.
14. Sherman, *Memoirs,* 2:129; idem, *Memoirs* (rev.), 1010–16; Sherman to Hood, *OR,* 2, 7 (Serial #120), 791. Clare's report (*OR,* 1, 38, iii [Serial #74], 993) gives a grand total of 1,168 persons who were transported to the neutral zone he supervised at Rough and Ready. This included 98 men, 395 women, 605 children, and 70 servants. If Clare's account is accurate, the number of imprisoned Atlanta males whose fate is unknown was approximately 900.
15. Hood to Sherman, *OR,* 1, 39, ii (Serial #78), 421.
16. Sherman, *Memoirs* (rev.) 1,026.
17. Hood to Sherman, *OR,* 2, 7 (Serial #120), 784.
18. Sherman to Halleck, *OR,* 1, 38, v (Serial #76), 839. In this telegram Sherman referred only to captured Confederate soldiers.
19. Hood to Samuel Jones, ibid., 971–72; Hood to Bragg, ibid., 1017, 1028; Hood to Davis, ibid., 1023.
20. Sherman to Hood, *OR,* 2, 7 (Serial #120), 791; Hood to Sherman, ibid., 799.

Chapter 21 • An Empty Town, Barely Occupied

1. Sherman to Calhoun, Rawson, and Wells, *OR,* 1, 39, ii (Serial #78), 418.
2. Sherman, *Home Letters,* 309.
3. Sherman to Calhoun, Rawson, and Welles, *OR,* 1, 39, ii (Serial #78), 418–19.
4. Shavin, *Atlanta Century,* October 16, 1864; Sherman to Maj. Gen. James B. Steedman, *OR,* 1, 39,ii (Serial #79), 447–48.

5. Sherman to Slocum, *OR,* 1, 39, iii (Serial #79), 125; Sherman to Corse, ibid., 134.
6. Dayton, Special Field Orders, No. 87, ibid., 144; Sherman to Howard, ibid. 207.
7. Sherman, *Memoirs,* 2:147–50.
8. *Augusta Daily Chronicle and Sentinel,* October 7, 1864.
9. Boney, "Joseph E. Brown," 228–30.
10. Sherman, *Memoirs,* 2:138, 142; Sherman to Lincoln, *OR,* 1, 39, ii (Serial #78), 395–96.
11. Stephens to King, *OR,* 1, 39, iii (Serial #79), 778.
12. Corse to Sherman, ibid., 188.
13. Sherman, *Home Letters,* 304–5.
14. Ibid., 307–8.
15. Sherman to Grant, *OR,* 1, 38, v (Serial #76) 408.
16. Sherman to Thomas, *OR,* 1, 39, iii (Serial #79), 190, 377–78; Sherman to J. D. Webster, ibid., 175; Sherman to Grant, *OR,* 1, 38, v (Serial #76), 408.
17. Sherman to John A. Sooner, *OR,* 1, 38, v (Serial #76), 305–6.
18. Halleck to Sherman in Sherman, *Memoirs,* 2:116–17.
19. Thomas to Stanton, *OR,* 3, 4 (Serial #125), 734.
20. Sherman, *Home Letters,* 253–56.
21. Sherman to Halleck, *OR,* 1, 39, iii (Serial #79), 203.
22. Sherman to Slocum, ibid., 305–6; Sherman to Thomas, ibid., 408; Sherman, *Memoirs,* 2:157–58.

Chapter 22 • Saltwater!

1. *Cump* was the customary nickname among relatives and friends.
2. Sherman, Special Field Orders, No. 1, *OR,* 1, 38, iv (Serial #75), 23–24; Sherman to Roswell M. Sawyer, *OR,* 1, 32, iii (Serial #59), 542.
3. Porter, *Campaigning,* 262; cf. Vetter, *Sherman,* 230.
4. Sherman to Halleck, *OR,* 1, 38, v (Serial #76), 482.
5. Sherman, *Memoirs,* 2:151; Hart, *Sherman,* 320; Nevins, *War for the Union,* 4:164–65.
6. Sherman, *Home Letters,* 124; cf. Sherman, *Memoirs,* 2:166.
7. Sherman to Grant, *OR,* 1, 44 (Serial #92), 726; Porter, *Campaigning,* 293.
8. Sherman to Grant, *OR,* 1, 39, iii (Serial #79), 658–61.
9. Sherman to Halleck, ibid., 357–58.
10. Grant to Sherman, *OR,* 1, 39, ii (Serial #78), 355; Sherman to Grant, ibid., 432.
11. Sherman to Grant, ibid., 355–56.
12. Sherman to Grant, 10:00 A.M., *OR,* 1, 39, iii (Serial #79), 202.
13. Sherman to Grant, ibid., 412.
14. Grant to Sherman, ibid., 202; Sherman to Grant, ibid., 174.
15. Grant, *Memoirs,* 2:376; cf. Sherman, *Memoirs,* 2:166.
16. Grant to Sherman, ibid., 202.
17. Hood to Bragg, *OR,* 1, 39, ii (Serial #78), 864.
18. Grant, *Memoirs,* 2:141; Sherman to Halleck, *OR,* 1, 39, ii (Serial #78), 517.
19. Sherman to Grant, *OR,* 1, 39, iii (Serial #79), 3; Sherman to J. D. Webster, ibid., 3; Sherman, *Memoirs,* 2:145; Sherman, *Memoirs,* 2:152.
20. Grant to Stanton, *OR,* 1, 39, iii (Serial #79), 239; Grant to Halleck, ibid., 239–40; Halleck to Grant, ibid., 267; Halleck to Meigs, ibid., 267–68.

21. Grant to Sherman, ibid., 222; Stanton to Grant, ibid., 222; Stanton to Sherman, ibid., 240; Sherman to Thomas, ibid., 333.
22. Sherman to Grant, ibid., 304; Sherman to Thomas, ibid., 365; Sherman, *Memoirs,* 2:156, 158.
23. Sherman to Thomas, *OR,* 1, 39, iii (Serial #79), 377–78; Sherman, *Home Letters,* 312.
24. Sherman, *Memoirs,* 2:163; Sherman to Thomas, *OR,* 1, 39, iii (Serial #79), 514–15.
25. Sherman, *Memoirs* 2:165–6.
26. Grant, *Memoirs,* 2:157–58, 166; Grant to Sherman, *OR,* 1, 39, iii (Serial #79), 594; Sherman to Halleck, ibid., 613–14; Sherman to James B. Steedman, ibid., 632; Sherman to Thomas, 647–48.
27. Ibid., 659–60; Sherman to E. D. Townsend, ibid., 679–80; Sherman to Corse, ibid., 682; Sherman to Halleck, ibid., 697.
28. Sherman, *Memoirs,* 2:171; Grant to Sherman, *OR,* 1, 39, iii (Serial #79), 679; Sherman to Grant, ibid., 660.
29. Grant to Stanton, *OR,* 1, 39, iii (Serial #79), 740; Grant to Stanton, ibid., 749.
30. Sherman, *Home Letters,* 211, 295, 243, 241, 227, 229; Sherman to Halleck, *OR,* 1, 39, iii (Serial #79), 203.
31. Sherman, *Home Letters,* 225–26.
32. Sherman to Knox, *OR,* 1, 17, ii (Serial #25), 894–95.
33. Sherman, *Home Letters,* 239–40; *New York Times,* March 27, 1864; *Mobile Daily Tribune,* March 5, 1864; *New York Herald,* March 15, 1864; *New York World,* March 14, 1864.
34. Sherman, *Home Letters,* 239–46.
35. Sherman, *Memoirs,* 2:117–29.
36. Sherman to Halleck, *OR,* 1, 39, ii (Serial #78), 502–3.
37. Ibid., 481.
38. Sherman to Halleck, *OR,* 1, 38, v (Serial #76), 638.
39. Sherman to Charles A. Dana, ibid., 727.

Chapter 23 • Atlanta Tipped the Scales for a Despondent Lincoln

1. *National Almanac 1864,* 78–79.
2. *New York Tribune,* October 24–November 30, 1864.
3. Basler, *Lincoln,* 7:164; Sherman, *Memoirs,* 2:116; Curtin to Lincoln, *OR,* 3, 4 (Serial #125), 753; 140.
4. *New York Times,* November 5, 1862.
5. *Philadelphia Inquirer,* September 20, 1862.
6. General Orders No. 24, *OR,* 3, 4 (Serial #125), 96–99; General Orders, No. 41, ibid., 209.
7. Basler, *Lincoln,* 8:11–12, 46–47.
8. Sherman, *Memoirs,* 2:168; Sherman, *Home Letters,* 315.
9. Some authorities suggest that these enforced political contributions were from employees of only three departments: Post Office, Treasury, and War.
10. Basler, *Lincoln,* 7:514.
11. Thurlow Weed to Seward, August 22 (ibid., 7:514n).
12. Sherman, *Home Letters,* 129, 142, 178, 190, 193, 197, 199, 200–201, 204, 210, 216, 224, 249, 271–72, 313, 315.
13. Sherman to Halleck, *OR,* 1, 38, v (Serial #76), 794.

14. Stanton to Sherman, *OR*, 1, 38, i (Serial #72), 86.
15. Table of Aggregate Votes in the States, *OR*, 3, 4 (Serial #125), 982.
16. Poe, Report of March 11, 1864 (*OR*, 1, 31, i [Serial #54], 303–15), 315.

Bibliography

Abbott, A. O. *Prison Life in the South.* New York: Harper, 1865.

Abraham Lincoln Quarterly. 15 vols. Urbana: University of Illinois Press, 1979–94.

Adams, Robert N. "The Battle and Capture of Atlanta." Minnesota *MOLLUS* 4 (1898): 144–62.

Anderson, Patton. "Report of Operations from 30th of July to 31st of August, 1864, including the Battle of Jonesboro, Georgia." *JSHS* 4:193–202.

Andrews, J. Cutler. *The South Reports the Civil War.* Pittsburgh: University of Pittsburgh Press, 1985.

Annals of the Civil War, The. Philadelphia: Philadelphia Weekly Times, 1879.

"Another Account," *RR,* 11:39–53, 205–8.

"Another National Account," *RR,* 11:60–64.

"Assault on Kenesaw, The," *RR,* 11:225–31.

Atlanta Appeal, July 1864.

Atlanta Intelligencer, June-August 1864.

Augusta Daily Chronicle and Sentinel, October 1864.

Badeau, Adam. *Military History of Ulysses S. Grant, from April, 1861, to April, 1865.* 3 vols. New York: Appleton: 1885.

Bailey, Ronald H. *Battles for Atlanta: Sherman Moves East.* Alexandria: Time-Life Books, 1985.

Baird, John A., Jr. "For Gallant and Meritorious Service." *CWT* (June 1976): 4–9, 45–48.

Barnard, George N. *Photographic Views of Sherman's Campaign.* 1866. Reprint, New York: Dover Publications, 1977.

Basler, Roy P. *Complete Works of Abraham Lincoln.* 9 vols. New Brunswick, N.J.: Rutgers University Press, 1955.

"Battle Near Atlanta," *RR,* 11:255–69.

"Battle of Peach-Tree Creek," *RR,* 11:249–54.

Beers, Fannie A. *Memories: A Record of Personal Experience and Adventure During Four Years of War.* Philadelphia: Lippincott, 1889.

Bernstein, Iver. *The New York City Draft Riots.* New York: Oxford University Press, 1990.

Boatner, Mark M. *The Civil War Dictionary.* Rev. ed. New York: David McKay, 1987.

Boney, F. N. "Joseph E. Brown." *CV* 1:228–30.

Boritt, Gabor S., ed. *Lincoln's Generals.* New York: Oxford, 1994.

Bowman, Samuel M. and R. B. Irwin. *Sherman and His Campaigns.* New York: Richardson, 1865.

Boyd, James P. *Life of General William T. Sherman.* n.p.: Publishers' Union, 1891.

Boynton, H. V. *Sherman's Historical Raid.* Cincinnati: Wilstach, Baldwin, 1875.

Breckinridge, W. C. P. "Opening of the Atlanta Campaign." *B&L,* 4:277–80.

Bright, John M. "The States in the Confederate War." *CV* 17:393–98.

Buell, Clarence C., and Robert E. Johnson, eds. *Battles and Leaders of the Civil War.* 4 vols. New York: Century, 1884–88. Reprint, Secaucus, N.J.: Castle, 1985.
Burch, C. V. "A Mother of Soldiers," *CV* 21:237.
"Campaign for Atlanta." *CWT* special ed. (July 1964): 3–50.
Carlin, W. P. "Journal of the First Brigade, Army of the Cumberland." *OR,* 1, 38, i (Serial #72), 527–34.
Carter, Samuel III. *The Siege of Atlanta 1864.* New York: St. Martin's, 1973.
Castel, Albert. *Decision in the West: The Atlanta Campaign of 1864.* Lawrence: University of Kansas Press, 1992.
———. "Union Fizzle at Utoy Creek." *CWT* (February 1978): 26–32.
Catton, Bruce. *American Heritage Picture History of the Civil War.* 1960. Reprint, New York: Wings, 1982.
———. "Famous Cyclorama of the Great Battle of Atlanta." *Civil War Chronicles* (Fall 1993): 4–19.
———. "Grant and the Politicians." *American Heritage* (October 1968): 32–35, 81–87.
———. *Grant Takes Command.* Boston: Little, Brown, 1968.
———. *Never Call Retreat.* Garden City: Doubleday, 1965.
———. *This Hallowed Ground.* Garden City: Doubleday, 1956.
"Cavalry Affair on Sherman's Rear, A." *RR* 11:65–68.
Century. 1887–88.
Chamberlin, W. H. "Hood's Second Sortie at Atlanta." *B&L,* 4:326.
———. "Recollections of the Battle of Atlanta," Ohio MOLLUS, 6:276–86.
———. "The Skirmish Line in the Atlanta Campaign," Ohio MOLLUS, 3:182–96.
Charleston Mercury, April-November 1864.
Chesnut, Mary Boykin. *A Diary from Dixie.* Edited by Ben Ames Williams. Boston: Houghton Mifflin, 1905.
Civil War. 1982–94.
Civil War Chronicles. 1991–92.
Civil War Times and *Civil War Times Illustrated.* 1959–94.
Clauss, Errol M. "The Battle of Jonesborough." *CWT* (November 1968): 12–23.
Clay, C. C., Jr., letter to J. P. Benjamin, September 12, 1864. *JSHS,* 7:338–43.
Clayton, H. D. "A Correction of General Patton Anderson's Report of the Battle of Jonesboro, Ga." *JSHS* 5:127–29.
"Closing Days of the Siege." *RR* 11:272–83.
Coburn, Mark. *Terrible Innocence.* n.p.: Hippocrene, 1993.
Columbus (Georgia) Daily Sun, August 1864.
Compton, James. "The Second Division of the 16th Army Corps in the Atlanta Campaign." Minnesota MOLLUS 5:103–23.
Confederate Veteran. 1893–1932.
Coulter, E. Merton. "Sherman's March to the Sea." *DAH* 6:278.
Cox, Jacob D. *Atlanta.* New York: Scribner's, 1898.
———. *The March to the Sea.* New York: n.p., 1882.
Current, Richard N., ed. *Encyclopedia of the Confederacy.* 4 vols. New York: Simon & Schuster, 1993.
Curry, W. L. "Raid of the Union Cavalry, Commanded by General Judson Kilpatrick, Around the Confederate Army in Atlanta, August, 1864." Ohio MOLLUS 6:253–86.
Davis, George B., et al. *The Official Military Atlas of the Civil War.* 1891–95. Reprint, New

York: Gramercy, 1983.
Davis, Jefferson. *The Rise and Fall of the Confederate Government.* 2 vols. New York: D. Appleton, 1881.
Davis, William C. *Jefferson Davis.* New York: HarperCollins, 1991.
Dawes, E. C. "The Confederate Strength in the Atlanta Campaign." *B&L,* 4:281–83.
Degregorio, William A. *The Complete Book of U.S. Presidents.* New York: Wings, 1991.
"Diary of Events." *RR* 11:258–68.
Dodge, Grenville M. "The Battle of Atlanta." New York MOLLUS 2 (1897): 240–56.
Downs, Alan C. "Vicksburg Campaign." *EC* 1:655–60.
Dupuy, Trevor M. et al. *The Harper Encyclopedia of Military Biography.* New York: HarperCollins 1992.
Dyer, Frederick H. *A Compendium of the War of the Rebellion.* 3 vols. Des Moines: Dyer, 1908.
Dyer, John P. *The Gallant Hood.* Indianapolis: Bobbs-Merrill, 1950.
Echoes of Glory: Illustrated Atlas of the Civil War. Alexandria: Time-Life, 1991.
Eisencheml, Otto. *The American Iliad.* Indianapolis: Bobbs-Merrill, 1947.
———. "Sherman: Hero or War Criminal?" *CWT* (January 1964): 7–9, 29–35.
Evans, Clement A., ed. *Confederate Military History.* 17 vols. Wilmington: Broadfoot, 1989.
Evans, David. "The Atlanta Campaign." *CWT* (Summer 1989): 3–66.
Ewing, Joseph H. *Sherman at War.* Dayton: Morningside, 1992.
Faust, Patricia L., ed. *Historical Times Illustrated Encyclopedia of the Civil War.* New York: Harper & Row, 1986.
"The First and Only Confederate President." *CWT* (July-August 1991): 36–40.
Foote, Allen. "Some of My War Stories." Ohio MOLLUS 9 (1993): 23–55.
Foote, Shelby. *The Civil War.* 3 vols. New York: Random House, 1958–74.
Force, Manning G. *General Sherman.* New York: D. Appleton, 1899.
Foster, A. B. Untitled letter. *CV* 6:585.
Foster, David C. "Gate City of the South, Farewell!" *Business Atlanta,* March 1987, 49–54.
Freeman, Douglas L. *Lee's Lieutenants.* 4 vols. New York: Scribner's, 1946.
Fullerton, Joseph S. "Journal of the Atlanta Campaign." *OR,* I, 38, i (Serial #72), 839–936.
Gallagher, Gary W. *Annals of the Civil War.* Philadelphia: n.p., 1878.
Gardner, Alexander. *Gardner's Photographic Sketch Book of the Civil War.* 1866. Reprint, New York: Dover Publications, 1959.
Garrett, Franklin. "Civilian Life in Atlanta During the Siege and Occupation." *CWT* (July 1964): 30–33.
Gay, Mary A. H. *Life in Dixie During the War.* Atlanta: Atlanta Constitution, 1892.
"General Sherman's Method of Making War." *JSHS* 13:439–53.
"Georgia in the Confederacy." *CV* 40:380–81.
Glumer, J. V. "Map Illustrating the Operations of the Army, under Command of General W. T. Sherman in Georgia." *OA,* plate 47, sec. 1.
Govan, Gilbert E., and James W. Livingood. *General Joseph E. Johnston, C.S.A.* Indianapolis: Bobbs-Merrill, 1956.
Grant, Lemuel P. "City of Atlanta and Line of Defenses." *OA,* plate 51, sec. 2.
Grant, Ulysses S. *Personal Memoirs of U. S. Grant.* 2 vols. New York: Webster, 1886.
———. Unpublished papers. Chicago Historical Society.
Hallock, Judith L. "Braxton Bragg." *CE* 1:203–06.

Harper's Encyclopedia of U.S. History. 10 vols. New York: Harper, 1901.
Harris, Brayton. "Military Relations with the Press," *Civil War* 15 (December 1988): 29–34.
Hart, B. Liddell. *Sherman.* New York: Dodd, Mead, 1929.
———. "Sherman—Modern Warrior." *American Heritage,* August 1962, 21–23, 102–06.
Hattaway, Herman. *General Stephen D. Lee.* Jackson: University of Mississippi Press, 1976.
Hay, Thomas R. "Atlanta Campaign." *DAH* 1:213–14.
Helmle, I. "Map Showing the Roads Followed by the Army of the Tennessee." *OA,* plate 57, sec. 3.
Hicken, Victor. "Hold the Fort." *CWT* (June 1968): 18.
Higbee, Chester G. "Personal Recollections of a Line Officer." Minnesota MOLLUS 4 (1898): 313–26.
Hinman, W. F. "The Fall of Atlanta." In *Conflict,* edited by Don Congdon. Reprint, New York: Konecku, 1992.
Hoehling, A. A. *Last Train from Atlanta.* New York: Yoseloff, 1958.
Hood, John B. *Advance and Retreat.* New Orleans: Hood Orphan Memorial Fund, 1880.
———. "Defense of Atlanta." *B&L,* 4:336–44.
Horn, Stanley. *The Army of Tennessee.* Indianapolis: Bobbs-Merrill, 1941.
Hornaday, John R. *Atlanta.* n.p., American Cities, 1922.
Howard, O. O. "The Struggle for Atlanta." *B&L,* 4:293–325.
Hughes, Robert M. *General Johnston.* New York: D. Appleton, 1895.
"Interesting Batch of Telegrams." *CV* 2:1110–11.
Irving, Buck. *Cleburne and His Command.* New York: Neale, 1908.
Johnson, Bradley T. *A Memoir of the Life and Public Service of Joseph E. Johnston.* Baltimore: Woodward, 1891.
Johnston, Joseph E. "The Dalton-Atlanta Operations." In *Annals of the War.* Pp. 331–41. Philadelphia: Weekly Times, 1878.
———. "The Defense of Atlanta." *B&L,* 4:336–44.
———. *Narrative of Military Operation, Directed During the Late War Between the States.* New York: Appleton, 1874.
———. "Opposing Sherman's Advance to Atlanta." *B&L,* 4:260–76.
Jones, John B. *A Rebel War Clerk's Diary.* Baton Rouge: Louisiana State University Press, 1993.
Journal of the Southern Historical Society (1876–1944). Edited by James I. Robertson, Jr. 49 vols. Richmond.
Julian, Allen P. "Atlanta's Defenses." *CWT* (Summer 1964): 23–24.
———. "From Dalton to Atlanta." *CWT* 7 (July 1964): 24–35.
Kane, Joseph N. *Facts about the Presidents.* 5th ed. New York: Wilson, 1989.
Katcher, Philip. *The Civil War Source Book.* New York: Facts on File, 1992.
Keller, Allan. "Johnston versus Sherman." *CWT* (December 1961): 18–22, 32–35.
Kellum, J. W. "Third Florida Regiment—Personal." *CV* 17:554.
Ketchum, Richard M., ed. *The American Heritage Picture History of the Civil War.* Reprint, New York: Wings, 1982.
Kirkland, Nell Felix, Elsie Lundeen, and Joan P. Kimble. *The Least of These.* Atlanta: Egleston Children's Hospital, 1994.
Kurtz, Wilbur, Sr. *The Atlanta Cyclorama of the Battle of Atlanta.* Atlanta: City of Atlanta, 1954–71.

———. "Battles Around Atlanta." *CWT* (July 1964): 8–17.
———. "The Ordinary Soldier in the Campaign for Atlanta." *CWT* (July 1964): 8–22.
Lewis, Lloyd. *Sherman—Fighting Prophet.* New York: Harcourt, Brace, 1932.
Long, E. B., and Barbara Long. *The Civil War Day by Day.* Garden City: Doubleday, 1971.
Longacre, Edward G. *Mounted Raids of the Civil War.* Lincoln: University of Nebraska Press, 1975.
Lorant, Stefan. *The Glorious Burden.* New York: Harper & Row, 1968.
———. *The Presidency.* New York: Macmillan, 1951.
Marszalek, John F. *Sherman: A Soldier's Passion for Order.* New York: Free Press, 1993.
———. *Sherman's Other War.* Memphis: Memphis State University Press, 1981.
Martin, Thomas H. *Atlanta and Its Builders.* 2 vols. Atlanta: Century Memorial, 1902.
Maurice, Frederick. *Statesmen and Soldiers of the Civil War.* Boston: Little, Brown, 1926.
McCormick, Edgar L., et al, eds. *Sherman in Georgia.* Boston: Heath, 1961.
McDonough, James L., and James P. Jones. *War So Terrible.* New York: Norton, 1987.
McElroy, John. *This Was Andersonville.* New York: Fairfax, 1957.
McMurry, Richard M. "Atlanta Campaign." In *Encyclopedia of Southern History.* Baton Rouge: Louisiana State University Press, 1968.
———. "Confederate Morale in the Atlanta Campaign of 1864." *Georgia Historical Quarterly* (1970): 226–43.
———. "Kennesaw Mountain." *CWT* (January 1970): 19–25, 28–33.
———. *John Bell Hood.* Lexington: University of Kentucky Press, 1982.
———. *Road Past Kennesaw: The Atlanta Campaign of 1864.* Washington, D.C.: National Park Service, 1972.
McPherson, James. *Battle Cry of Freedom.* New York: Oxford University Press, 1988.
Meredith, Roy, and Arthur Meredith. *Mr. Lincoln's Military Railroads.* New York: Norton, 1979.
Merrill, W. E. "Block Houses for Railroad Defense in the Department of the Cumberland." Ohio MOLLUS 3 (1890): 389–421.
Miers, Earl S., ed. *Lincoln Day by Day.* 3 volumes. Washington, D.C.: Lincoln Sesquicentennial Commission, 1960.
———. *The Web of Victory: Grant at Vicksburg.* Reprint, Baton Rouge: Louisiana State University Press, 1984.
Miles, Jim. "The Campaign for Atlanta." *Civil War* (January-February 1991): 12–25, 54–60.
———. *Fields of Glory.* Nashville: Rutledge Hill Press, 1989.
Miller, Francis T., ed. *Photographic History of the Civil War.* 10 vols. New York: Review of Reviews, 1911.
Mobile Daily Advertiser and Register, July 1864.
Moore, Frank, ed. *The Rebellion Record.* 12 vols. New York: Van Nostrand, 1868.
Morgan, George. "Assault on Chickasaw Bluffs." *B&L,* 3:462–70.
Munson, Gilbert D. "Battle of Atlanta." Ohio MOLLUS 3 (1890): 212–30.
Nashville Times, July 1864.
National Almanac and Annual Record for the Year 1864. Philadelphia: n.p., 1864.
Neely, Mark E., Jr., ed. *The Abraham Lincoln Encyclopedia.* New York: McGraw-Hill, 1982.
Nevins, Allan. *The War for the Union.* 4 vols. New York: Scribner's, 1959–71.
———, James I. Robertson, and Bell I. Wiley. *Civil War Books, A Critical Bibliography.* Baton Rouge: Louisiana State University Press: 1969.

New Orleans Picayune, August 1864.
New York Herald, July 1864.
New York Times, May-November 1864.
Nichols, George W. *Story of the Great March from the Diary of a Staff Officer.* New York: Harper, 1865.
Nicolay, Helen. "Lincoln's Cabinet." *Abraham Lincoln Quarterly* 5 (1983): 282.
Nicolay, John G., and John Hay. *Abraham Lincoln: A History.* 10 vols. New York: Century, 1886.
———. *Complete Works of Abraham Lincoln.* 12 vols. New York: Francis D. Tandey, 1905.
Nye, Wilbur S. "Cavalry Operations Around Atlanta." *CWT* (July 1964): 46–50.
Official Records of the Union and Confederate Navies in the War of the Rebellion. 22 vols. Washington, D.C.: Government Printing Office, 1894–1922.
Osborn, Thomas W. *The Fiery Trail.* Knoxville: University of Tennessee Press, 1986.
Overly, Milford. "What 'Marching Through Georgia' Means." *CV* 18:444.
———. "Williams's Kentucky Brigade, C.S.A." *CV* 13:460–63.
Petersburg Daily Express, 1864.
Phisterer, Frederick. *Statistical Record of the Armies of the United States.* New York: Scribner's, 1883.
Pickering, W. A. "The Washington Artillery." *CV* 17:250.
Poe, Orlando M. "Report of April 11, 1864." *OR,* 1, 31 (Serial #54), 303–15.
Polk, William M. *Leonidas Polk.* 2 vols. New York: Longmans, 1983.
Porter, Horace. *Campaigning with Grant.* New York: Century, 1897.
Randall, James G. *The Civil War and Reconstruction.* Boston: Heath, 1953.
Ransom, John. *John Ransom's Andersonville Diary.* Middlebury, Vt.: Paul S. Eriksson, 1963.
"Recruiting in the Rebel States." In *RR,* 11:188.
Reed, Wallace P. *History of Atlanta, Ga.* Syracuse: D. Mason, 1889.
Richmond Examiner, July-August 1864.
Ridley, B. L. "Camp Scenes Around Dalton," *CV* 10:66–68.
Robinson, Leigh. "General Joseph E. Johnston." *JSHS* 19:327–70.
Roller, David C., and Robert W. Twyman. *Encyclopedia of Southern History.* Baton Rouge: Louisiana State University Press, 1968.
Rowland, Dunbar, ed. *Jefferson Davis, Constitutionalist.* 10 vols. Jackson: Mississippi Department of Archives and History, 1923.
Roy, T. B. "General Hardee and the Military Operations Around Atlanta." *JSHS* (August-September 1880): 337–87.
Royster, Charles. *The Destructive War.* New York: Knopf, 1991.
Ruger, Edward. "Map Illustrating the Second Epoch of the Atlanta Campaign." *OA,* plate 58, sec. 1.
———. "Map Illustrating the Fourth Epoch of the Atlanta Campaign." *OA,* plate 60, sec. 1.
Schafer, Elizabeth D. "Jaded Mules, Twisted Rails and Razed Depots." *Civil War* (January-February 1991): 40–46.
Sea, Andrew M. "An Incident of Rocky Face Ridge." *CV* 6:318–19.
Secrist, Philip. "Life in Atlanta." *CWT* (July 1970): 30–38.
Seitz, Don C. *Braxton Bragg.* Columbia, S.C.: State Co., 1924.
Shavin, Norman. *The Atlanta Century.* Atlanta: Capricorn, 1965.
Sherman, William T. "The Grand Strategy of the Last Year of the War. *B&L,* 4:247–59.

———. *Home Letters.* Edited by M. A. DeWolfe Howe. New York: Scribner's, 1909.
———. *Marching Through Georgia.* Edited by Mills Lane. Savannah: Beehive, 1974.
———. *Memoirs.* 2 vols. New York: D. Appleton, 1875. (Unless otherwise noted, citations are from this edition.)
———. *Memoirs.* New York: Library of America, 1990. Material not included in the original appears in appendices.
———. Report of September 15, 1864, *OR,* 1, 38, I (Serial #72), 61–85.
———. Report of September 15, 1865. *RR* 11:300–315.
———. *War Is Hell!* Edited by Mills Lane. Savannah: Beehive, 1974.
———. "The War of the Rebellion." Parts 1 and 2. *Century* (July 1887) and (February 1888).
"Sherman in Georgia." *RR* 11:24–39.
"Sherman's Atlanta Campaign." *RR* 11:203–322.
Sifakis, Stewart. *Who Was Who in the Civil War.* New York: Facts on File, 1988.
"The Situation." *RR* 11:219–24.
Smith, Gustavus W. "Georgia Militia Around Atlanta." *B&L,* 4:331–35.
"Speech of Jefferson Davis at Macon." In *RR* 11:148.
Stepp, John W. and I. William Hill, eds. *Mirror of War.* Washington, D.C.: Washington Evening Star, 1961.
Stern, Philip Van Doren. "Doctor Gatling and His Gun." *Civil War Chronicles* 2 (Winter 1993): 42–49.
Stevens, O. B. *Georgia: Historical and Industrial.* Atlanta: Harrison, 1901.
Stiles, John C. "Some American Huns." *CV* 28:265–66.
Strong, William E. "The Death of General James B. McPherson." Illinois MOLLUS 1 (1891): 311–43.
Sutherland, Daniel E. *The Confederate Carpetbaggers.* Baton Rouge: Louisiana State University Press, 1988.
Symonds, Craig L. "Atlanta Campaign." *EC,* 1:111–14.
———. *Joseph E. Johnston.* New York, 1992.
Taylor, Tim. *The Book of Presidents.* New York: Arno, 1972.
The Mountain Campaigns in Georgia. Buffalo: Matthews, 1886.
Thompson, Holland. "Exchange of Prisoners." *PH,* 7:24–151.
Thompson, William C. "Memoirs, Part 2." *CWT* (February 1965): 40–44.
Tuthill, Richard S. "An Artilleryman's Recollections of the Battle of Atlanta." Illinois MOLLUS 1 (1891): 293–309.
Van Horne, Thomas B. *The Life of Major-General George H. Thomas.* New York: Appleton, 1885.
Vandiver, Frank E. "Jefferson Davis." *EC,* 448–53.
Vetter, Charles E. *Sherman.* Gretna, La.: Pelican, 1992.
Walton, J. B., et al. "Sketches of the Washington Artillery." *JSHS* 11:210–47.
War of the Rebellion: Official Records of the Union and Confederate Armies. Washington, D.C.: Government Printing Office, 1880–1901.
Ward, John S. "Responsibility for the Death of Prisoners." *CV,* 4:10–12.
Warner, Ezra J. *Generals in Blue.* Baton Rouge: Louisiana State University Press, 1964.
———. *Generals in Gray.* Baton Rouge: Louisiana State University Press, 1959.
Washington National Republican, July 1864.
Watkins, Sam. *Co. Aytch.* Chattanooga: Times, 1900.

White, Joseph F. "Social Conditions in the South During the War Between the States." *CV* 30:142–44.

Whitney, Grady. *Braxton Bragg.* New York: Columbia University Press, 1969.

"Why General Sherman's Name Is Detested." *CV* 14:294–98.

Wiley, Bell I. "Billy Yank and Johnny Reb in the Atlanta Campaign." *CWT* (July 1964): 18–22.

Williams, T. Harry. *McClellan, Sherman, and Grant.* New York: Rutgers University Press, 1962.

Woodworth, Steven E. "How to Lose a City." *Civil War* (January-February 1991): 28–33.

———. *Jefferson Davis and His Generals.* Lawrence: University of Kansas Press, 1990.

Index

Illustrations are listed in **boldface.**

Webb Garrison is a veteran writer who lives in Lake Junaluska, North Carolina. Formerly associate dean of Emory University and president of McKendree College, he has written forty books, including A Treasury of Civil War Tales, A Treasury of White House Tales, *and* Civil War Curiosities.